Discovering
Choices

Our Recovery in Relationships

 Al-Anon Family Groups
Hope and help for families & friends of alcoholics

For information and a catalog of literature write to:
Al-Anon Family Group Headquarters, Inc.
1600 Corporate Landing Parkway
Virginia Beach, VA 23454-5617
(757) 563-1600   Fax (757) 563-1655
www.al-anon.alateen.org/members
wso@al-anon.org
©Al-Anon Family Group Headquarters, Inc., 2008

Al-Anon/Alateen is supported by members' voluntary contributions and from the sale of our Conference Approved Literature.

Library of Congress Catalog Card No. 2008926304
ISBN -978-0-9815017-3-4

Approved by
World Service Conference
Al-Anon Family Groups

Al-Anon books that may be helpful:

Alateen—Hope for Children of Alcoholics (B-3)

The Dilemma of the Alcoholic Marriage (B-4)

The Al-Anon Family Groups—Classic Edition (B-5)

One Day at a Time in Al-Anon (B-6), Large Print (B-14)

Lois Remembers (B-7)

Al-Anon's Twelve Steps & Twelve Traditions (B-8)

Alateen—a day at a time (B-10)

As We Understood . . . (B-11)

. . . In All Our Affairs: Making Crises Work for You (B-15)

Courage to Change—One Day at a Time in Al-Anon II (B-16), Large Print (B-17)

From Survival to Recovery: Growing Up in an Alcoholic Home (B-21)

How Al-Anon Works for Families & Friends of Alcoholics (B-22)

Courage to Be Me—Living with Alcoholism (B-23)

Paths to Recovery—Al-Anon's Steps, Traditions, and Concepts (B-24)

Living Today in Alateen (B-26)

Hope for Today (B-27), Large Print (B-28)

Opening Our Hearts, Transforming Our Losses (B-29)

Preamble

The Al-Anon Family Groups are a fellowship of relatives and friends of alcoholics who share their experience, strength, and hope in order to solve their common problems. We believe alcoholism is a family illness and that changed attitudes can aid recovery.

Al-Anon is not allied with any sect, denomination, political entity, organization, or institution; does not engage in any controversy; neither endorses nor opposes any cause. There are no dues for membership. Al-Anon is self-supporting through its own voluntary contributions.

Al-Anon has but one purpose: to help families of alcoholics. We do this by practicing the Twelve Steps, by welcoming and giving comfort to families of alcoholics, and by giving understanding and encouragement to the alcoholic.

Suggested Preamble to the Twelve Steps

Serenity Prayer

God grant me the serenity
To accept the things I cannot change,
Courage to change the things I can,
And wisdom to know the difference.

Contents

Preface

There are no simple answers to the difficult and complex challenges of relationships affected by alcoholism. As Al-Anon members, we have a wide range of experience in dealing with every type of difficulty that results from our relationships with problem drinkers. Yet as we share our experience, strength, and hope in the mutually supportive environment of Al-Anon meetings, we often discover possibilities and positive choices. In applying the principles of the Al-Anon program to our own lives, many of us find an inner strength that has a positive effect on all of our personal relationships.

This book brings together a cross-section of the wisdom and insight that many of us uncover in Al-Anon as we search for understanding, integrity, harmony, and love in our relationships. In this book, we share how we use the tools offered by the program to learn about ourselves and discover spiritual resources we didn't know we had. Our opportunities for progress depend only upon how well we keep our focus on what is within our power to change. As one Al-Anon member shares in this book, "My family is doing the best they can. As I gradually let go, however, I find that their view no longer makes the sky any less blue for me."

In Al-Anon Family Groups we discover these choices are available to all of us, provided that we're able to put our relationship problems in perspective and open ourselves to whatever each day offers. By putting our own lives on more solid footing, we can have a positive effect in our interactions with others, ultimately improving the quality of all of our relationships. While there's no instant solution, we discover in Al-Anon that there are more choices available to us than we had thought. This book shares with you some of those possibilities.

Chapter One

We Start from Where We Are

We come to Al-Anon because of the problems caused by someone's drinking. Some of us are primarily concerned about a relationship with a spouse or partner who has a drinking problem, while others have alcoholic parents or children. Sometimes an alcoholic situation in the workplace brings us to Al-Anon. Regardless of the particular relationship, there is one common denominator: the effect of someone else's drinking on us. Al-Anon gives us an opportunity to look at ourselves and understand how alcoholism has distorted our perspective, hurt our self-image, and affected our ability to develop and maintain healthy relationships.

It isn't unusual to enter the doors of an Al-Anon Family Group in a state of distress. Despite the confusion and chaos we may be experiencing, the program offers us hope that by improving our attitudes, we can live better, happier lives. In Al-Anon meetings we meet people who have had experiences similar to ours. They share how much their lives have improved. They show us that our past failures don't have to limit our future growth as long as we are willing to learn new approaches.

An Al-Anon Family Group also offers opportunities to understand our own feelings better, and how to reach out to other people for support. Before we began attending Al-Anon meetings, many of us ignored our feelings and felt isolated by our problems. We focused primarily on trying to fix the alcoholic relationship or coping with the crisis of the day. We tried to keep things as "normal" as possible by taking on responsibilities that the alcoholic neglected. It was all up to us, or so we believed. We felt we had to keep up the appearance that everything was okay, even if that meant making excuses or lying for the alcoholic. Under these circumstances, it can be painful or confusing to pay attention to our own feelings. When we hear other people share in the meetings, however, we begin to recognize how much we have in common with them. As we relate, we begin to feel connected—sometimes for the first time in our lives. Trust begins to grow.

An Al-Anon meeting is a safe place to share our feelings. We learn that we're not the only ones whose point of view has been twisted by the strain of living with the effects of someone else's drinking. As we listen to other people's stories, we discover things about ourselves that we may have never suspected. We can begin to admit to ourselves how we feel and come to understand ourselves better. With the love and support we find in an Al-Anon meeting, we're able to recognize—and accept—who we are.

Wherever we may be in our search for healthy relationships, we have to begin where we are today. It may be painful to think how much better our relationships could have—or should have—been. There's no point in criticizing ourselves when we did the best we could with what we had. We can gain peace of mind by putting aside what we could or should have done and by accepting who and where we are right now.

The Al-Anon program offers a range of tools that can help us. As we continue to attend meetings, we learn that it is possible to let go of old companions like failure, shame, and guilt. In time we can make progress, but we can only make it "One Day at a Time." The Al-Anon tools help us realize that the ability to start over is always within our reach, and that there's always more hope than we may have thought.

Personal Stories

I was full of anguish when I first arrived at Al-Anon. Real progress came when I understood that I am responsible only for the consequences of my own behavior and choices. In time I came to understand that much of my family members' lives was none of my business. I had no right to judge them as right or wrong, much less interfere with their lives, even if they asked for my opinion.

My greatest progress in overcoming the urge to get involved in others' lives came when I recognized that I don't always know what's going to turn out to be a good thing. As I listened at meetings, I realized that many an idea that I thought would be the best possible solution turned into a complete disaster. On the other hand, things I thought would surely stigmatize and ruin lives turned out to be someone's salvation.

If I can't recognize whether the consequence of an action will turn out good or bad, how can I possibly make a reliable judgment for others? My only responsibility is to put the focus on my behavior, understand my family, and try to be non-judgmental. I stopped judging my family, and I now accept them for who they are. I do my best to give unconditional love.

❧

My first Sponsor asked me how I felt, but I didn't know. Ever since I was a little boy, I had been told how to feel by my family. I took a consensus—and that's how I felt. It took a lot of courage to begin to feel my own emotions. I heard a man say that for most men, emotions are the slimy things you find when you lift up a rock. That really rang true for me.

My Sponsor said my feelings are mine and I have a right to feel them. What is really important is what I do with them. I have the right to be angry, but I don't have the right to be verbally or physically abusive. I often find that the root of my anger with someone else is a problem I have yet to address within myself.

In Al-Anon I have learned that the guilt I feel is like a brick I carry in my pocket—I choose to carry it. I can let it go through honesty and amends. I can deal with my fear by living today, "One Day at a Time." That cuts my problems down to a manageable size. Now I can choose to feel joy and happiness. There is no charge for feeling them.

⌐✎⌐

I recently spent ten days on a trip in a motor home with my grown daughter. We had a great time. We both applied the principles of this program to our lives. We gave each other space and time alone. We could disagree without being disagreeable. It was the most memorable trip I have ever taken.

It wasn't always like that. When my three children were young, I was still sick from the effects of alcoholism. The day my daughter got married, she told me she would never come back into our crazy hell-hole of a home again. She said she never wanted to see me or her father again. A year-and-a-half later, she gave me a cigarette lighter as a holiday gift. It was engraved: "To Mom, from your daughter." I knew that inscription meant that she wanted to be my daughter again. Because of my years in Al-Anon, we are friends today. She calls me and we go to plays or movies together.

When we came home from the trip, people asked me if we were still speaking. I just laughed. My daughter is the joy of my life and a wonderful friend.

⌐✎⌐

Growing up in an alcoholic family, I was a very angry person. I had no friends, no self-esteem, and no ability to trust anyone. I had no idea how to love myself. I didn't know how to take responsibility for my thoughts, words, or actions. I didn't know the difference between honesty and dishonesty. I was just like my alcoholic dad. In Al-Anon I learned that the only difference between us was that I do not have a compulsion to drink.

I am a grown man who has been around alcoholism all of my life. I didn't realize how much the disease had affected me. I ended up getting married, having children, and treating them the same way I had been treated. Through Al-Anon meetings I learned that I only need to take care of myself. Other things will take care of themselves.

My wife was in Al-Anon for 12 years before I began in A.A. She started getting better while I got sicker. She used detachment with love. I got sick enough to hit bottom; I got into A.A., and our relationship started to get better. We both got involved in service. But ten years later, I was still making bad choices and trying to fix them all by myself. Things kept building up until I just wanted to end it all. Then one day an Al-Anon member asked if I would like to come to an Al-Anon meeting. That first meeting was on self-esteem.

My relationship with my wife is better today than it has ever been. We say "I love you," and we do things together. We also let each other do things and go places on our own. We work our own programs. I thank God as I understand Him for helping me find Al-Anon and A.A. and for keeping our family together. Our house has become a home again.

As an active member of Al-Anon, I continue to experience startling spiritual awakenings. Recently I was disappointed in several family members who did not do what I wanted. The disappointment became so intense and painful that I finally sought God and surrendered myself and all my old ideas about how my life should be. I experienced sorrow and grief in letting go of expectations. I stayed with the grief until God revealed the truth to me. It was time to know and accept the truth about myself.

Both of my parents were alcoholics and impaired by the disease. They ignored my needs, which they discounted or dismissed as unimportant. My family practiced denial daily. Keeping secrets was very important, and anyone who broke that rule was punished.

I tried to guess what normal was. I was suffering from distorted attitudes, perceptions, and beliefs. I felt that I was unwelcome and unappreciated. I was consumed with shame, fear, and immense loneliness.

When I married and began a family of my own, I was only vaguely aware that I was trying to create the family I never had. I wasn't aware that I wanted and expected my new family to make up for what I missed as a child. Instead of seeing my children as beautiful souls in their own right, I used them to try to fill my own unmet needs.

Thanks to this awareness, I have the opportunity to choose healthier beliefs and values. I want to accept and appreciate my loved ones as they are and to let go of expecting them to fit my distorted ideas. I now know they don't exist just to make me happy. They don't owe me anything. I owe them amends; I am seeking God's guidance on how and when to make amends. I know that forgiveness is an ongoing change in attitude that is manifested in my behavior.

I finally understand my motivations with other people. In my blindness and denial, I thought others were responsible for the quality of my life. I had burdened myself with a belief that I can now let go. My disappointments were always the result of my perceptions and attitudes. I have been on a quest for meaning and fulfillment in my years in Al-Anon. Letting others off the hook is a big step forward for me in that quest.

~⊗~

I entered Al-Anon while my husband was in treatment for alcohol and drug abuse. My daughter was still a preschooler, and it was many years before I would see how much she had been affected by alcoholism and my reactions to it.

One day after my daughter had left for college, she called to say she had been admitted to the hospital for cutting herself. I felt fear, pain, and hurt. I was truly distraught. When she returned home, she was not very talkative at all. Then the day came when she admitted she had a problem. She said she was a cutter, had an eating disorder, and was both bulimic and anorexic. She needed long-term care and went to a treatment facility. My heart cried in shame, guilt, and pain. What had I done to my daughter?

Without my Al-Anon program, I don't believe our relationship could have been healed. Healing our relationship wasn't about her changing; it was about the changes I needed to make, especially letting go and letting God. I believe God loves her as much as I do and that she has her own Higher Power. Today we have a closer relationship than I ever dreamt possible. Today I believe I have experienced a miracle. Our relationship has gone from one of hopelessness and despair to one of love, respect, support, forgiveness, and acceptance of each other as we are.

―――✖―――

I tried Al-Anon three separate times during a 12-year period of living with active alcoholism. For one reason or another, I didn't stay in Al-Anon the first two times. I always thought that my situation was different from other members.

As the family disease of alcoholism progressed in my home, I gave up on any notion of God. If He did exist, I didn't think He knew that I existed. I felt abandoned by God. All I ever prayed for was that the drinking and unhappiness would stop. It was a very confusing time in my life, emotionally and spiritually.

In spite of all my attempts to help my husband, he reached out to A.A. for help instead. He was changing, but so was I. I was still getting worse. By this time, I was so full of anger and confusion that I could hardly live with myself anymore. After praying all those years for his sobriety, I wanted nothing to do with the alcoholic or sobriety. I had learned how to live with alcoholism: how to live separately in the same house; how to stuff feelings; how to project the perfect family image to those outside our home; and how to build up anger and resentment. I needed help, but didn't know where to start.

One day, I dropped to my knees and with a soulful plea I cried, "Dear God, please help me." I emptied myself of all my old ideas of what my life should be. Without really knowing it, I had done Steps One, Two, and Three right there. Finally I was ready and willing to do anything I had to do to achieve some sort of emotional and spiritual sobriety.

I decided to try Al-Anon one more time. I felt like such a loser, but this time I was willing to surrender my will and my life over to the care of a God I really didn't understand. This time I had no more answers. I was willing to "Listen and Learn." No more being different—no more denial. This time I totally surrendered myself to this simple program. Here was a group of individuals who seemed to have found a solution to their problems. They were not problem-focused people; they were solution-focused people. This group provided me with a calming approach to life.

⌒⌘⌒

I married again after a 27-year engagement. We're both male adult children of alcohol-affected parents, and we're recovering— not an uncommon match as a basis for a strong marriage. Thanks to Al-Anon, we're finding great hope by seeing our parents in the new light of compassion and understanding. Our relationships with them have improved in countless and miraculous ways since we started applying the principles of the program.

⌒⌘⌒

I developed friendships and relationships with people who used emotional terrorism and alcohol to ease the pain in their lives. I took pride in the power I gained through anger.

When my parents divorced, I began to fear for my mother's health. Her anger seemed to escalate in an attempt to control the young men my sister and I brought to the family. Strangely, I was more concerned about my mother's anger affecting her health than I was about it affecting our relationships. Yet as I neared the age of 40, I couldn't see the part *my* anger had in my own deteriorating health. The only danger I could see was in other people's anger and in the over-use of alcohol in all of our lives.

I came to Al-Anon because of my desire to help my sister—and the realization that so far my attempts to help her were pushing her away.

After just eight Al-Anon meetings, I accepted that I was powerless over the lives of my loved ones. As I "Let Go and Let God," I felt a great relief, most evident in the release of the physical pain I'd developed over the years. I began to focus on my own characteristics and became willing to let go of what no longer served me. I was even noticing that it was easier to avoid giving advice when I practiced "Live and Let Live." This progress was a real feat for me, after having been the self-appointed family advisor for so long. I learned how to ask for what I want, to recognize what I need, and to get it without feeling guilty.

As I strive to become the person I want to be in my marriage and in my family, Al-Anon is helping me develop healthier relationships with myself and my Higher Power. I feel blessed for the support from the people in Al-Anon who helped me love and let go of my beautiful mother during her last six years with us. I came to understand that her anger, like alcohol, initially seemed to provide her with the power to gain a certain strength and freedom, but eventually consumed her. I could detach from that, love her through it, and learn from it, being grateful for the lesson.

───❦───

Before I came into Al-Anon, my relationship with my wife had deteriorated to the point that we could not communicate with one another. The only discussions we had were heated arguments, and there was little communication in those. I treated her like a child, trying to manage all aspects of her life and sort things out when there were problems.

In Al-Anon I learned that my managing and helping were preventing my wife from facing the consequences of her actions. I was allowing her to carry on in the same way without any reason to change. I learned that letting go and letting God was the best thing I could do. Without my interference, my wife found sobriety, and gradually our communication has improved. I am grateful that through our programs our marriage has gotten better.

$\sim\infty\backsim$

I'm the fourth son in a family of five children. My father was an alcoholic before he ever met my mother. He continues to drink to this day.

I was born in denial and remained that way until I began regularly attending Al-Anon. I have never known my father outside of alcoholism. The constant presence of his disease faded into a background blind spot of my life, like the drone of a refrigerator.

It wasn't until I developed alcoholism myself and found A.A. that I realized I was also sick from growing up in an alcoholic home. I remember a lot of guilt, shame, and embarrassment. I remember anger that I couldn't understand and fear that kept me always on edge, never sure when I would say or do the wrong thing. I still suffer from mild paranoia, always wondering if someone might be insinuating something or dropping subtle hints, never quite sure when to take things seriously.

Meetings are the key for me to deal with this part of my disease. Whether we are reading from the literature or sharing in an open discussion, there is a clear and direct quality to it all that I find very reassuring. Simple sayings such as "I didn't cause it, I can't cure it, and I can't control it" cut through my confusion and help me to see what is right before my eyes.

Learning to respond rather than react has made it possible for me to separate my father from his sickness. I used resentment to pretend that I did not love my father, which made it easy to believe that he didn't love me. Today I realize that his disease does not come from a lack of love. Today I know I can love him completely without endangering myself or enabling him in any way. Through Al-Anon, I'm learning to encourage the person without encouraging the problem. More and more often, I find ways to bring happiness into my father's life, sharing what I can of the ease and comfort I find in the fellowships. Working my program has proven to be the most helpful thing I can do for my father. I can see how my efforts are making his life easier.

One of the gifts this program has given me is the ability to keep in mind all the good things I see in my father. In fact, one day when I was feeling down, my father—beer in hand before noon— was able to cheer me up.

I see that he needs to know there is something deeply good about who he is. I'm beginning to understand that with the help of a Higher Power, I might just have a chance to show him how meaningful and valuable his life really is. This way, maybe one day he'll find the strength and courage it takes to get help.

⌒⧓⌒

Growing up in an alcoholic family and later marrying an active alcoholic, I felt so alone while being around so many people. I wanted so much just to be loved and to be able to show my love for family members who were around me.

Before I came to Al-Anon, I walked away from people before they could get too close and find out what was really missing in me. I would find excuses to get angry at other people and justify ending a relationship. Didn't these people understand that if they saw who I really was, they wouldn't want anything to do with me? I thought I would save other people the trouble and heartache of finding out how crazy and empty I was. I would put on my "I'm fine" smile and chat with them when we saw each other, but I wouldn't work at having a deeper relationship. My solution would be to walk away and never come back. Yet I felt angry and sad that I had no friends. Why wouldn't I feel sorry for myself, since it seemed no one wanted to be around me?

When I met my husband, I thought I had found someone who was different. Here was someone who seemed to have it all together—someone who really understood how mixed-up and confused I felt. Since he wanted to marry me, I thought that maybe I had been wrong. Maybe I wasn't so bad after all. Perhaps I could have a good relationship with another human being.

But through the years, I kept getting worse at trying to share my feelings. I shared less and less of what my true feelings were. I spent my time and energy on pointing out how he wasn't trying hard enough to understand what was going on inside me. How could he when he had his own demons to contend with?

When my husband went into treatment, I was advised to try Al-Anon, where I learned how to define who I was and how to appropriately share that with others. Today, after almost seven years, I think I am getting better at that. I look at my role in my relationships and ask, "How can I make my part better?" I'm grateful for all the people in my life who love and care about me. I couldn't have made this progress on my own. I don't ever want to stop and go back to being alone; that just hurt too much.

⌒◯◯◯⌒

I knew something was terribly wrong with me when I went to family week at the treatment center to see my son. I thought my whole world had fallen apart.

All my dreams and hopes for his future were gone. He celebrated his 21st birthday at the center. I just couldn't figure out how to climb out of the pit I was in. His drinking and drug use had affected me profoundly. I desperately tried searching for answers to cure him. Nothing worked. He became more and more resentful, and I became depressed. As I went through family week, I kept hearing, "Go to Al-Anon."

My first meeting was in a small room with a couch that had broken springs, but I noticed the people there were smiling and laughing. Oh, how I longed to be able to do that. Nobody seemed to notice the shabby furniture.

I learned the phrase, "Give the alcoholic the dignity to fail." As strange as it sounds, by learning to let go of my son, I got my life back. Today he is sober, and I have been in Al-Anon for three years. I am indeed a very grateful member.

⌒✹⌒

After my alcoholic wife divorced me and another problem-filled relationship failed, I began to realize in Al-Anon that I tended to get involved with women who had more problems than I could imagine. I was drawn to them by the prospect that I could save them from their problems, since I obviously had the solution.

Later, I reconnected with a woman I had casually met where I work. She had many positive qualities. After a couple of dates, I said to her, "But you don't need me for anything!" She had a good job, a nice condo, nice things, and was totally capable of taking care of herself without intervention by anyone. She said that two people can have a relationship just because they want to be together. All of my past relationships were based on pity and the belief that I could fix their problems—that I was all that was needed to improve their lives.

The more I got to know this lady, the more I discovered other beautiful qualities. I eventually married her and embarked on a wonderful new life—one that I would have never found without the awareness I found in Al-Anon Family Groups.

For Thought and Discussion:

1. How healthy are the relationships in my life?
2. What am I doing to grow and mature?
3. If I were not so worried about someone else's situation, what would I be doing?
4. How have my ideas about a Higher Power changed?
5. What are some of my favorite things to do?
6. How would I like my relationships to develop?
7. What positive qualities do I contribute when I interact with others?

Chapter Two

A Solid Foundation

In Al-Anon we learn that alcoholism is an illness, not a moral choice. None of us would choose to have an illness, and neither do alcoholics. It would be short-sighted to blame them for something that was not their choice. When we begin to look at alcoholism in this way, it is easier to have compassion for those who suffer from it. Alcoholism has psychological, social, and spiritual aspects that impact the family, as well as affect how the alcoholic relates to other people.

Like the alcoholic, few of us would choose to be affected by an illness. Just as we can learn to have compassion for the alcoholic, we can also learn to have consideration and understanding for ourselves. There's no need to blame ourselves for something that we didn't cause. There's also no need to accept any blame that anyone—including the alcoholic—might try to place on us. We don't have the power to make someone else drink—or not drink—any more than we have the power to cause or cure any other illness.

Whether or not we think we're somehow responsible for someone's alcoholism, many of us are slow to recognize the impact it has had on us. Some of us were raised by alcoholic parents or by the adult children of alcoholics. It's hard to know how our assumptions about relationships were affected by the illness, since most of these beliefs were shaped by our experience with unhealthy alcoholic relationships. For others, the progress of our loved one's illness was so gradual we didn't recognize how the alcoholic relationship had also changed our perceptions and attitudes. Just as the active alcoholic tends to minimize or deny the alcoholism, it's not unusual for us as the friends and families of alcoholics to minimize and deny how the illness affected us. We often mirror the drinker's behavior in a complex dance in which the drinking may seem to be the only issue.

At some point, we find someone else's behavior greatly disturbing to our peace of mind. We want to help them because we believe that is the best way to help ourselves. We think if only they would stop drinking, everything would be well again. Our effort and energy have shifted almost exclusively to what we can't control—someone else's drinking. As a result, we lose touch with what we *can* control—ourselves and our attitudes. With the focus off ourselves, we lose a balanced perspective on life without realizing quite how it happened.

Trying to fix someone else's problem is like stepping uninvited into someone else's shoes. The shoes don't fit—they pinch or they're too loose. As difficult as it is to walk in them, we remain determined to make it work. We don't realize that we have choices. It doesn't occur to us to take the shoes off and look for a pair made specifically for us.

For those of us with relationships affected by alcoholism, nothing fits quite right from day to day. We know confusion, pain, and despair. Days are often spent reviewing the past where nothing can be changed, or rehearsing a future that hasn't yet happened. Meanwhile, we completely miss the present moment. As the effects of the illness progress, we become increasingly out of touch with ourselves and isolated from others.

It took more than one day for this situation to develop, and it will take more than one day to find a solution. With the acceptance, understanding, support, and friendship we find in Al-Anon meetings, however, we can begin to feel better today. There's more to the Al-Anon program than can be absorbed in a day, yet its elements are simple enough that there's always something that can help right now—the Serenity Prayer, a slogan, Al-Anon literature, or a conversation with a program friend.

At meetings we find people who have discovered that happiness is a choice they can make at any moment. Contentment is no longer seen as an accidental mood created when someone else does what we want. We see people who are able to find peace and serenity even when the outward circumstances of their lives are chaotic. We're able to listen to them share, and we find that their experience of living with an alcoholic has much in common with ours. As we hear about the relationships in their lives—healthy or unhealthy—we come to understand that everyone in Al-Anon is on a similar path. Peace of mind and healthy relationships are possible for all of us.

Personal Stories

I had always considered myself to be the stable person in my marriage. I thought my husband was a person adrift without direction. I hadn't been in Al-Anon long when we had another argument. His response to my criticism was, "Well, you're not easy to get along with either!" Imagine the nerve of that guy to attack me. Al-Anon helped me become receptive to the idea that I didn't have all the answers, and that wisdom can come from the least expected sources if I am willing to hear it.

⌐⊗⌐

I was reeling from the changes in our lives that my wife's recovery in A.A. was causing. It was wonderful that she'd been sober for months. Her commitment to recovery meant that she was more present and honest than she'd ever been, but I didn't like what came with her recovery. She wasn't using alcohol to numb her feelings anymore. Instead, she was venting years of hurt through anger and violence within our family. I still thought that I was the cause for so much that was wrong.

I had a lot of guilt about my own violence in the relationship. I was confused about my part in the emotional nightmare we lived. At Al-Anon meetings I heard others speak honestly about similar experiences. I learned that I didn't cause my wife's problems and wasn't responsible for fixing her. I could put guilt and shame aside and begin to look after myself. Only by nurturing and loving myself first could I love and nurture those around me. This looked "selfish" to my wife. As my Sponsor told me, it was only in being "selfish" in this way that I could detach and learn to be compassionate and supportive.

I no longer live with my wife. But my children are still affected by the disease, and I have many friends who are not in recovery. There are still many opportunities for me to lose perspective. It's easy for me to feel guilty or to think that I am being selfish and unreasonable. Recovery isn't a place where everything turns out the way I want it. Being in Al-Anon did not "recover" the family of my dreams. I still find myself feeling trapped by old choices and patterns. I still find it hard to deal with the recovering alcoholic's slips into unhealthy patterns of thinking and behavior.

Recovery does mean, however, that I am learning to love and nurture myself. I am letting go of fears and resentments that keep me from enjoying this wonderful life. I make small steps toward compassionate detachment so that I am better able to enjoy the gifted—and flawed—individuals who are part of my rich life today. Recovery means that I can be happy today if I choose to be.

⌀

I watched my mother endure my father's rage without showing any emotion. She showed no response to his outrageous behavior. We, the children, had no protection from our father's anger. I realized at an early age that we were beaten not because of what we had done, but because of bill collectors, money problems, and unpleasant phone calls.

At age nine, I watched my mother walk out of our house on a dark, rainy evening. She didn't say she was leaving. She didn't say why she was leaving or how long she would be gone or even if she'd ever be back. I watched her come home several months later and still not say a word about why she left or whether she would ever leave again. I learned not to trust others or myself.

Later, when I became a mom and found myself struggling with the disease of alcoholism, I didn't understand what was wrong in my marriage. I saw myself as a victim.

I allowed my mother to rescue me over and over. She took me away on vacations and bought me wonderful career clothes. I couldn't even say I liked something without getting it within days. By then, I had been in and out of Al-Anon like a revolving door. I never saw it as the solution to the hell I was experiencing. I didn't listen. I didn't attend regularly. I just came when I was hurting and expected everyone else to fix me.

Consequently, when my mother remarried and moved away, I felt that same abandonment at age 44 as I felt at age nine. Before she remarried, my mother had been my lifeline out of hell. Now she didn't want to be away from her husband. She didn't even talk to me about what was going on in her life. I lost the mother I had depended on to rescue me.

Then I started attending Al-Anon regularly. A loving member gently told me that maybe now I was ready to start working the program. I got a Sponsor who began working through the Steps with me. I started attending multiple meetings each week. I have become involved in service and am learning to be one among others.

I have learned that my parents were devastated by the effects of my grandfather's alcoholism. I did not cause my father's rage, I couldn't cure my mother's pain, and I couldn't control the disease ravaging our home. My mother does the very best she can. Retreating emotionally when she is in pain is just one of her survival tactics.

I choose to live today. I know that in order for me to live, I have to practice the Twelve Steps in my life, to share with my Sponsor, and to be willing and open to do things differently. I practice keeping my life in the shape of the Al-Anon triangle—recovery, unity, and service.

⌒⟊⟆⌒

I grew up in a home where the abuse of alcohol was not visible, but the effects were rampant. We learned how to keep secrets and not to make friends. Everything in our home was a crisis; violence and anger were a way of life. Mom specialized in the most painful torture—the silent treatment that lasted for weeks, along with the threat of "wait until your father comes home." As a result, my three siblings and I learned how to avoid being the target, even if it meant sacrificing each other. Dad would explode at one of us, but then calm down and be so loving and tender.

I learned to anticipate what others wanted, to be seen and not heard, and to avoid conflict at all cost. I held everything within for many years, letting it wear me down from the inside out. Eventually the tension boiled over as anger. There came a time when all four children were cast out from the family. We became strangers to each other.

Today I have a relationship with only one of my siblings, and that is only because of what I learned in the Al-Anon program—to mind my own business, give my opinion only when it is requested, think before I speak, respect other people's opinions, and the slogan, "How Important Is It?"

I recently had major surgery, and the sister that I didn't have contact with for so long flew up to stay with me. She's a clean freak— I'm not—and we both laughed at the expired condiments when she started cleaning out the refrigerator. We enjoyed hugs, laughs, tears, and most of all love, thanks to what I have learned in Al-Anon.

⌑

I coach a junior football team. Before coming to Al-Anon, my coaching style was instructive and dictatorial. My relationship with my six other coaches and 30 team members was full of anger and control issues. Although we were a winning team, many of us were not having fun.

It is no wonder that it was this way, since I had only one identifiable emotion—anger. Learning in Al-Anon to surrender control over the alcoholic and to develop a real relationship with God has changed the way I live life.

I now work with seven other coaches and 30 children, and we are all having a blast. We work hard and we condition harder, but I now have the ability to let go of control and to let the other coaches do their jobs. I still manage what goes on with the team, but I'm more interested in everyone learning and letting every coach and team member become all that they can be.

As a result of all of the work I've been doing on myself, this season a number of parents got together and wrote an article about me, nominating me for "Coach of the Year." I cried when I heard. No one would have ever thought of doing that prior to Al-Anon and now this has happened. It's not the big changes in my life that have made the difference. It's the daily influence of this program that has made the changes possible.

⌐∽⌐

I walked into my first Al-Anon meeting because of a request from my recovering alcoholic partner. She explained to me that the program would enrich our relationship. I was in a lot of pain. In my confusion, I thought, "What have I done? Why do we argue? Why can't she understand me and why can't I understand her?" Drama, chaos, and crisis were the norms in our relationship. She acted, I reacted, and the pattern didn't change until Al-Anon.

I came to these rooms with resentment because I didn't see myself as the sick one. I just wanted a manual on how to fix the alcoholic and then I'd be on my way. Instead, you suggested that I focus on myself. How could I do that? I was too busy focusing on everyone else's problems. Members also suggested that I "Keep Coming Back" and wait for the miracle. I wondered what they were talking about. I came back and complained about the alcoholic instead. They listened without interruption and suggested I attend at least six meetings and get a Sponsor.

I learned slogans, and the first one I grasped was "Let Go and Let God." I had been the people-pleaser and the fixer. I took care of everyone else around me. I allowed them to use me, put me down, and take advantage of me. The other members let me know about boundaries and that I had choices. I didn't know that.

It was hard for me at first to let the true me come out. I am a gay woman; because of my fear of rejection and criticism, I kept silent or I referred to the alcoholic as just that—the alcoholic—without gender. However, the more meetings I attended, the more I experienced unconditional love. Today I am open about my partner.

I make choices today, and I'm responsible for the consequences. My relationships with my family, partner, and friends have all changed for the better because I have changed. I only hope I can give back to Al-Anon as much as it has already given me.

My mother is a difficult woman to get along with. She is not an alcoholic but is affected by others who are. She was always there physically—three square meals a day were always on the table, the laundry was always done, and the house was always clean. But try as I might, nothing I ever did was good enough.

I grew up afraid of her because she was emotionally explosive. Sometimes she was calm and easy-going, but I couldn't relax at those times because I never knew when the next explosion was going to happen. When I was a teenager, I stopped trying to please her. In fact, I went to the other extreme of doing things deliberately so that she would disapprove. I chose a husband she didn't like—an alcoholic—partly because I knew she didn't like him.

After we were married, we moved a long distance away from my mother's home, and our lives came to revolve around drinking, kids, drinking, debts, drinking, worry, and not enough of anything else. Appearances were important to me, and once or twice a year I wrote to my mom to tell her the lie that all was well in my house. Once a year I took the kids for our week-long annual holiday to visit their grandparents—partly because I thought I should go, and partly because it was the only place we could afford to go. Getting ready for the trip, I packed my resentments along with my toothbrush and socks, so I was already angry by the time we arrived at my mother's door.

On one visit, I screamed at my kids for almost no reason at all. My mother made an excuse for me, saying I must be tired. I assured her I was not tired, that the kids deserved my tirade, and that she shouldn't interfere. At the end of that visit, she told me that I had changed. I knew she didn't mean for the better. That was one of my first moments of clarity.

It took a few more years, and quite a few more horrible incidents, but eventually I made it to Al-Anon. For the first few years, I started praying a couple of weeks before our annual visit to Mom's that she would find Al-Anon and take a crash course, so she would be easier to get along with while I was there. I was missing the point, wasn't I? After I realized that I needed to change for the relationship to change, I got to work.

The first tool I used was prayer; just a few simple words—"Dear God, please make me different." I prayed it many times a day and I slowly began to change, and not just in my relationship with Mom.

⌐◦∞◦⌐

I was devastated when my alcoholic wife told me she was leaving. I was fully aware that our marriage was in trouble, but separation wasn't an option for me. We separated anyway.

My mother-in-law, a member of A.A., suggested I go to Al-Anon. I went to my first meeting hurt, angry, and almost paralyzed. My recovery began when, after years of thinking it was my wife who had the problem, I learned that I was sick and needed to heal.

Tradition Five states that Al-Anon Family Groups have one purpose—to help the families of alcoholics. They have helped me. I learned that I wasn't the cause of my wife's drinking and that I couldn't control it. Other members shared their experience, strength, and hope with me. My hurt and anger gradually gave way to a sense of peace I hadn't experienced in years.

My wife soon found recovery in A.A., and each of us focused on our own programs, occasionally sharing insights we had in our own growth. After a year of recovery, my wife and I rediscovered the things in each other that had initially brought us together but had been buried in the disease. We reconciled with a stronger relationship and we are closer than ever.

⌐◦∞◦⌐

I had exhausted every avenue I could find to save my son from alcohol and drugs. He started down that destructive path at an early age, which increased my panic and fear. I had no hope. I truly believed that the only relief from this suffering would be his death—and there are no words that could express my horror at the thought of that. I shut my life off. I chose to stop doing anything beyond going to work and coming home. I was too afraid to do anything else. I tried everything—begging, pleading, threatening, and pushing—to get him to change. I became more distant, hostile, fearful, and needy in my relationship with him. I made all the other relationships in my life subordinate; this one was all-important. Everyone in our family became more isolated—from each other and those around us.

At first I held on to the hope I received in Al-Anon literature, especially the phrase, "When one member is thinking sanely, the whole family situation can improve." I learned how to apply the tools I learned to my own life.

Soon I was learning about detachment with love, though I wasn't sure if I was actually abandoning with contempt. I have heard detachment with love being compared to building a bridge. All I needed to do was build my side of it. I prayed for God to reveal how to proceed. I discovered that to have unconditional love, I have to practice it first. I needed to see beyond the surface and look to the heart. I decided to reach out to my son, who I knew was still there hidden behind all of the effects of the disease. Deep inside, I knew I wanted my words to him to be words of love, just in case they happened to be the last words he would ever hear.

My son was in the habit of doing what I called "fighter passes." He stayed away for the most part but rushed in now and then for food, a change of clothes, or other things. Then he rushed out again, jumping into someone's car and speeding away with other sick people. Each time, God moved me to hug my son as he was about to leave the house without any comments other than "I love you," "Take care of yourself," or "See you later." I looked beyond his glazed eyes, need for a haircut, the smell of alcohol, and the reek of marijuana. I let go of the anger at seeing him come home wearing someone else's clothes, or finding things missing from my home. What a tall order!

That first hug was one of the most awful experiences of my life. It was cold, wooden, one-sided, and filled with tremendous emotional hurt. Nonetheless I did it and bit my tongue to keep from crying. After that I didn't think I could do it again, but with God's help, I did. Hugging him got easier until it became a part of me again—even though he didn't respond. One day my son came flying through as usual and went right back out again so quickly that I was not able to give him my usual hug. I heard a car door slam and the car pull out of the driveway. Then I heard the car pull back in and another car door slam. My son rushed in and said he had forgotten his hug. We hugged before he flew back out again.

This moment was the beginning of a new relationship for us. It is still fragile, even after my years in Al-Anon and his attempts at sobriety. Recently my son was telling me of a conversation he had with another A.A. member. He told the person she needed to go to Al-Anon because that was what helped his parents continue to love him and respect him no matter what he was doing in his life. That sharing is my evidence of a recovering relationship.

I don't know what the future will bring, but I have real hope and peace now. I've learned that the issue was never about love. The love was there all along. It was the loss of hope that led me to believe I had lost my son's love and God's love for me. Today I know to "Let Go and Let God" by taking care of myself. I know deeply in my heart that my loved ones are completely safe in God's hands, just as I am. God is trustworthy and faithful even when my circumstances don't look like it.

⸙

After my wife and I divorced, I embarked on the dating scene with some reluctance. I was certain not to date any women who were alcoholics. My first serious relationship, however, showed me that although alcohol was missing, the same unhealthy patterns of my marriage were still there—as well as the arguments, the rage, and the shouting. Since there was no alcohol involved this time, the common factor had to be me. I was in a judgmental, controlling state of disarray. I thought that if people would just follow my suggestions, their circumstances would improve.

I realized that I really needed to work on me. I was angry and possessed low self-esteem that made me constantly critical of others. One day, part of the Al-Anon Preamble hit me like a ton of bricks: "We do this by following the Twelve Steps, by welcoming and giving comfort to families of alcoholics, and by giving understanding and encouragement to the alcoholic." I had never done that. Every time I picked up the kids, my ex-wife and I had to fight about something. I had to criticize how she parented our kids.

So, for once I went to pick up the kids and instead of fighting I told her a joke. She laughed, we smiled, and I took the first step in my recovery. I accepted her for herself, including her disease. That led to my accepting me, and now I have no malice toward her at all. This critical step paved the way for me to have a normal relationship and to improve my way of life.

⸎

Looking back, I can see why my 25-year marriage with an alcoholic ended in divorce. I realize now how destructive that relationship was. Of course at the time, I thought that he was the only one who needed to change his ways.

I believe that the family I grew up in led to my becoming a very insecure, possessive, and controlling woman. Inevitably I chose an equally immature and irresponsible husband whom I tried to mold into the person I thought he ought to be. I was attracted to the loveable rogues of this world who would naturally rebel against being controlled.

I don't think I could have had a good relationship with anyone else until I had a good relationship with myself and my Higher Power, both of which I have found through Al-Anon.

I waited four years before getting into another relationship. This time was crucial for me to learn how to take responsibility for myself, emotionally and financially. I knew I had no one else to blame for my past misery and mistakes. In Al-Anon I learned to take responsibility for my own happiness.

I am now in a 13-year relationship with a reliable, long-time friend. I don't behave the way I did in my marriage. Gratitude is now on my agenda. There is trust between us. We don't take each other for granted. I have established boundaries.

We are honest without the fear of rejection or put-down, and we can share our feelings and problems. We value each other's opinions. I am not responsible for his happiness or for his diabetes and its limitations; he is not responsible for my happiness either.

The relationship is a bonus to my life and not a necessity. I no longer think that I'm nothing without a man. The Al-Anon program has changed my relationship with myself and with my Higher Power. I see the benefits reflected in better relationships with other family members and friends as well.

When I came to Al-Anon, I was just dropping in to find out if the program could help my life partner. Imagine my surprise when it began to dawn on me that I needed help, regardless of what my partner might be doing or not doing, thinking or not thinking.

I began to realize that alcoholism had affected my relationships with all of the people in my life that I'd been trying to fix. It was at once a shock and an embarrassment, but also an odd kind of relief.

After I overcame my astonishment enough to be able to start using the slogans and working the Steps, I actually began to feel better a tiny bit at a time. I never dreamt I could find a way to make changes in myself that would benefit all of my relationships.

I'm still driven to focus on others, but now I can hold myself in check more often. The positive results make it easier to make the right choice more often.

I came to Al-Anon because of my husband's drinking, but something completely unexpected has happened: My relationship with my father has improved.

As a child, I was afraid of my father. As I grew up, my fear subsided, though I began to feel superior and judgmental. In Al-Anon, however, I learned that alcoholism is a disease. How can I feel superior to someone because they suffer from an illness?

I took a look at my own actions, and realized that my relationship with my father was strained, in part because of my behavior. Today I make every effort to act as a kind and loving daughter. This change in my behavior is reflected back to me in the way my father acts toward me. I've given up my childhood fantasy of thinking either one of us has to be perfect. Today I choose to enjoy every little step of progress.

For Thought and Discussion:

1. What are some traits I believe are important for a healthy relationship?

2. What traits have I judged in others? Are they a part of my personality?

3. How do I react when someone expresses negative emotions?

4. What are my favorite foods, activities, or styles? How do these preferences differ from those of my partner or spouse?

5. When have I been reluctant to ask for what I want or desire?

6. How could I be more direct about expressing what's right for me?

7. Am I more—or less—trusting than I used to be?

Chapter Three

A More Positive Perspective

Whether we grew up in an alcoholic home or encountered alcoholism later in life, the effect on our lives can be traumatic. Some of us may have become so overwhelmed by the challenges of alcoholism that we lost touch with our sense of what is healthy in a relationship. Others never saw any examples of healthy relationships from which we could learn. We lacked a positive frame of reference.

Life with an alcoholic is often centered on the drama that accompanies the illness. Infidelity, bankruptcy, violence, homelessness, and abuse—emotional, physical, and sexual—are all possible companions for those of us who live or have lived with an alcoholic. We can become so distracted that our worries crowd out all notions of a sane relationship with ourselves or others.

For those of us who encountered alcoholism as adults, recovery can mean restoring some of the nourishing relationships we once had or creating new ones built on a firmer foundation. For those raised in alcoholic homes, recovery in Al-Anon gives us an opportunity to better understand what healthy relationships are and to begin developing them, perhaps for the first time in our lives.

If we're afraid of being alone, we might keep holding on to a relationship that has been important to us for many years, even if it is harmful to us now. While denial often serves the purpose of helping us to cope with the effects of alcoholism, it blinds us to the true nature of our approach to relationships. Without the use of the Twelve Steps and the support of other Al-Anon members, many of us feel lost and distracted. We may have come to Al-Anon not knowing that alcoholism is an illness or what part our behavior has played in making the alcoholic situation worse. Our vision of life can become very narrow. Much like the alcoholic, we don't realize how much alcoholism has changed us, and we don't understand how much we need to recover.

Living with an alcoholic, drunk or sober, can be a mind-altering experience. We are often told not to believe what we see. We begin to doubt ourselves and learn to mistrust our own instincts. In time we may feel that our perceptions and beliefs are invalid, and that we shouldn't feel the way we do. As we adapt ourselves to an unhealthy environment, we become sick too. Our bearings are lost. At times we may even begin to worry about our own sanity.

This uncertainty and confusion can carry over into every aspect of our lives, including matters of sex and intimacy. Our ability to have healthy sexual relationships can be hurt by the effects of alcoholism in our lives. Some of us even feel angry that we've been denied what we have longed for: the opportunity—and for some, even the ability—to share emotional intimacy with a loving partner. However, just as we reacted to the illness and learned unhealthy responses, we can also learn new, productive patterns. If we can learn how to trust, and then to open our hearts in safer, healthier ways, our personal growth can prepare us for participation in healthy relationships.

As we attend meetings, we begin to discover or regain our sense of balance. As we listen to other members share their stories, we learn that we always have choices. Gradually we start to see how we can choose different attitudes and behaviors, and consequently we can enjoy different outcomes. We embark on an exciting voyage of self-discovery as we learn who we are—and who we can become.

Personal Stories

I used to have an idea of how my family should look, act, and feel. More times than not, one of them would say or do something outside the limits of what I wanted. My insides would plummet to the bottom of my toes. Didn't they know what they were doing to me?

Al-Anon showed me how to let go of my image of how everyone else should be. I have released a lot of unpleasant turmoil that was living inside of me. By letting go of my rigid standards, I have been able to love my family for who they are—not who I want them to be. I can now accept that everyone is entitled to their own feelings.

⌒⟗⌒

Al-Anon has helped me learn that successful relationships depend on what I'm thinking and the attitudes I choose. It's ironic that even though a relationship requires at least two people, it all comes down to one person—me.

I used to think I had to take care of my mom. I saw her as a fragile creature who needed to be protected. I believed her happiness was totally dependent on my behavior, as if her world would fall apart if I made a mistake. I can pinpoint the very first time I challenged my thinking about Mom. She asked me to do something and I said no. To my surprise, she didn't collapse. That was the beginning of my recovery.

⌒⟗⌒

If someone had asked me what my problem was, I wouldn't have been able to tell them. I didn't recognize the role alcoholism played in the arguments with my wife. I thought we had a normal family, and that it was normal for a married couple to disagree from time to time. I underestimated how angry I was. I didn't have expectations for anything better, because I thought I was living a normal life. Over time, that sort of conflict was, in fact, normal for us. I underestimated how bad it was because I never had anything more positive to compare it with.

Years later, a psychiatrist asked me why I put up with all this misery and frustration: "Don't you feel you're entitled to anything better than what you're getting from your marriage?" I didn't find that question helpful, because all my focus was on trying to fix my marriage, not find something better. In fact at some level, I had no idea how I could feel any better than I did. All my energy was centered on changing someone else's behavior.

In Al-Anon I heard stories from people who had struggled with the same frustrations that I had with my wife. They understood my problem in a way that the psychiatrist could not. I found hope in Al-Anon because I saw examples of people who had been in my situation, but had achieved peace of mind. I saw that a better way of life was possible.

⚬◦⚭◦⚬

I knew I was in trouble when, while driving down a busy, two-lane highway, I started hitting my husband. My anger was out of control.

For a long time I was angry that I had a husband who did not see what I saw, could not act the way I wanted him to, and was so badly afflicted by the disease of alcoholism. But what really made me angry was how the disease had affected me.

⚬◦⚭◦⚬

The home I grew up in was very strict and authoritarian. Dad had all the control. After being in Al-Anon, I realized that my dad was affected by growing up in an alcoholic household. Dad didn't drink, but he wanted everything to be perfect.

I was afraid of him and never talked with him. I just showed him respect and stayed out of his way. As the second youngest of a very large family, I felt that I didn't matter and didn't count. I coped by doing what I was told and not making waves. I often had ulcers and was known as a nervous person.

Al-Anon has helped me learn how to be myself and express what I am really feeling. Overall, I feel better now. Sometimes I am even relaxed and calm. My fear of men lives on, but I try to see that some men are nice people too.

⌒⌾⌾⌾⌾⌾⌾⌒

Recently I saw a movie about World War II. The main character spent quite a bit of his time hiding from the enemy. I found myself identifying with his need to look for safety in the midst of a battlefield.

I realized while watching the movie that Al-Anon has become a safe place for me. In Al-Anon I have become aware of my tendency to hide my feelings, even from myself. It was easier for me to care for my children, spouse, and friends to the detriment of my own emotional well-being. I didn't want to face my feelings of shame, low self-esteem, and sadness that came from growing up in an alcoholic home. I had used denial as a survival tool, but it was no longer serving me well. It prevented me from experiencing the joy of being alive.

My spouse of 30 years and I have separated. I have lived alone this past year and have experienced sadness at the loss of our relationship, even though it was rocky. I have been able to find serenity by removing myself from unexpected—and at times irrational—behavior. I am left with the tools of the program and the comfort of the members who help me reevaluate where I've been, where I am now, and where I am going. I no longer need to hide.

⌒⌾⌾⌾⌾⌾⌾⌒

I remember how uncomfortable I was the first and only time I heard someone frankly discuss sexual relationships at an Al-Anon meeting. She spoke of how she was looking for someone or something outside of herself to give her what she felt was missing in her life. She found that other people couldn't give her the love that she didn't have for herself. She thought she was getting love, though she later came to realize that she had had sex with people who didn't love her. All I could say was, "You have a lot of courage in speaking about this issue." In that way, I kept the focus on her story and away from mine.

I felt a lot of shame because of my wife's alcoholism. The sexual aspect of our relationship was a more private, deeply felt level of shame. I didn't know what a healthy marital relationship would be like; I just knew that I was confused, embarrassed, and not comfortable enough with myself to want to talk about it with anyone.

My wife ran hot and cold on sexual intimacy. Sometimes she was passionate, far in excess of what I thought was appropriate for the time and place. I was excited but embarrassed when she wanted sex in semi-public places, probably because of the drinks she had just had in a restaurant. However, that excitement didn't always carry over to the privacy of our bedroom. There she would get sick because she had too much to drink or claim that my sexual interest in her made her feel uncomfortable. She wanted sex at times when I was ambivalent about her drunkenness, and she was remote when I wanted intimacy.

My wife blamed me for the problems in the sexual aspect of our relationship, but I'm learning that I don't have to be ashamed of myself because my attempts to love her failed. My wife acted the way she did because of the illness, not because of anything that I did. It took me a very long time to recognize how the illness of alcoholism had deeply hurt my self-esteem.

꩜

I had been in and out of Al-Anon for ten years when I decided to get back into the program to make sure I had my feet on the ground before I divorced my husband. One word I heard at meetings that caught my attention was "courtesy." That was something I felt I could do.

Our relationship had deteriorated to such a state that my effort to be more courteous soon got my husband's attention. He said my words sounded nice, but that he didn't believe that I meant them. I told him he was right. I didn't really feel the kindness that

A More Positive Perspective   45

I was expressing in words. I was practicing what I had learned in Al-Anon about how to behave in a relationship. I got pretty good at it too, and slowly I began to feel the kindness I expressed. It was a humbling experience for me because I had thought my husband was the problem.

Today things are far from perfect, but I have grown enough to be able to enjoy all the good there is in my life, including my relationships. My kids' rooms are still messy, but we enjoy expressing the love we feel for one another. Even my husband isn't the ogre I thought he was. He is who he is, and often I'm even glad of that. We laugh together at our imperfections and make plans for our future.

I no longer get in the way of the good things. The good in my loved ones now shines through for me to enjoy.

⤔⦿⤕

My mother was the alcoholic—sometimes hitting, often blaming. My father was cold, absent, and sexually abusive. I have not seen either of them for years.

I was desperate when I came to Al-Anon just a few months ago. I was spending a lot of time trying to decide if I should kill my father in order to stop him from raping other children. I wondered how I could hurt my mother as much as she hurt me. I was also trying to decide how to kill myself in the most painless and effective way. What I really wanted was a way to live.

As a child, I was not allowed to show my feelings. I still don't understand how it works, but in Al-Anon there are people who can listen to me. There are people who tell parts of my story and express their feelings.

The other night my feelings caught me by surprise as I was drifting off to sleep. I was thinking, hoping, and praying that one day Mum would find peace, comfort, hope, and goodness in her own way, as I have found in Al-Anon. I still cannot visit her—it's too crazy and too dangerous for me—but it is worthwhile to fix, ease, and heal myself.

My wife was the drinker, but I was the absentee father during the last 15 years of her drinking, when it was really bad. Being at work 12 hours a day and in graduate school many evenings, I seldom saw my three children, except on weekends. Even then, I was busy with home projects and had little patience with my girls and their childish questions. I was obsessed with my work and education, oblivious to my children's needs for parenting. I didn't realize that my wife was becoming increasingly impaired, and I was not keeping up my role as a father.

Toward the end of my wife's drinking, only my youngest daughter, then in her early teens, was left at home; she was increasingly rebellious. In my blindness, I did not see that she was practically motherless and was lacking a supportive father.

I was far away on business when the worst happened—a serious physical conflict between mother and daughter. Rushing home as soon as possible, I found out that my daughter had run away to save herself from bodily harm. I was upset, but concentrated on finding her, which I did. I was very angry with my wife and could hardly speak to her. How did we get into this mess?

I had just been in Al-Anon a short time. With my daughter safe, I concentrated on my work and my program. My wife attempted suicide on two occasions before she started her long-term recovery in A.A.

The first year of her sobriety was very wild, with great swings of mood and emotion. By the end of the second year, we were beginning to settle down and relate to each other better using the principles embodied in the Twelve Steps. Gradually our daughters came back into our lives, and we began to rebuild our family structure. After four years of recovery, we began to have family holiday gatherings with a small degree of politeness. There were even signs of healing, and expressions of caring were exchanged.

It was such a relief for me to see my family members loving each other again after the long history of bitter conflict. We no longer approached family get-togethers with dread. My relationship with my wife was healing, and things were really looking up.

But at six years of recovery, I found I was lazily expecting my spouse to read my mind, putting a heavy and unfair strain on her. With the help of a therapist, progress in our individual programs, and God's help, we began to communicate much better and our relationship became better than ever.

We now have 24 years of continuous recovery in A.A. and Al-Anon, and life is good. Our three daughters who were damaged by growing up in an alcoholic home now enjoy a loving relationship with us and have long since forgiven us for our insane behaviors. We are truly blessed.

⌐✖⌐

I try to make every day a day of gratitude. This morning I woke up feeling especially grateful because my husband is sober. Last night he turned to me for comfort and fell asleep while holding my hand, from tiredness rather than from the side effects of an empty bottle. Without A.A. and Al-Anon, that would not have been possible and we wouldn't be together today.

We met when we were 11 and 12 years old. I was attracted to him because he was the first person to understand the chaos I was growing up with. Everyone else I knew seemed to have a normal family with a mom and a dad, sisters, brothers, and a dog that all lived together.

I remember when my husband took his first drink. My stepfather gave it to him as part of his initiation into manhood. That was the day both our illnesses began to spin out of control. I knew fairly early on that he had a problem, but I thought I was being a good friend by ignoring it and staying quiet. Besides, we were young, irresponsible kids. I thought we were supposed to be out drinking, smoking pot, and having a good time.

After I left for college, it became harder and harder to pretend that my friend didn't have a problem. One night when I was home on a break, he called me while extremely angry, drunk, and depressed because his girlfriend had dumped him. He had a gun, and told me there was one bullet in the chamber. He said he was going to leave it up to chance whether or not he should continue living. I threatened to call his father or the police, but he knew my words were empty threats. He eventually passed out and we didn't speak about what happened that night for a long time. When I finally confronted him years later, I realized that he had no memory of it and probably never would. However, I could no longer deny that he had a problem, or that his problem was having a profound effect on me. Regardless, I continued to enable him by tolerating inappropriate behavior.

Eventually I got to the point in my early 20s where I couldn't cope with his problems on top of my own, and I walked away from our friendship. I was never honest with him about how his drinking and drug abuse affected me. Therefore he thought I had severed our friendship to appease the possessive man I was involved with at the time.

The whole time we were estranged, I continued to worry about him. Several years after being apart and still not being able to let go, I decided to try and make amends by sending a letter stating I was sorry. His response made it apparent that he still had a problem. I made the decision to walk away a second time, but this time I was going to be honest about it. Before I had the chance, however, he showed up at my door newly sober.

Unfortunately, while he was beginning his recovery, my illness was still affecting my life. I mistakenly thought that since I no longer lived with my alcoholic relatives and he was sober, I was no longer affected by alcoholism. The next couple of years turned out to be rough for both of us. He struggled with his sobriety, and I struggled with the unhealthy patterns that had become my life. By then, I was in a second marriage that was falling apart, and my grandfather was dying due to complications from alcoholism. Although I lived several hours away from my grandparents, I was the one being asked to make difficult decisions, commuting every weekend with my infant in tow. I was taking care of business that really wasn't mine.

As my health started to deteriorate, I realized that something had to change. I also didn't want my daughter to grow up with the insanity I had experienced and be unable to form or maintain healthy, meaningful relationships with others. I went to an Al-Anon meeting.

Ironically, this man was the main reason I kept going back. When our friendship evolved into something more, I was jealous of his A.A. program. I was angry that his sobriety came first because I wanted to be first. I hated the fact that he could share things with his Sponsor that he wouldn't share with me. Through Al-Anon I've learned that we wouldn't be together if his sobriety didn't come first. There are things about my husband he can't share with me because I wouldn't understand. I'm not an alcoholic. I've also learned in Al-Anon that there are things about me, as a result of my experiences with alcohol, which he will never understand. And that is okay.

We wouldn't be happily married today if we weren't active in A.A. and Al-Anon. I still have a lot of work to do. I recognize that recovery is a lifelong process, not the three months I originally anticipated (Twelve Steps at one Step a week equals three months). Although I am far better off today than I was two years ago, I'm finally able to acknowledge that parts of me may never be put back together just right. "Progress Not Perfection" was a very hard concept for me to grasp, but it has become the key to my ongoing recovery, as well as the success in my marriage.

⌐⧠⌐

A few months ago, I had the opportunity to get to know an old acquaintance from high school who had moved out of town shortly after graduation. I was quite fond of her back then, a little obsessed even, but never really got to know her. It was something I regretted, and I had promised myself that I would make it right if I had another chance.

We went out for coffee and movies and got to know each other a little better. After awhile I began to realize one of the reasons I was so drawn to her—she was an alcoholic. Instantly a million flags went up in my mind about how bad it would be to get into a relationship with an alcoholic who was still drinking. At meetings I had heard others share about being raised in an alcoholic home, as I had been, and then going on to fall in love with an alcoholic. I thought that was silly and absurd. I surely wouldn't do that myself. Yet there I was, completely in love with this woman whom I knew would drive me mad if I got together with her. So after talking with my Sponsor, I let it go "Just for Today" and it worked.

Several weeks later something totally unexpected happened. The young woman realized she had a problem and reached out to me. I wondered if I had been lucky enough to meet her right as she was sobering up, and I took her to her first A.A. meeting. Unfortunately, I expected far too much from her, and took on her recovery as my responsibility. The next week, we met in a pub and she ordered a beer. She asked me if I was disappointed in her and I quickly replied that I was impressed that she even went to a meeting in the first place, which I was.

I now realize that everybody who needs the program has to come to it in their own time. No matter how much I love them or how much I want them to stop drinking, I will only drive myself mad trying to do it for them.

I still call her to see how she's doing and to let her know that I still care. I would like to get into a relationship with her, but realize now is not the time. We both still need time to work on ourselves.

⌒⟨⟩⌒

From an early age, I witnessed my violent, abusive, alcoholic grandmother mistreat my mother. I was so grateful that my mother was sober. By the time I was ten, my older sister developed the same alcoholic tendencies as my grandmother. I watched my sober mother tangle with my sister just as she had with her own mother. I was just grateful that I did not have a desire to drink or use drugs and that I wasn't giving my mother trouble the way these other women were. In time my way of coping became ongoing despair.

For a long time I stayed away from Al-Anon because I believed that I wouldn't be wanted. My problems were too small and meaningless. I had visions of the members laughing at me and throwing me out the door into the streets because I was too full of self-pity. I didn't think that my problems mattered. I feared being trapped in a room full of needy, victimized women like my mother. I also feared recreating the emotional dishonesty that has been a characteristic of my relationship with my mother. Within the first week of Al-Anon meetings I felt a kind of loving support I had never had.

I attended an open A.A. meeting and discovered that I felt an all-encompassing revulsion toward female alcoholics—even though they were in recovery. I decided to look at that feeling. I began to see the women who attended both programs as a bridge. I started to see how linked our situations were and made a heartfelt connection with an older woman who had been working the A.A. program for 20 years. I was a child again, ready to latch onto her apron strings and follow her anywhere. She was so wise and loving. I started to quiz her about what meetings she went to so I could start going to those meetings too. She gently touched my arm, smiled, and told me that if we were meant to be together, we would find each other. I haven't seen her since, but I think of her every time I look into the face of a woman struggling with alcoholism—in any of its manifestations.

I no longer find it necessary to label women as either alcoholics or enablers. I no longer feel revulsion for such women—a revulsion I had transferred to all women. I no longer have to shut out all women for fear that they will use my emotions against me. I have developed better judgment about whom I can or cannot trust. I can see beyond the human flaws that we all share; I can see the woman within, struggling for freedom.

After a lifetime of feeling that I don't belong and not knowing why, I have been able to bring down the walls I built and release myself from the bondage of false attitudes and expectations.

⟡

My life spiraled out of control about four years ago. At least that's when I became aware of it. Things began to fall apart when my daughter decided she would leave her husband and bring her children to live with my husband and me.

Since I thought my way has always been the right and only way, I expected my daughter to always listen when I was trying to tell her what to do and how to do it. Somehow she just wasn't getting it and continued doing what I knew was wrong. I persisted in yelling, screaming, belittling, shaming, and threatening her. She continued on the path of alcoholism.

It all came to a crisis one night when she angrily told me to get out of her life and get a life of my own. She also informed me that everything bad in her life was my fault because it was all about me. In my despair I went with my husband to a counselor, who told us to look into Al-Anon. We went because we wanted to learn how to get our daughter to stop drinking. To my surprise, I've come to realize that after spending too much of my life trying to fix everybody and everything else, I was the person I needed to fix.

⟡

My relationship with my daughter had steadily worsened through her preteen years. By the time she was 12, we were in an unending battle of wills. She became depressed. I had grown up in an alcoholic home, and I had been depressed at her age. I told myself it was normal and she would grow out of it. She was suicidal, but so was I at her age. I loved her and desperately wanted to fix things for her, but didn't know how. The situation steadily worsened.

After one argument, my exasperation was too much for me. I was out of control, screaming over and over, "It's just like living with a drunk!" My explosive reaction forced me to see that my relationship with my daughter felt just like my alcoholic mother's relationship with me.

I turned to my brother for help. He listened to me and told me that going to Al-Anon meetings would help. Things stayed tough with my daughter for a long time, but I found hope even from my first meeting. I heard that if you say something once, you are communicating. If you repeat yourself over and over, you are no longer communicating; you are trying to manipulate and control. I did that constantly with my daughter. I never said something once, even something as simple as "Brush your teeth." I didn't see my harping for what it was until I heard another person talk about it at a meeting.

At home I tried my best to stop nagging. Sometimes I had to bite my tongue or put my hand over my mouth after I had said something the first time. I didn't always know why the tools would work, but I knew my old ways had failed me, and I was willing to try anything.

I had always tried to solve my daughter's problems. Somehow I had just assumed that my role was to make everything right in the lives of everyone around me. I stopped, shut up, and just listened. I was amazed to see that the simple, sincere act of truly listening to my daughter was worth more than all the advice I had ever tried to give her.

After quite a while in the program, it occurred to me that I ought to start sharing the hugs I got at meetings with my family members. This took a lot of courage. We had never hugged in my family while I was growing up, and it was not a common practice in my home with my daughter. At first when I hugged her, she just stood still, unmoving and unresponsive. She even stiffened, as though to repel my touch. I had also heard at meetings that I should have the courage to do what I think is right and let go of the reactions of others. I let go of my daughter's silent, subtle revulsion, and just kept giving hugs.

It took years, but one day, to my surprise, she hugged me back. It was a weak hug, a tentative hug, but a hug nonetheless. I look back at that hug as symbolic of the repair that had been taking place in my relationship with my daughter as a result of my focusing on myself, my actions, my words—and just trying to focus on doing the next right thing. I knew I felt better about myself, and as my relationship with my daughter steadily improved, I had tangible proof that when one person starts to recover, there are beneficial effects on all family members.

Today, nine years later, my daughter is one of my best friends. When she's home from college, she'll sometimes walk up to me and give me a big, long hug—for no reason except that I'm Mom and she loves me.

For Thought and Discussion:

1. What areas of my life have I been neglecting—or worrying about too much—out of shame or embarrassment?
2. What beliefs do I have about the roles of men or women that are no longer serving me in a healthy way?
3. What words would I use to describe the quality of my emotional intimacy with my loved ones?
4. What emotional needs do I have that I'm reluctant to face directly?
5. How has my ability to have healthy sexual relationships been affected by alcoholism?
6. What are some of the ways I can take care of myself?

Chapter Four

We Begin to Know Ourselves

The Al-Anon program asks us to keep our attention on our own lives and detach with love from the drama and turmoil created by alcoholism. When we first hear these words, the meaning may escape us. Old feelings of anxiety might arise, but we don't have to hold on to these fears. Guided by the Serenity Prayer, we can find some stability when we detach from what we can't control and sharpen our focus on what we can change within ourselves.

Many of us have kept our focus on the problem drinker for so long that we have forgotten about ourselves. We may find it easy to list the details of the drinker's issues, but have neglected our own lives to the point where we are out of touch with our personal needs and preferences. In filling our minds with mental chatter about someone else's business, it is easy to lose focus on ourselves and ignore the present moment. Our obsessions keep us trapped in the past, and our fears throw us into a future made purely of our worst imaginings. We can exhaust ourselves without moving a muscle. While there might be spiritual resources available to us, we are usually too distracted to notice.

Through sharing our struggles with other Al-Anon members, we can begin to gain some perspective on our problems and some detachment from our self-created dramas. When we begin to listen to other members share honestly about themselves, we can reflect on our own situation. We have the opportunity to become more aware of how we feel in the present moment.

The Al-Anon program reminds us that whatever arises—problem or opportunity—there are people who can help us with their stories of courage, strength, and hope. Instead of focusing on our disappointments and anxieties, we can read Conference Approved Literature or call an Al-Anon friend who has faced similar challenges. Reaching out to fellow members is a safe way to learn skills for building healthy relationships. These contacts can be helpful and supportive—and some of them evolve into genuine friendships. We are also encouraged to study the Twelve Steps with a Sponsor—a trusted Al-Anon member who has also walked along this path.

Genuine care for our new Al-Anon friends might cause us to question our old attitudes about friendship and love. We are urged to notice the difference between love and control. There is a tremendous freedom to be experienced when we "Let Go and Let God." By allowing others to decide for themselves how to live their lives and face the consequences of their actions—good or bad—without our interference, we become free to concentrate on what is truly ours to change.

When we're caught in negative thoughts about someone else's problem drinking, gratitude for anything—much less gratitude for anything about ourselves—may be the last thing we feel we have time to consider. But taking five minutes to begin a gratitude list is an excellent first step in a time of crisis. Starting a gratitude list puts the focus on ourselves, even if only for a short while. It also puts the negative aspects of our situation into a broader framework that also includes positive factors. Writing a gratitude list can be the beginning of a lifelong process of learning how to see our lives in a more positive light. It only takes a few minutes to start, but ultimately it can have profound benefits. Our gratitude list will keep growing the more we add to it. When we adopt an attitude of gratitude, there is less room in our lives for self-pity, control, and despair. If we are no longer trying to change others, it is possible to see the good qualities they have to offer.

While our gratitude allows us to begin to appreciate the good qualities that we already have, in time it can also reveal to us the parts of our lives that we are capable of changing. As we change, our gratitude increases even more. We can create a new foundation for our lives, based on looking for the best life has to offer instead of the worst. As we do so, our attention shifts further and further away from things we can't control.

It's much easier for us to mind our own business when we have clarity and understanding of who we are. Al-Anon shows us that it is possible to be satisfied and happy, no matter what is going on around us, including whether or not the alcoholic is drinking. With each day, we can learn how to define who we are without waiting for others to agree. We can begin to develop and enjoy a new perception of ourselves. We take small steps, try different options, and get used to different outcomes. Slowly we learn that it's okay to take care of ourselves. When we are being good to ourselves, we are better able to make a positive contribution to the lives of all those we love, including the alcoholic.

We can look at what we can do "Just for Today" and let that be enough for now. As we grow in the Al-Anon program, our list of positives can keep growing.

Personal Stories

It was a stormy night. I stood at the window staring out at the dark street, trying to "will" each pair of headlights into our driveway. I focused on my missing alcoholic husband. Occasionally one of our four children would try to speak to me. I brushed them off, ignoring their hunger as well as my own. I remember saying, "Can't you see that I'm busy?" and didn't think how incongruous it was to expect that I looked busy when I was staring out a window.

Suddenly what I call an Al-Anon miracle occurred. I realized that I was focusing on the alcoholic and not on my own responsibilities. I went downstairs, prepared supper, and discussed plans for the next day with my children. We had shopping to do in a nearby town, and with my new focus I realized that we would do it, whether the alcoholic came home or not. And so we did.

During the following months, I grew in my strength of focus. I no longer became angry at the children when the alcoholic didn't behave as I wanted. My relationship with our children improved because I was no longer the unpredictable person I had been. I began to practice the Twelve Steps at home.

My children, now adults, love and respect me, and they even ask for my advice sometimes. I love and respect them, and I am careful to keep the focus on myself. I do not to try to control anyone else's life.

⌒⤳✖⤳⌒

My Sponsor suggested that I start a gratitude list that would have no ending. Each day I would write down at least three things that gave me some measure of gratitude. At first I sat staring at the page, trying to come up with anything more than "still breathing." My Sponsor laughed and said, "That's always a good beginning."

I still found it difficult to stop thinking about what the alcoholic in my life might be doing right at that minute. I felt discouraged by my inability to change my way of thinking and do my simple task. My Sponsor smiled with kindness and asked me, "If you were the new person on a job, would you be expected to know everything in the first few months?"

That helped me gain some perspective and I went back to my task. To refocus my wandering attention, I found a small rock with rough edges to remind myself that anything grasped too tightly can begin to cause pain. I carried the rock loosely in my hand as I walked around my neighborhood, looking for reasons to be grateful. Every time I thought about the rock, I looked for something right around me that could fill me with appreciation.

I still noticed the crabgrass along with the flowers, but at least the flowers were finally in my view. Along the way, I found out my neighbor was rebuilding an antique car and the people down the street were adopting a child. I admired the Asian garden around the corner with the small waterfall, and I helped an older neighbor carry groceries from her car. Her gratitude for my small service filled me with joy. Suddenly I had more than three things to write down on my never-ending list of gratitude. It was getting harder to keep track of the details that didn't belong to me. I was building my own life.

I had become willing to stop and notice what was already there. Problems and challenges still came up; there were moments when I forgot everything that I had learned, but they didn't come as often.

A day came when the alcoholic created his own crisis, and I was able to step back and let him handle it as he saw fit. I was no longer in charge of the outcome because I had my own life. I took out my never-ending list and added something new—gratitude for the people in my life who live with the disease of alcoholism.

⌐◦≫◦⌐

I would always describe my relationship with my son as the best that life had given me. From the day he was born, we clicked. He was truly the light of my life. I always felt like a good mother when dealing with my son. Our son loved Alateen and attended faithfully. I felt we were saving him from the possibility of the disease of alcoholism by driving him 45 miles each way to a weekly Alateen meeting for three years. All would be well by our own hands, I thought.

At age 15, my son had his first brush with the legal system. My husband and I felt that this was just a one-time incident, a small matter that we could deal with by hiring a good attorney. We knew this good kid wasn't really to blame; he had just been influenced by some bad kids that night. We just knew the drinking that occurred was accidental. This kid knew and understood the disease of alcoholism.

Small incidents continued over the next two years, and we still felt it was a normal teenage experience. We made use of all the help available. We felt that we just had to navigate him through the teenage years and that it was all up to us and within our power, if we just did the right things. The tough times really began when, because of drug and alcohol use, he decided to drop out of sports and school at the beginning of his junior year in high school. He was still underage, and we decided to put him into treatment. Our son turned 18 while in a halfway house. He came home a few months later.

Little did we know that this was the beginning of a long, sad, heartbreaking time. Within 24 hours of returning from the halfway house, our son chose drugs and alcohol again. We watched as he did everything in his power to destroy the life we would have chosen for him. We learned as parents what powerlessness really was.

My Sponsor also has a son. With her help and guidance, I learned that I needed to see my son as the young man he was and not as a helpless little boy. I learned that the word "using" meant not only drugs and alcohol, but people—myself included. I learned that when I chose to stop enabling him, he would find someone else to do the job.

No one enjoys watching a much-loved son choose homelessness rather than living drug- and alcohol-free in a secure, safe home. No one enjoys having a son disappear for months only to reappear over the holidays asking to stay in his old room or to sleep in the garage. No parent dreams of her gentle, sensitive child joining a gang in an attempt to meet his needs or choosing drugs or alcohol over high school and college. No one wants the heartbreak of seeing her child after a stretch on the streets, sitting before her, dirty, grimy, and broken. No one wants to hear that her child has been sleeping on a park bench. No one understands this except another parent who is walking this path.

I came to realize that no matter what I wanted or dreamt for this child, it was what he wanted for his life that mattered. I learned that I was powerless.

My only healthy choice was to focus on me and what I needed in my life. At first I took up swimming because it was easy to swim and cry. No one notices the tears with water all over your face, and no one hears the sobs under water. In time, though, I learned the valuable lesson that I would be okay, no matter what happened outside me. I learned that I would not die of a broken heart.

The most powerful lesson I received was how to depend on a Higher Power. So many miracles happened during this time. At times we would not hear from our son for several months. Most of the time, I would live by the adage, "No news is good news." At other times, I would feel I could not stand it anymore and I would ask my Higher Power to let me hear from him. Always, at this point, I would receive a phone call from our son within 24 hours and feel the strength to do what was before me.

My Higher Power brought so many people into my life to take my hand and walk with me. I learned that good could come out of this situation if I looked for it. And it did. I learned that I have a life to be lived and I have a right to live it without all the pain and destruction that other people's choices bring into their lives. I learned to love unconditionally for the first time in my life.

Our son is now 26. I love him dearly and we have a good relationship. He works and supports himself in a city four hours from us. I still wonder sometimes if he is okay, but I work to remember that he has a Higher Power guiding his life and it isn't me. I trust in his Higher Power's plan for his life and live my life "Just for Today." I have learned that it is okay to take care of myself. I have become used to experiencing joy and peace—and I like it.

⌒⟨✕⟩⟁

Today I visited my brother at the prison. As I listened to him, I saw the effects of alcoholism. He was blaming everyone and everything else for why he was in prison. I didn't feel the need to confront him, fix him, or make it easier for him. I just listened. I didn't take responsibility for the way he was feeling. I was just there.

His feelings didn't ruin my day or make me terribly sad. I was just grateful that by the grace of God, I had been given a chance to change the way I view my life through the blessings of the Al-Anon program. I didn't feel angry that my brother was in prison. I felt grateful that there is such a place for him to be where he can't hurt anyone else and where maybe, just maybe, he will finally reach out for help from the recovery programs that are offered through the prison.

I walked away from the prison full of hope, gratitude, and the comforting knowledge that I am doing all I am supposed to do. I can pray to my Higher Power on behalf of my brother. I know that no matter where I am, the best gift I can give others is my presence, a listening ear, and a prayer. Today I know that I can have healthy relationships.

⌒⟨✕⟩⟁

I married a woman raised in a home with an alcoholic father. Al-Anon has proven to be a valuable resource to me in the way I relate to my two children, who are now both young adults.

My son would often tell me about his problems, and my reaction would be to try to help fix them. About ten years ago, I came to believe that wrestling my son's responsibilities away from him was not helping him and was unhealthy for both of us. Now when he shares a problem with me, I am able to say, "Yes, that is a big problem you have, but I believe you can handle it." Our relationship has improved since I started giving my new responses.

When I first heard about Step One in Alateen, I realized how much it applied to me. My father is a recovering alcoholic. When I was about ten, he went into a rehab center. About a year later, he relapsed. As he drank more and more, my life became uncontrollable. I constantly told myself lies so that I wouldn't have to face reality. My father's drinking got to the point that my mom sent me to my older sister's house. My mom was going to decide whether or not she was going to leave my dad. I had to admit that my father's drinking had made my life unmanageable and that no matter how much I loved my father, I couldn't make him stop drinking.

My relationship with my daughter was always close, but it changed for the better as I worked on my recovery. In the past, I would vent and confide in her when I was upset with my husband's drinking. She was a good listener and always took my side. As I learned new ideas in Al-Anon, I began to see that this was inappropriate because she was just a teenager.

I began to let go of my husband's actions and stopped venting to my daughter. Instead, I explained to her about alcoholism being a disease. I told her it was best for her father to make his own decisions about his drinking. She and I could start to find other things to enjoy. We are still close, but our focus has changed. We leave the alcoholic out of our conversations unless it is a positive thing we want to share about him. We discuss our successes, dreams, and mistakes. We try to mind our own business and share only what's appropriate for a mother and daughter to share.

After my divorce, I was certain that I would never date another problem drinker. In time, however, the woman I was dating admitted that she had had a problem with drinking several years before, shortly after her own divorce. Eventually she admitted that she had attended A.A. meetings—as a social opportunity, she said, to meet people who were in recovery. Perhaps that reason for attending A.A. should have been a warning sign that she had some level of denial about her own drinking, but by that time I already liked her very much and wasn't looking for reasons to stop seeing her. Then one day she had some drinks at a business meeting, and our evening plans changed. She got drunk, which I enjoyed since she was far more physically affectionate to me than she had been previously. She drank several times after that, and was always more amorous with me than she was without drinking. I enjoyed the affection, such as it was, but it got me wondering about how much she actually liked me or whether it was just alcoholic behavior that had nothing to do with me.

At one level, it was a replay of my relationship with my former wife: Once again I found myself loving an attractive, exciting woman with some serious personal problems that would have sent someone else running for the nearest exit. At least this time I could clearly see that I didn't cause her drinking, and I understood that whether she drinks or not is entirely her issue, not mine.

My life is better when I can give love and encouragement to someone without any ulterior motive, whether for their own good or not. Giving love and wanting to control someone else are two different things. I take my relationship with this woman "One Day at a Time." It will be time to leave if I start wanting to change things I can't control.

⌀

My daughter recently returned from her sixth rehabilitation treatment program for drug and alcohol abuse. She came home sounding strong and hopeful.

One night, my cell phone rang. When I answered, the caller hung up. I immediately thought the worst. I created numerous scenarios that could have prompted the call, including that my daughter was dead. After all these months in Al-Anon, I suddenly forgot it all. I took the cell phone into my bed and lay there, praying and meditating all night. No return call came. In the light of the morning, I checked the phone number and realized that it was unknown to me. A voice in my head asked, "What if it wasn't bad news about my daughter?"

Within the hour, my cell phone rang again. This time I answered it in time to hear a kind, male voice saying, "I called you by mistake last night. I was trying to reach a friend of mine. His number is only one digit different from yours. I apologize and hope that I didn't cause you any concern." I was amazed. I thanked the young man for his thoughtfulness. I told him that indeed I had worried about my daughter, who must live near him, but that I was wrong to have worried.

Within another hour, my daughter called to talk about how things were going—a routine call. Finally I told her what had happened the previous night. She said she could understand why I reacted the way I had, and said she had heard similar stories from others in her A.A. group. Then she said, "Mother, I think your Higher Power was trying to tell you something." I had to laugh. In fact, we both laughed. Here was the voice of reason and wisdom coming from my alcoholic daughter. Here I was the sick one, having created an insane situation from one misdialed phone call.

<hr />

At my first meeting, someone mentioned that I didn't cause my wife's drinking, I can't control it, and I can't cure it. It was a relief to know that I didn't cause her to become an alcoholic, but the control part took a lot longer to grasp. It took a while for me to really understand that I can't control her or her behavior. However, I did remember from the Serenity Prayer that I could change myself. I accepted that it is not my right to tell other people how to conduct their lives. I don't know what is best for them, nor is it my right to decide that for them.

I also finally acknowledged that my wife was going to die if she did not quit drinking. It was extremely difficult to sit back and watch her spiral ever deeper into some sort of darkness that I didn't understand. But I could accept that it was her decision, not mine. My son kept asking me to stop her from drinking. I tried without much success to explain to him why I couldn't do that. Now I don't attempt to explain, which avoids useless arguments and a considerable amount of frustration on my part.

$\sim\!\!\infty\!\!\sim$

I came to Al-Anon feeling totally alone, completely helpless and hopeless. I felt like I must be the only mom of an alcoholic. My pain had reached the point where I didn't think I could take anymore. How could someone I loved so much, my youngest son, put me through this misery? It seemed that all of my help made matters worse. How could my loving intentions turn out to be so wrong?

I thought I was helping when my husband and I cruised up and down unfamiliar, dangerous, big-city streets looking for his car. I thought I was helping while we checked out his car that was pulled over to the side of the street. I thought I was helping when our son finally telephoned, and I kept talking to him as his dad drove miles away to pick him up.

I've come to realize that the disease of alcoholism can be fed by the good intentions of loved ones. Consequences were not allowed to happen, because I was too busy helping.

Alcoholism is a progressive disease. All the love in the world could not stop the disease from growing worse. There came a time when we didn't hear anything from our son for eight months. When he called, he was extremely consumed by alcoholism. He gave me a phone number, which I put in a box for God to handle. That kept me from checking to see if my son needed my help. Putting that phone number in my God box kept God in charge and not me.

When my husband and I went to an Al-Anon International Convention, it was all I could do to keep from issuing an all-points bulletin to ask the thousands of people there to look for a small gray pick-up truck. Our son was waiting for us when we returned home. It had been more than a year since we had actually been able to hug him. He stayed three or four days, and once again the disease of alcoholism took him out of our lives for another seemingly endless period of time.

A few months later, I got a call from him. He was in jail 1,500 miles from our home. We did not go to help this time. I increased my meetings and took my first three-year service position. Being a District Treasurer kept my focus where I really could be of help.

My term as District Treasurer ended just a few days before our son was released from prison. He came home the way his Higher Power intended—as a member of Alcoholics Anonymous. He came home healthy and whole—without my help.

Today my son, my family, and I have a relationship in recovery that far exceeds the relationship we had within the family disease. We love, respect, admire, and value each other and our time together as a family. We support one another's activities. We are there for one another in the challenges and the opportunities life has to offer.

⌒⌒⌒

Mum left everything to Dad when she died, which turned into a long lesson in detachment for me. Mum had only been dead a year when he helped out a pregnant, alcoholic, marijuana smoker by moving her into her own house in another town three hours away. Both their names were on the title, but Dad paid for it all. He hoped she'd look after him too. A month later he left and came back to his own home. She eventually took off with a lot of our mother's furniture that Dad had left behind.

It was really difficult to accept that as old as he was, my dad was just a beginner. He had never been given the opportunity before to run his own affairs. Here he was at 68 years old, having to act like a grown up who knew how to do his own budgeting, when he had very little experience.

I had been expecting my dad to know what to do simply because he was older than me. It set me up for many disappointments and restless nights of worry and frustration. Even though I wanted to, I didn't have the right to tell him how to run his life. I kept going back to my meetings. I kept talking to God and to my Sponsor. It is in those trying times that I have to break the days into "One Day at a Time" and let my dad live his life, without my interference.

Dad is now 74 years old and I think he has learned a lot of things since my mum died. It doesn't mean I agree with the decisions he makes. I have even been candid enough to say so.

I can recognize that Dad's intentions toward anyone he has helped were honorable. My father has a generous spirit. Maybe he is practicing unconditional love better than I am.

Without my Al-Anon program, I would have a totally unmanageable life. I need Al-Anon's way of life every day to enjoy and be grateful for what I do have. It's too easy for me to slip back into old behavior.

I am a 45-year-old single man and the son of an alcoholic mother. Ten years ago I left an unhealthy marriage and began attending Al-Anon Family Groups. I have had three relationships since my divorce. I've grown through each of them, but I am having a really hard time letting go of the most recent one. I obsess about her, which was a problem in my marriage as well. We often get locked in a conflict of wills. This is still better than my marriage, when I didn't feel that it was okay to have a will of my own. Then I expressed my desires in absolutes, such as, "We need to visit my parents every year," or in fits of rage that would end in sarcasm or with my slamming the door and going for a long walk.

Now I'm working on praying for the people I resent as well as for the people I love. This type of prayer is a wonderful tool, freeing me from obsessing about what is none of my business.

After having been in Al-Anon for a while, I became a bit smug. I thought I had my problems with an alcoholic relationship under control. Then God saw fit to put another alcoholic in my life—my son. I was on my knees and back at Step One. During an especially difficult period, I was sure my son would die. My Sponsor soothed me and suggested that I plant some seeds. I said to her, "Do you mean plant Al-Anon seeds and call a newcomer?" She replied, "No, I mean plant some flower seeds." I asked how that would help my son and she said it wouldn't, but it might just help me. So I did it. Each year since that time, my son and I watch the columbines grow and bloom.

The year he was in prison, I sent him a picture of our columbines. Thank you, God, for allowing me to continue this new loving relationship with my adult child. I told him the story of the seeds. Whether he is still drinking or not, we are able to hug one another and smile in the warmth of God's love.

I crawled into Al-Anon completely obsessed with my lover. The people in these rooms suggested that I show up for the next six meetings. I learned that my pain could be the motivation to love myself.

I learned that detachment is neither kind nor unkind. I learned to be courteous and to have warm, personal regard for all people at all times. I learned that setting boundaries protects me and helps me to create space just for me. I learned how to separate from her by focusing on my problems and finding my solutions. I heard about how to be honest, open-minded, and willing. I sought to truly get off her back, get out of her way, and get on with my own life. My obsession with her life and then the detachment was very painful. I went through withdrawal after withdrawal seeking answers by listening carefully to the stories in these rooms. I worked the first three Steps over and over and then asked myself, what is my part in this?

My job is to take care of myself, step out of the drama and chaos, breathe while saying the Serenity Prayer, "Keep it Simple," and take "One Day at a Time." This keeps my feeling of being overwhelmed to a minimum.

For Thought and Discussion:

1. What is the difference between a relationship based on love and one based on control?
2. What three things can I be grateful for today that don't depend on another person?
3. How do I feel in this present moment?
4. Do my thoughts distract me from my feelings or do they keep me focused on certain feelings?
5. How does the Serenity Prayer apply to what is worrying me now?
6. What is one positive thing I can do for myself today?

Chapter Five

Recognizing that a Better Way Is Possible

As we recover from the effects of alcoholism, we begin to notice that our feelings provide information that can help guide our actions, regardless of how we judge those feelings. Feelings are not positive or negative. It is our reactions to them that make us consider them so. When we pay attention to the particular feelings we have, we can begin to learn from them and bring our attention back to the simplicity of the present moment.

In the past, we may have felt locked into feelings of guilt, suspicion, or fear. We reacted automatically, as if our feelings were unavoidable facts rather than our interpretation of facts. Yet often there are more possibilities available to us than we immediately recognize, and our perception of the facts may be only a partial view. If we can begin to recognize that our feelings at any one moment may not be the final answer, we are better able to accept them as a source of useful information that could lead us in a positive direction. We don't have to avoid our feelings. Instead, we can let them teach us more about ourselves.

Many of us are afraid that the past will repeat itself. We base future expectations on our difficult past experience. This belief can be a great source of pessimism and anxiety for us, even though we're not really in any position to know for sure what the future will bring. Only a Higher Power could know that. Our certainty that a negative past will repeat itself, however, can become a self-fulfilling prophecy. We don't have to cling to negative beliefs such as "Things just never work out for me." Instead we can "Let Go and Let God."

How we react to our feelings is ultimately a choice. Almost everyone has had some discouragement or disappointment in relationships with other people; that's not a reason to conclude that there is no hope for something better. We have the opportunity to make amends when we've made an error and the freedom to learn a positive lesson from a negative situation.

The recognition that we have choices opens the door to hope—hope that despite the effects of alcoholism on our lives, we can find a more positive way of relating to other people. Once we realize that we are not permanently blocked by these negative effects, we can admit that there is a range of other possibilities. Even if we don't yet know what these positive possibilities could mean for us, we can begin to open our eyes to the many resources in Al-Anon available to help us broaden our vision.

If we choose, we can find ways to fill our moments with comfort, joy, and serenity. With the support and understanding that is always there for us in Al-Anon, we can find a different way to look at ourselves and others, leaving behind fears that once seemed insurmountable. As the Suggested Welcome to our meetings tells us, "We, too, were lonely and frustrated, but in Al-Anon we discover that no situation is really hopeless and that it is possible for us to find contentment, and even happiness, whether the alcoholic is still drinking or not."

Just as the Second Step informs us that sanity is indeed possible, it is also possible for us to have higher expectations about our lives and our relationships. It may take time to focus our efforts and attention on what we can change instead of what we can't. With help and guidance, however, we can see, first, that positive developments are possible, and second, that there are many ways to learn how to make this possibility a reality in our lives.

We can learn to open our hearts and be still. Growth often occurs in the quiet space between what has been and what is yet to come. When we start to listen, it becomes less tempting to fall back into old patterns. We can become aware that something else just might be possible. Some of us begin to turn our attention to a Power greater than ourselves and begin to trust that this Power will guide us. This trust requires us to accept that we don't always know what is best for us or what will happen next. We can't even be sure that we will always like everything that is headed in our direction. We might swing back and forth between the known and the unknown, wondering just how long we have to wait for answers. We know that solutions are possible, but we don't have to know what they are right away. Today we can allow them to unfold in their own ways, without our interference.

Good things take time. An acorn doesn't become an oak tree overnight, but its growth is certain though barely perceptible while it is happening. The roots of the oak tree find their way, growing around the rocks and sending off smaller shoots as needed. Obstacles are no surprise, and other routes become possible.

We can focus on growing strong and healthy each day. By keeping our focus only on what we can do today, we don't need to worry about how long it will take to achieve our goals. As we get to know ourselves better, we begin to establish our own healthy roots. We learn how to grow around our fears and challenges. We receive the tools necessary to grow stronger and more confident, standing a little taller each day. Life can become a journey to be enjoyed day-by-day.

Personal Stories

About a year after my wife and I were divorced, I went to a local bar to celebrate St. Patrick's Day. I was there for five minutes when I approached a young lady and started having a simple conversation with her. She told me she had just broken up with her boyfriend the prior evening and had been fired from her job that morning! Before Al-Anon, I would have stuck around to see if maybe I could help. Instead, I excused myself to the bathroom and escaped by the back door!

I wondered how I could have chosen the person with the most problems, and I began to see that I was unknowingly drawn to someone in pain. I was looking for people with sadness in their eyes and tended to avoid those who were having fun. No wonder I was meeting people who I thought needed fixing. This experience showed me a behavior I wasn't aware of before.

I tend to fear the future and lament the past. I take a situation I'm facing and project myself into the future, using my vivid imagination to turn a little incident into a full-blown science fiction horror movie with absolutely no basis in fact.

Sometimes I relive a painful memory from my past. I go through all of the same emotions and feel the anguish, anger, shame, and guilt that I did back then. Once I get done with that memory, I tell myself how stupid and foolish I was.

I use the tools of Al-Anon to help me. They include asking myself where my feet are at this very moment—in the here and now. I take a deep breath, ask my Higher Power to help me regain my serenity, and I take the time to become quiet and listen for my Higher Power's strength and wisdom. I do my best to "Keep It Simple."

While working my Ninth Step, my first amends were to my alcoholic wife, but I couldn't see that I also owed amends to my oldest son. Even though I was oblivious to his situation, he had clearly felt the brunt of the family disease of alcoholism. Eventually, I tried to make amends to him. I asked him how I could be a better father, but he couldn't tell me.

A month later, during a campfire meeting at an Alateen campout, the teens shared about the physical and emotional abuse they suffered in their alcoholic homes. In story after story, I heard the teens say what my son couldn't tell me. The awareness hurt so badly, I felt like crawling out of my skin.

These kids told my father's story of emotional abuse, my story, and my son's story. My son is at least the third generation who suffered this abuse. I prayed, and then shared with them. I told how I felt while listening to them and then hearing my son, knowing that I, the sober one, was the abuser. It hurt; I needed to start the healing process and I made amends. My son and I both cried.

I'd like to say that all is well at this point and that I'm now the perfect father. But like the slogan says, it's "Progress Not Perfection." We continue to work on our relationship today, and a lot of the healing comes from doing service together in the program.

⌐⟡⌐

A few years ago, my cat had a peculiar habit. When I opened the apartment door, he would slip through my legs into the public hall. I reacted by chasing him throughout the entire building. I must have been a sight: a 140-pound woman pursuing a 12-pound white cat. I hunted him up and down the halls on every floor of the building. One day it occurred to me not to follow the cat. I left my apartment door open and my cat returned after five minutes.

After this episode, I realized that I did not need to react to my cat. It represented how I interacted with people. I allowed my gut to rule without thinking.

In Al-Anon I learned that I don't need to react. I can wait, think things over, and make a decision that is best for me. I find that when I do not react quickly, I can act rationally. My cat still slips through my legs on occasion, but I don't chase him. I leave my apartment door open, and he comes back on his own. Today I don't quickly react to other people's actions. I allow myself time to make choices.

One day I was talking to a friend, telling her that I had been married 15 years and never had a fight with my partner. She said she didn't believe me. I thought it was something to be proud of. Some time later, I was talking to another friend about how hurt I was that my partner was drinking so much. I wondered why he was drinking day after day. She told me there was a place where she was going, and that I could come and listen to what they had to say.

I didn't believe what I was hearing at those first few Al-Anon meetings, but I thought, "My husband will never do that to me." But he did try to stop me from going to meetings; he hid the car keys from me. I didn't see his need to control as abusive. After a while, I realized that I didn't have a life. I never did anything without asking permission, and I only did what he wanted me to do. No wonder we never had a fight.

Now I can say I live for myself and do what I want—how, when, and where it is convenient for me. I don't depend on anybody for my happiness and have picked myself up off the floor. I love the person I've become. I am honest and generous. I speak my mind without being mean. I am a simple person. I am still with my partner, though we have had ups and downs. He doesn't have a program and the drinking only stopped in the last few years. There are still slips once in a while, but I know now that it doesn't have anything to do with me. I love the person, not the illness.

Before the Al-Anon program, my focus was entirely on the comfort of others. All my feelings about myself were demanding, demeaning, and derogatory. The slogan "Easy Does It" became my tool for change.

When I was in a quandary about a situation, an Al-Anon member would ask, "What would you suggest for me to do if I were in your shoes?" As I stepped back from the situation and viewed it from a different perspective, I was able to give myself the same care and consideration I had been giving away to others. My thoughts could gently turn to thinking kindly and respectfully about myself.

⎯⎯⎯∝⋙⎯∝⎯⎯⎯

Marrying an alcoholic satisfied my need to be needed. Yet I still had the feeling that I lacked something. I knew that I based my self-esteem on what I did for others, and I didn't have a good understanding of who I was. I learned to manipulate, control, and belittle, but beneath these behaviors was the belief that I couldn't live or support myself without my husband. I saw myself as a victim.

My denial was powerful. I blamed others and took everything too seriously. If someone was too happy, I found fault with that. Rather than tell my family or friends that my husband drank too much, I blamed my dissatisfaction on work and changed jobs a lot. Then my husband became sober, and I believed all our problems were behind us.

As it turned out, I wasn't ready to change—and my problems stayed with me. I continued to see him as the one with the problem. Six years later, my life was still unmanageable and I was angry, sad, and depressed. I knew I couldn't go on this way. At last, there was nothing left to blame for my unhappiness but me. A counselor lovingly suggested Al-Anon, and I began attending meetings. I am more aware of myself now, and can see areas of my life where I can improve. I now have a personal relationship with my Higher Power. I'm relieved to know that I don't need to know the way, because God does.

I have learned to respect my spouse and to show it. I let him be who he is and don't try to change him. The things I liked about him early in our relationship, which later became irritating, are once again endearing. We laugh together, work together, and sometimes play together. I have gratitude for the situation I'm in, which is living with an alcoholic. It has turned out to be my path to learning how to love myself.

⌒✄⌒

When my wife and I had reached a rocky point in our marriage, it scared me because I had already been through one divorce. My tendency was to run from problems. I didn't know how to talk and reason things out. When a problem arose between my wife and me, I would just freeze up. I couldn't think, let alone be reasonable. I was more concerned about being right than working things out. I insisted on my way or else.

Before Al-Anon, I had thought of my wife and daughter as possessions. They must do as I say, not as I do. I thought I was God and that somehow I knew what they should do and think. Growing up with alcoholism, I never learned how to build a healthy relationship of trust and mutual respect. I learned in Al-Anon to place principles above personalities. I also learned, "You may be right," and "How Important Is It?" The tools are endless.

Today I know that with God's help, my wife and I can reason things out. If my motive is right, God will give me the words. Problems are now opportunities to deepen our relationship, mature as a couple, become even closer, and learn new relationship skills. My marriage is where I first noticed Al-Anon working in my life. Our marriage isn't perfect, but it's so much better than anything I ever knew. As I get better, my world gets better.

⌒✄⌒

I don't know when I became my daughter's chief demon. I suspect it was a gradual process. By the time I found my way to Al-Anon, we barely spoke. When we did, we often raised our voices and did our dance of anger. After I separated from her father, my daughter grew even more distant.

I knew with all my heart that I wanted to heal this relationship—but that my daughter had choices in the matter. When I called her, she ended every conversation with tears. It broke my heart. I knew that not communicating with her would reinforce her belief that I didn't really care.

With the help of what I was learning in Al-Anon, I recognized that I needed patience and perseverance to change myself, not my daughter. I let go of my expectations and did the only thing I could see to do. I looked at how I could begin to make amends to her, and changed the way I communicated.

Since we couldn't talk without tears, I decided to begin a letter-writing effort. I didn't want to cause her any pain with phone calls, so I started sending her notes that she was free to open or not. The notes were short—sometimes only a thought for the day. I found many cheerful cards that I included in my effort. For six weeks, I sent something almost every day without any expectation of a response. Then one day the phone rang. My daughter wanted to talk.

The conversation wasn't an easy one, but the joy of it was that she trusted me with her feelings. She told me what she thought was wrong with our relationship. I listened and I heard her. I didn't try to justify my actions or take on more than my share. I fought those urges and stayed open to her words. The conversation cleared away a great deal of pain. Most important, it gave me a great deal of information that I could work with to change me. I was able to thank her for the courage it took to say what she had to say.

It was the beginning of a new chapter in my relationship with my daughter. Now I can happily report that we're not only close, we're friends. I've learned to listen to her with respect and treat her with dignity. I don't try to solve her problems or interfere in the things that are hers to work through. I can cheer her on, support her choices, and most important tell her I love her every chance I get.

On a recent Mother's Day, I got a card from my daughter. In it she said I was her teacher, her mentor, and her friend. She thanked me for my love and guidance. What an amazing gift. My heart is so full.

⌒⋙⋘⌒

My damaged relationship with my mother brought me to Al-Anon. Although we both had to cope with the disease of alcoholism in loved ones, over the years a wall of hurt feelings built up between us. I perceived her frustration with my stalled marriage as a condemnation of me, and I reacted defensively. The more I tried to stand my ground, the more sensitive I became to her criticisms and the less aware I became of her love.

In Al-Anon I discovered that I had a part in the breakdown of communication with my mother. It was freeing to realize there were some things I could change. I started by being open to the idea that my mother hadn't turned against me, and I prayed for God to help me re-establish a loving relationship with my mom.

God was bringing about spiritual changes in her life, too, that allowed us to share our faith in a deeper way than we had before. Still, I felt rejected whenever my mom offered any suggestions about my relationship with my husband. After all, I thought, I didn't need her to tell me that my marriage was unmanageable, my house was a mess, and my workload was overwhelming.

What I really needed, it turned out, was the courage to face my difficulties, turn them over to my Higher Power's care, and wait for His guidance. I told my husband about my needs and he agreed to seek counseling with me. My reactions to my mom have changed from defensiveness to honesty and openness. Both relationships are improving, thanks to the principles I've learned in Al-Anon.

Best of all, I am hopeful that I am growing closer to God, and closer to accepting and loving myself as I take responsibility for my part. I'm grateful.

⁓

I have been in relationships where I totally sacrificed myself to make someone else comfortable and happy at the expense of my own comfort. Now I'm becoming someone who takes care of herself and can still love her partner.

I have taken my focus off trying to make him believe that I'm wonderful. I have let go of my fear of being abandoned by him. If he chooses to go, that's his choice. He is an adult and he can do what he wants. I am also an adult, and I no longer need him to see that I'm wonderful in order to survive. What he thinks or believes does not make me who I am. I am wonderful just because I'm me. What he does has nothing to do with me.

Since I have let go of the need for his approval and turned it over to God, my partner is letting me know he does think I'm great. Now I am also free to love and accept him as he is. It's been a great experience.

⁓

I grew up in an alcoholic family as the oldest daughter of eight children. My father was an alcoholic and my mother was the daughter of an alcoholic.

Before my father passed away, he spent a month in a nursing home. My mother and I attended a few Al-Anon meetings together during that time. Since I'd already been attending Al-Anon regularly and was a Group Representative, I was very comfortable with sharing my feelings in an Al-Anon group. I was much more reserved about sharing my feelings with my mother. During the meetings that we attended together, however, I found myself forgetting that she was there and I shared openly.

A strange feeling came over me when I remembered that my mother was sitting right next to me. Then I realized that she, too, grew up in an alcoholic home and experienced the same isolation, verbal abuse, and negativity that are common to alcoholic homes. I no longer looked at my mother as a person who tried to make life worse, but as a sister in Al-Anon. This new understanding allowed me to be gentler with her and to love her more than before I saw her as an adult child of an alcoholic.

⌒◯✕◯⌒

I separated from my first wife after six years. She was the child of an active alcoholic. I have since come to realize that I had family problems, too, although I am not sure alcohol was among them. Without recovery, our protective walls were so thick that there was no real relationship.

After that marriage ended, I tried to find someone more interesting. I succeeded—I married an alcoholic. I didn't search out an alcoholic. I didn't even know she was an alcoholic for the first ten years of our marriage, largely because I didn't really know what alcoholism looked like. Heavy drinking was a normal way of life for us as young naval officers.

As the years went by, however, her drinking became more of an issue. Since I was working and she was not, it was easy to protect her from the consequences of her drinking. Finally, the physical consequences of the disease caught up with her and she almost died. After two weeks in intensive care and two more weeks in the hospital, she ended up in treatment. I was directed to Al-Anon.

We were both still crazy. Although we were each trying to work our programs, we still had all the problems of a 17-year marriage that wasn't working. After two and a half years of sobriety, she relapsed and I relapsed right along with her. I somehow thought it was my fault, and I was ashamed to go back to Al-Anon.

Over the next few years, there were several more treatments and several more relapses, and I was up and down with all of them. However, as time went by, I was able to focus on my own program and realize that whether or not she found sobriety, I could find serenity.

We both have more than five years of continuous recovery. Things are by no means perfect. We both still suffer from this disease. She is only a thought away from a drink and only a drink away from getting drunk. I don't even have that extra step—I am only a thought away from being crazy. If I don't work the Steps daily and turn my will and my life over to my Higher Power, I will rapidly become as crazy as I was when I first came into the program. My problem now is that I can't blame it on her drinking!

When I began dating someone in A.A., I didn't think alcoholism had affected my life. I wasn't an alcoholic nor was anyone in my family. I was in a lot of pain from a previous alcoholic relationship, but I didn't see the connection. As long as my new dreamboat kept out of trouble, his problem didn't concern me. I was curious, however, whenever he mentioned snippets of A.A. philosophy. It seemed so sane, so much more accepting than my preconceptions had led me to believe. Six months into our honeymoon-like relationship, he slipped back into drinking. I raised my eyebrows, but still considered it his business until the night he didn't come home for three days. I was hysterical.

For me, this slip was a blessing in disguise. The craziness of alcoholism was pushed up to my face where I couldn't deny it. I saw how it possessed the person I loved, and through him, how it possessed me. He sobered up and got a Sponsor. I admired his courage—and was envious because I wanted someone I could share my confusion and pain with too. He suggested I go to Al-Anon, but I didn't think I qualified. Even though my boy-friend was an alcoholic, I thought going to Al-Anon would be cheating. I'd be getting a Sponsor for free when I should pay for therapy. I still have a hard time believing I deserve it. I agreed to go to a meeting anyway, thinking it would help me understand him better.

I expected to hear a bunch of gory stories at my first meeting—tales of the dark side of alcoholism. Instead, I heard people simply state their experience, strength, and hope. I was baffled, but I still felt better afterwards. I went to more meetings and was blown over by the sincerity and the humility of members sharing their stories. I slowly began to realize that my thinking, in every area of my life, was marked by fears and resentments. My relationships at work were the first to change as a result of my new understanding. I quit challenging my supervisor's every decision and stewing over his inconsistencies. It wasn't easy, but it felt so much better that I kept trying.

My family relationships began to shift next. As I released resentments I'd clung to for years, I began to appreciate my mother. She immediately noticed the change in my voice when she called because I was happy to hear from her. This miracle alone would have made Al-Anon a worthwhile program to me, but it didn't stop there. Working with a Sponsor, I began to consider the possibility that just maybe there could be a Power greater than myself somewhere in the universe. Although I deeply doubted this, I wished it were true, since I had made such a grand mess of my life. What a relief it would be to turn it over to someone else's care.

The loving examples of my Sponsor, my boyfriend, and members at meetings caused me to question my stubbornness. I decided to act as if I believed in a God-Allah-Buddha-type Power. Sure enough, one blessing after another convinced me. Even though my faith is new—barely a green bud at the tip of a stem—my Higher Power welcomed me with a warm blast of sun and is coaxing me to open up.

Finally, my relationship with my boyfriend benefits from my Al-Anon program work. We still stumble against old behaviors, but we choose to trust our Higher Power to guide us past them. Trust is new territory for me. I would never have believed it possible. I thank my Higher Power every day that He led me to recovery via such a handsome and willing partner. While I started going to meetings to understand him, I found myself and, incredibly, a Higher Power instead.

When I was younger, I was a people-pleaser. It made me happy to make other people happy, and I strived to do that. I remember my father telling me that it was impossible to make everyone happy. I always thought that he just didn't want to try hard enough. I had determination, and I was going to make everyone in my life happy.

When I was in a relationship with an alcoholic, I first thought it didn't take much to make him happy. Drinking alcohol made him happy. So I was always first in line to purchase alcohol for him. I finally realized two things. First, that it's not a good idea to have my happiness dependent on his alcohol intake. Second, that I could buy him all the alcohol I could afford, and he still wouldn't be happy and neither would I.

After coming to Al-Anon, I realized that I couldn't make another person happy. I ended up trying so hard that I would lose myself and my own happiness in the process. I have realized that I can only change myself and learn how to be happy. Others have been able to see my change in attitude and have responded, giving me more happiness in return.

I am currently in a different relationship. We both realize the issues that each of us has. We also realize that we are responsible for working on those matters ourselves. I am not responsible for the issues that he carried into this relationship. He is not responsible for those I brought with me. I have a relationship now where we can be two separate people and still enjoy each other's company. That is a great gift.

I first came to Al-Anon Family Groups because I was yelling at my 16-year-old daughter, who is the closest to me. I realized she didn't deserve such behavior from me and that I needed help.

I am an adult child of an alcoholic. When I joined Al-Anon, I was fully aware that I needed something—that my life was unmanageable. I soon learned that change was possible—and even probable—if I would do my part: attend meetings, read the literature, and get a Sponsor. Then I needed to "Let Go and Let God" do for me what I couldn't do for myself. It was really the first time I actually became aware that I didn't have to do it alone—that support from others in the program and from my Higher Power was available to me.

In my early days, I was so ecstatic and grateful for the program that I wanted everyone to have it. I practically preached it, especially to my daughter. For a number of years, I encouraged her to go to Al-Anon, but she declined. I have since learned that the program is based on attraction rather than promotion. I was trying to control her and be her Higher Power, which I am not.

I'm happy to report that my daughter has become involved in another Twelve Step program and has even started a new meeting where she lives. She is married now and has a family of her own. I'm still trying to work my program and stay out of her stuff. I finally learned to respect her life as just that—her life. We have a very close and loving relationship, which I attribute to the growth I've had over the years. Now I actually have a life and I keep the focus on myself.

For the first time in my life, I have chosen a partner who allows me to be me. In my past relationships, I was hypersensitive to the other person's needs and oblivious to my own. With the help of working the Steps and, more significant for me, the Traditions, I have learned how to keep peace and to ask myself "How Important Is It?" Would I rather win or be happy?

I had to get to know and accept myself (and be unconditional in my acceptance) in order to fully love myself just the way I am. When there are issues to discuss, I do my best to remain open and respectful in my listening, which is not always easy. The old triggers from the past rear their ugly heads and that childhood belief comes back again: If I am not right, I am unlovable, and if I am unlovable, I will be abandoned and I will die. When I am able to separate myself from my partner, and allow her to be exactly like she wants to be, I enhance intimacy and set a tone of mutual sharing. I used to think that a healthy relationship had to be a lot of work. I now believe that when I choose the right people, my relationships are balanced and full of grace.

For Thought and Discussion:

1. What are some possible positive things I can find in a situation that I have so far considered to be entirely negative?
2. If I stop trying to fix certain relationships, how could I benefit?
3. What have I noticed lately that someone in my life was doing right?
4. How can I apply Step Two to my relationships?
5. Do I pause to listen to a Higher Power, instead of reacting immediately to someone else? How can that change my relationships?
6. In what way has the slogan "How Important Is It?" helped me choose a different reaction to a personal situation?

Chapter Six

Risks and Rewards

When affected by alcoholism, our hopes for a loving relationship can bring us pain, disappointment, and loneliness. We tend to isolate ourselves from other people as we become absorbed in a situation that we find shameful and that we're convinced no one else understands. Without realizing how it all happened, we find ourselves vulnerable and afraid. In these circumstances, who would feel comfortable presenting themselves to a room of strangers? They already know each other, but we don't know them and they don't know us. With a history of relationships gone bad, what reason would we have to believe that our relationship with these strangers could result in something positive?

It seemed to some of us that meetings are for people who are comfortable talking with others, enjoy meeting people, and are socially confident. That's why attending an Al-Anon meeting is the very last thing many of us wanted to do. It's not unusual to find Al-Anon members who say they finally went to a meeting because it *was* the last thing for them—they were at a dead end and could see no other alternatives.

Paradoxically, Al-Anon meetings are for people who don't like meetings and who may even be fearful of interacting with people. An Al-Anon meeting is a safe place where healing and recovery can begin. No one judges us at an Al-Anon meeting. Our social status or career accomplishments are irrelevant there. No one criticizes us or our mistakes. If we don't feel comfortable enough to share, we can simply say, "I pass."

Over time this environment nurtures our self-confidence and builds our social skills. We come to understand that we can share our innermost feelings at meetings without having to worry about criticism or having to respond to unsolicited advice. For many of us, it may be the first time in a long while that we've been able to speak without interruption, contradiction, or conflict. No one, no matter how well intended, is telling us what to do or how to feel. At the same time, we learn how to listen to other people with respect. We share a safe environment that is healing for those who speak as well as for those who listen.

Al-Anon meetings give us the right to be heard, but not the right to dominate a meeting. Everyone has an equal voice. By practicing this simple principle, we begin stepping outside the familiar but constricting limitations of our old way of thinking. We start to see each other differently. Our minds and hearts begin to open, and we slowly develop acceptance of ourselves and others. While an Al-Anon meeting isn't an instant solution to our problems with relationships, it's a positive step in the right direction.

Many of us find one meeting that we attend most frequently, where we feel the most connection to the other members. We often begin to feel close to that group because the members are as supportive to us as we would have wanted our own family to be. We come to consider that group as our "home group."

An Al-Anon meeting cannot take the place of a loving relationship with a spouse or partner, parent or child, friend or relative. It's a place where we can learn something about how the disease of alcoholism has affected us and our relationships. At meetings we can learn—and practice—some skills in developing healthier relationships. As other members share their experiences, they often hold a mirror to our lives. Each story shared by other members is an opportunity for us to learn from their successes as well as from their mistakes. Yet hearing members speak about themselves is not threatening to us. We don't have to be defensive because they speak only for themselves about their own experiences—not for us, or to us. We have the freedom to take what we like and leave the rest. There are lessons to be learned, but it's up to us to determine for ourselves what those lessons are.

Communicating with an alcoholic is frustrating and discouraging, and it affects how we communicate with everyone, alcoholic and non-alcoholic alike. It only makes sense that getting along with other people is often the subject of an Al-Anon meeting. So in addition to the safe environment that an Al-Anon meeting offers, the meeting topic is also helpful to us in our efforts to have more positive relationships with other people. No one can say in advance what we'll learn at a meeting. It may be a lesson that's unique to our situation or one appreciated by the entire group. It's not unusual to hear at least one person say at every meeting, "That's exactly what I needed to hear."

Many of us come to Al-Anon without clear boundaries of any kind. Decisions that affected us have been made without our input or understanding. We weren't given the opportunity to ask questions or offer opinions. As a result, some of us learn to be silent, helpless victims, never fully participating in our relationships. Others grow angry and resentful from these situations. We jump at any chance to tell our boss, our spouse, or the cashier at the dry cleaners exactly how we feel about everything, and just how unfairly we are being treated. We don't give ourselves the time to think before we speak, and we often wear out our relationships.

Al-Anon works for us through a system of substitutions. We are encouraged to replace each painful thought with a more positive alternative. Hope replaces disappointment. Confidence replaces fear. Stubborn pride gives way to acceptance. Focus on ourselves replaces frustration with someone else. We learn to take care of ourselves, and in the process we learn how to build better relationships with others.

As each member shares personal strengths and hopes, we find wisdom that we can apply to our own lives, and we can begin to replace unhealthy patterns. Adherence to Al-Anon's three Legacies—the Steps, Traditions, and Concepts of Service— ensures that every meeting is consistent with Al-Anon principles and welcomes everyone. We do our best to keep the focus on ourselves. Although we are individuals in our own unique situations, we start to notice all that we have in common with each other. Accordingly, even as we learn to be independent, we also become better able to work together as a unified group. These are the first steps toward building or repairing relationships with others.

As we take part in informed group conscience discussions at our meetings, we learn how to peacefully decide matters that are important to the group. This process give us the opportunity to examine all sides of an issue, ask questions, share our opinions, and then accept the decision of the group as a whole, whether or not our opinion prevails. We learn good communication skills, without the drama.

Through the support of the Al-Anon fellowship, we continue to give voice to thoughts that we previously kept to ourselves. In time we begin to practice our new attitudes and actions in the world. We know that if we stumble or even fall, there is a safe place where we can return to revitalize our commitment.

Whenever we come to an Al-Anon meeting, we know we are among people who understand. We can be ourselves, bringing all our struggles and triumphs with us, and be met by others who have had similar experiences. Through regular attendance, we stop being afraid of how the relationships in our lives define us, and we learn to accept ourselves and others exactly as we are.

Personal Stories

Emptiness and gloom filled my entire being. My life was in chaos and I felt utterly unloved and unlovable. My misery brought me to Al-Anon. Although everyone greeted me with warmth, I was suspicious of the concern that they demonstrated. I interpreted their smiling faces as evidence that they were a bunch of frauds. I recoiled at their hugs and rejected their warm invitations to join them for coffee after the meeting. How could anyone really care about a fat, ugly, stupid, worthless piece of garbage?

Although my doubts almost kept me away, something deep within urged me to keep coming back. Week after week as people shared their experience, strength, and hope, I gradually began to "Listen and Learn." At times I felt awestruck that I could actually feel the presence of God among us. As I immersed myself in the program, I was introduced to a caring God who loved me unconditionally.

Through the nurturing that I received, I felt like a rosebud gradually blossoming into a magnificent flower. With each unfolding petal, I banished the old negative images of myself and began to recognize all the unique talents and gifts that God has bestowed upon me. I was learning how to love myself as God loves me. As this positive attitude blossomed and grew, I discovered that my relationships with others also improved. It was so much easier to love and accept others when I loved and accepted myself.

This new attitude brought me so much joy that I expanded my horizons to my seventh and eighth grade students, many of whom were struggling with the same low self-esteem that once tormented me. I wanted to reach out to them and help them shed their negativity. I wanted them to blossom, grow, and see themselves and each other as lovable human beings. My new silent mantra was to look at each person through the eyes of God and celebrate the beauty that He sees in each of them. With each affirmation that they received, my students began to recognize my classroom as a safe environment in which to share their unique talents and gifts.

My students' response to my affirmations has been beautiful and contagious. It's truly a pleasure to be greeted each day by a sea of smiling faces. Because they know that I'm looking for their best qualities, this is exactly what they bring into my classroom. Because they know that I celebrate what is special about each of them, they in turn demonstrate love and concern for me, helping me recognize my own unique talents and gifts. Each day brings a new celebration of God's love.

⌒✥⌒

As a child, I was subjected to physical violence from my mom's boyfriend. He would come home drunk and abuse me on a regular basis. As a result, I became very afraid of people and their potential to hurt me. I built many walls of protection that later became my confinement. I grew to enjoy being alone because I saw it as safe. However, my gnawing sense of loneliness and disconnection also grew. I knew, inside of me, that I needed to be with people— not be continually isolated from humanity. I didn't feel safe with people, yet I needed them. My dilemma grew into acute pain.

I went to my first Al-Anon meeting nervous and unsure of what to expect. To my amazement, everyone treated me kindly and with consideration. I listened in awe as people took turns openly sharing their hearts and baring their souls. I had found a place to be with people and safely interact with them. Since that time, I have learned how to open up my heart, quiet my head, and share my soul too.

I still have a difficult time reaching out to people in general, but I always know I have a place where I can be with nurturing people. I am learning to open up to people and give them a chance to communicate with me. I see now that it's possible for people to treat each other with loving kindness and respect. I watch as we all heal, grow, and learn how to feed and strengthen the relationships with ourselves and with each other. Today, I understand gratitude.

Before Al-Anon, I only had relationships within my immediate family. I had too many secrets and didn't want to talk about what was going on in my life. I was the queen of isolation. At my first meeting, I was horrified at the friendliness and hugs shared between members. I liked my isolation and aloneness. However, I heard something at my first meeting that made me return. I wanted to hear more.

It felt wonderful not to be judged in Al-Anon meetings. I started reaching out to others, which was something I had never done before. I started taking down all the walls I had built around myself to keep everyone else out. They had been built out of fear of judgment.

Today I have many friends in Al-Anon. I have shared my problems and secrets—and still I'm loved. My recovery is connected to these relationships. The alcoholic in my life has moved on, but I have stayed with Al-Anon and my Al-Anon friends.

When I first came to Al-Anon Family Groups, I was often the only man at the meetings I attended. The women encouraged me to feel my feelings—something I had never learned to do as a boy. Yet I wondered why I had trouble connecting to others. The more I listened to other members share their own feelings, the more I began to get in touch with my own. It proved to be a great advantage in all my relationships.

I struggled for 11 years to make my husband quit drinking. I had tried everything from the silent treatment and threatening to leave, to screaming and crying. Then I gave up. I had hit bottom. I finally went to an Al-Anon meeting and brought a list of questions intended to help me change my husband. The members were gentle with me and told me to keep coming back.

I did. I learned to focus on myself and provide care for myself and my children. Unfortunately, my marriage ended in divorce. Soon after, my ex-spouse entered treatment. He has now been sober for 15 years. After ten years of sobriety, we remarried, but I had fallen away from attending meetings. Then our son was in trouble with the law and had an addiction. I felt myself slipping again into the dark tunnel of loving someone with a disease, but I knew of a way of life to manage myself. The Al-Anon program allows me to live the life I choose.

⌐⊶⊃ ⌐

I was angry when I went to my first Al-Anon meeting two years ago. I had been in therapy before, read numerous self-help books, and even tried church. Nothing gave me any significant relief. That first time I went, I was so angry—angry with clients at work, coworkers, and my partner of two years, who was very active in A.A.

I was always angry and thought others were just being unreasonable. I was frustrated with my partner, who went to her meetings almost daily. I would call my friends, who were not in any program, and they would agree with me. I had every right to be resentful.

Initially I just went to Al-Anon in order to learn how to nag less at my partner and to be more supportive. The more I went, the more I became aware of my fears and my expectations that my partner meet my needs. A year into Al-Anon, I was talking to a longtime member, complaining about my partner attending so many meetings. She told me I needed to "get a life." She said the more I had a life, the less I would rely on my partner to meet all my needs.

It has been hard to not sit at home and wait for her to come home while I put on my victim face. Instead, I go to three or four Al-Anon meetings per week, call my Sponsor, and actively work the Steps. I blame less and accept more. Since I don't rely on her to meet all my needs, our relationship has improved. It isn't based on fear and neediness so much, but on a mutual respect where two people can have a life separate from the relationship. I continue to learn from others and to learn about me.

I have been married 28 years. I was angry much of that time. I thought that if I had children, we would make a happy family. I thought that if my husband would just stop drinking, I would feel better. I told him many times how inconsiderate and selfish he was. I felt that I had to do everything—look after the kids, shop, do the housework, and manage the finances. I would sit up half the night and try to explain to him how I felt. But I still didn't really know.

In Al-Anon I learned detachment, and then detachment with love. I learned to look for the good and not to wallow in all of the bad stuff. I am learning to be good to myself.

I am able to communicate reasonably well with my husband these days, even though he continues to drink daily. Al-Anon has also helped me with my relationship with my children, who are all adults now.

My initial reason for attending Al-Anon meetings was in order to have a common language with my girlfriend who was in A.A. She thought if I began going to Al-Anon I might be able to understand her better, and so I agreed to go. This was one of a long line of choices I made in order to please the alcoholic with whom I was in a relationship.

I spent several months mostly listening. I never heard anything about pleasing the alcoholic. Instead, I heard people talking about what they had done in the Al-Anon program to help themselves. The idea of keeping the focus on myself in an intimate relationship, or any relationship for that matter, was an entirely new concept.

I was married to an alcoholic for 30 years. I had unhealthy relationships with everyone. I was a nagging, fault-finding shrew. I taught my children to join in as we maintained a façade to the outside world that we lived a normal—even happy—life. My actions ensured that the problems in our family would continue on to the next generation. With my wider family, my parents and siblings, I was the classic people-pleaser, willing to do anything for anyone at any time, except for myself.

I knew I was unhappy, but I didn't know what to do about it. It had been so long since I had to be honest with anyone that I was very surprised at the love and support shown to me at Al-Anon meetings. It was my dear friends at that first meeting who showed me that I could have and sustain relationships just by being myself.

Just before his death, my husband told everyone that the last years of our marriage were the happiest of his life. This was all due to Al-Anon, because he had not stopped drinking. Now I allow my children to be themselves and make their own mistakes without my interference. I have a life of my own—full of friends.

⌐⧔⌐

I am a grown man who has been around alcoholism all of my life. I didn't realize how much the disease had affected my entire life. I ended up getting married, having children, and treating them the same way I had been treated.

Through Al-Anon meetings I learned that I only needed to take care of myself. Other things will take care of themselves.

⌐⧔⌐

Having grown up with alcoholism, I felt that I never learned how to have normal relationships. I came into Al-Anon because I did not know how to carry on relationships with the alcoholics in my life.

Other people seemed able to handle their relationships without the struggle I had. I always tried to be nice to other people, but still ended up hurting them and feeling awful about myself. I was trying desperately to keep the peace with everyone around me. Somehow I had decided this was my role.

When I walked into the rooms of Al-Anon, I found people who talked about their feelings, which was scary territory for me. As I listened, others spoke of feelings that I had. When I finally found the courage to share, no one laughed or ridiculed me. When I asked someone to be my Sponsor, I was not turned away as I had feared. That relationship was the beginning of my learning how to have healthy relationships.

It was a miracle to learn that I could share the real me—my real feelings, not just what I thought someone wanted to hear. I began to stand up for myself and take responsibility for my actions—or lack of action. I began to be honest with myself and with others. I learned to confront those who hurt my feelings. I learned that if others continued to treat me badly, I did not need them to be a part of my life, no matter how much they professed to love me. I got to try out new behaviors in a safe environment before I tried them out in the world. I received support and gentle redirection when I needed it.

I began to stop questioning my ability to have relationships with others. I came to recognize that I already had several successful relationships with people that spanned many years. I didn't always do everything perfectly in those relationships, but those people still loved me. I began to learn to trust my heart in relationships.

Right now I am learning how to have a good relationship with myself, something that has been lacking for many years. I am learning to treat myself more like I would treat a friend or a loved one. I am convinced after sharing and living the Al-Anon program that if I learn to have a good relationship with myself, my relationships with others will seem almost effortless too.

꒰꒱

Before Al-Anon, I always stayed busy and had little time to do things with anyone else. I took care of others and neglected my own needs. I kept to myself at parties. I feared intimacy, sure that others would see how flawed I was. I became lonely, resentful, paralyzed, and isolated. I never suspected that these were simply the effects of what I was doing—and had always done.

In Al-Anon meetings I learned to do things differently. I found a connection with a Higher Power that is a source of comfort and strength. I'm able to express myself honestly in relationships, to accept others as they are, and to see the gifts others have to offer me.

⌒⫸⌒

I was an active member of Al-Anon with five years in recovery before my husband and I relocated to another state. Once we moved, I planned to get to meetings and find a new home group, but there was so much to do. I had to unpack and set up a new home. Things were going well, and although we weren't connecting with other people, we were happy with each other.

It was right before Thanksgiving that my husband was diagnosed with lung cancer. I had been in my new job for seven months, and we had been in our new city for almost 18 months. When the cancer was discovered, it had already spread to the lymph nodes. What followed was a barrage of doctors' visits, treatments, and major and minor crises. Our lives were driven by hospital and medical schedules. Plus, I had to keep working to maintain the health insurance that had become so necessary. My best efforts were to no avail, and my husband passed away after ten months of treatment.

The grief was overwhelming; suddenly I didn't have anything to keep me busy. I was in an empty house with no close friends or family. I went to an Al-Anon meeting because I was desperate. I don't remember much of that meeting except that I got out the words, "My husband died," and I started to cry.

Two exceptional women who were widows themselves immediately took me under their wings. They gave me their phone numbers and told me to call. They told me to keep coming back and

I did. One of these women started meeting me for coffee in the morning. We talked, and she shared her experience in the program and with the death of her husband. I started cooking with the other woman I had met, who also shared her experience, strength, and hope with me. We got together at least once a month and made a meal that we had never made before. After the first try, we needed people to experiment on, and we started inviting other group members to eat the experiment du jour.

I wound up being invited to a series of social events given by members of what was now my home group. When the holidays came around, I had a different Al-Anon member's home to go to from Thanksgiving to New Year's Day. We grew from members of the same group to friends.

Since then, the members of my home group have truly become my family. As with any family, I am closer to some than others. I have incredibly strong relationships with the two women who originally reached out to me. I am close to another member in a way I would not have thought possible. We have supported each other through illness and surgery. We share our triumphs and our failures—and we go to meetings. For me, Tuesday nights feel like a family reunion with everyone having to check in, connect with each other, and give and receive hugs.

Members of my group have changed. I have learned people will always come and go in my life, but the core group that I consider my family remains the same. I went to that meeting in such unbelievable pain that all I wanted was for it to lessen a little somehow. What I received was a family that truly loves me, a recommitment on my part to my Al-Anon program, and growth in my recovery.

For Thought and Discussion:

1. How does sharing at a meeting enhance my recovery?

2. How can my participation during meetings help me to learn how to speak to others in my life?

3. Why do I consider one group my "home group" rather than another?

4. Have I ever asked for a group conscience meeting when there was conflict among members of my group? How did the group deal with the conflict?

5. When I feel frustrated during a meeting, what is the problem? Is there a lesson I need to learn?

6. What types of changes, if any, have I noticed in the ways I interact with people outside of meetings?

Chapter Seven

Creating Balance within Ourselves

Those of us who have lived with the effects of alcoholism can become obsessed with the behavior of others. We spend time analyzing behavior, figuring out motives, and identifying what we deem is wrong with the people in our lives. In Al-Anon we learn that excessive scrutiny of others can be counter-productive. From the first meeting, we are reminded to keep the focus on ourselves, not on the alcoholics in our lives. We soon discover that we can't build healthy relationships until we know who we are.

Steps Four and Ten, the inventory Steps, are Al-Anon tools that help us to know who we are. With Step Four, we make "a searching and fearless moral inventory of ourselves." With Step Ten, we continue to take inventory on a regular basis, promptly admitting when we are wrong. These Steps help us look within ourselves to see what we have done that we can feel good about, as well as the things we regret. We become willing to create a balanced picture of ourselves.

Many of us discover when taking our inventory that we possess the same character defects we have recognized and resented in others. These flaws may not be exactly what we observed in others, but if we put aside excuses and justifications, we may find that the qualities we dislike in others are part of our character makeup too. In time we no longer see those we resented, despised, or gossiped about as any less worthy of respect than we are. We are better able to see them as equals because we are now aware of our common ground.

Step Four and Step Ten are very important to our efforts to improve the quality of our relationships with others. If we're confused about who we are, how can we understand what we want in our relationships? An unbalanced self-image could create problems in how we behave. If changing ourselves is crucial to enjoying our relationships, how else could we know what we can change without a thoughtful inventory of our strengths and weaknesses?

The inventory Steps bring us gently back into balance with ourselves, and eventually in our relationships as well. The effects of alcoholism may have twisted our beliefs, attitudes, thinking, and feelings. A searching inventory of ourselves helps us recognize distortions in our self-image and shows us how to reshape what no longer serves us well. As our self-awareness changes, we may find an increase in self-esteem, a diminished sense of guilt, and a greater peace in our lives. Whether or not others continue the same behavior as before, our reactions change and the outcomes are different. We make new choices when we let go of the warped ideas that have colored our perceptions. Gradually, as we replace old patterns with new ideas, we begin to change. As a result, so do our relationships.

As our inventory progresses, we become ready to ask ourselves tougher questions—about finances, parenting, sex, love, or intimacy, for example. Honestly answering these questions can be a monumental step. Being apprehensive at the beginning of the process is natural, but proceeding at our own pace can prove to be highly rewarding.

Many Al-Anon members have worked with a Sponsor on the Steps. A Sponsor can offer a deeper level of support, encouragement, and guidance than can be found at a meeting. The gentle but equally honest feedback of our Sponsor can help us see what lies behind our anxiety and reactions. A Sponsor can encourage us to break old patterns and help us admit to new truths.

Each of us is in charge of our own recovery—not our Sponsor. A Sponsor should be someone whom we choose because we believe we can work together comfortably and productively. A Sponsor does not tell us what to do, but merely offers suggestions. It is up to us to put them into practice or not. As always in Al-Anon, we can take what we like and leave the rest. It's not appropriate for a Sponsor to direct us in our personal affairs, and it's not appropriate for someone else to select a Sponsor for us.

We learn from our Sponsor's gentle guidance that intimidation, control, and humiliation are not part of a healthy relationship. Working with our Sponsor on our inventory is a chance to design a relationship built on honesty and trust. For many of us, it is a first attempt that becomes a blueprint for the other relationships in our lives. Just as we need to find balance in other relationships, we need a balanced relationship with a Sponsor.

Personal Stories

I was worn out, full of fear, and angry over situations and people in my life. I was trying desperately to hide my insides from everybody. Negative and crazy feelings were rampant in my life. I forced my true feelings down, giving myself uneasiness in the pit of my stomach. I could cry just watching a show on television or reading a book. I always told myself that my feelings really didn't matter. I had no self-esteem. Everyone else was more important than I was.

When I got to Al-Anon, I was told to put the focus on myself. I had no idea who that was. I had usually been whoever someone else wanted me to be. I didn't know myself.

I have to accept myself as I am—not as the person I wish I were. I work constantly to be positive and take useful actions as I continue to learn who I am. I feel I am gaining, changing, and rearranging my relationship with myself. My self-esteem has improved. I have stopped—most of the time—rationalizing, justifying, and explaining. I am continuing on this journey of finding the real me.

⌒◁▷⌒

The disease of alcoholism left me filled with anger, resentment, and hate during my first marriage. At the end of my marriage, I was left with despair and confusion about what went wrong and why it happened. A beautiful relationship ended in a divorce.

Everyone had noticed the excessive use of alcohol, but very few noticed the loss of trust, loyalty, and unconditional love. I did an excellent job of hiding these losses from everyone. Like many men, I don't discuss my feelings as easily as I show my anger, frustration, and a strong desire to be the guardian of my family.

Al-Anon was the first place I noticed unconditional love. It was like finding an oasis in the middle of a desert. I was accepted just the way I was, and no one appeared surprised or dismayed about what alcoholism had done to me. They said they had been where

I was, but they offered me hope. They did not guarantee that my marriage would survive, but told me that if I worked the Steps, my life could continuously get better. I had nothing to lose, and nothing I had tried had worked, so I committed to do the Steps. Every meeting I went to I left feeling better. In the early days, it did not last too long and most of the time I slipped back into depression and anger, which was what I felt most of the time. I finally understood why my counselor kept insisting that I attend three to four meetings a week.

Step Four turned out to be the turning point of my life. I finally understood why I acted, reacted, and responded the way I did. Acting out of anger, fear, and resentment brought me more pain. Clearing all these negative feelings gave me the clarity to make the right choices out of kindness, compassion, and hope. I began to feel spiritual growth, and as I continued to stay focused on working the Steps, my depression and anger slowly melted away. I was filled with hope of a better life ahead. My marriage did not survive, but I did.

⌐⟨⟩⌐

Growing up in an alcoholic home played havoc with my relationship with my mother. Due to my father's drinking, my mother was the controlling, dominant figure in our home. I grew up fearing and resenting her. I saw her as an unfair, mean, bossy nag. Then I came into Al-Anon.

After I worked Steps Four and Five, my mother and I slowly started tearing down the wall between us. Over time our relationship started to change. My mother never did come to accept that both her husband and son in-law suffered from alcoholism. In time, however, we were able to talk about almost anything else. We became able to laugh and have fun. I learned to respect her for all the strength that I never knew she had, and she had a lot. The last three years before she passed away, she became my best friend. She encouraged me and I encouraged her.

⌐⟨⟩⌐

It used to bother me when my Sponsor would respond to my deepest, darkest problems and secrets with the statement, "That's okay." I would think to myself, "Aren't you listening?" So I would tell her something worse and she would respond, "That's okay too." I used to think I was so bad and needed so much fixing. After several months of hearing "That's okay" and experiencing unconditional love, I began to realize that I *was* okay. The dreams I had for my future—the future that I would get to experience when I was healthier—were waiting for me and had been waiting for me for a long time.

The job that I wanted, the relationships that I desired, the love I longed for were all within reach. I've learned to erase those old tapes that used to say, "Someday you'll be ready for this" and replace them with the truth: I'm exactly where I'm supposed to be, experiencing the exact experiences that my Higher Power wants me to experience. I'm more than just okay—I'm God's perfect child. It took me a long time to learn that lesson, but that's okay.

⌐◦◦✥◦◦

I used to complain about everything my wife would say when she called me on my cell phone. I'd get so angry. Finally my Sponsor asked me if my phone had caller identification. He also asked if my phone would take messages. I said yes to both. He told me, "When your wife calls, and you see that it's her, don't answer it. Let the phone take a message. Then if it's something that angers you, talk about it with me before you call her back." I've had tremendous success by practicing this technique.

⌐◦◦✥◦◦

Growing up with an alcoholic father, I was angry much of the time. I never confronted my dad with my feelings, though, because I was too scared. I just kept quiet, but I was really angry.

Many years later, I suspected that my unexpressed but still vivid anger was spilling over into other relationships in my life. I was taking out my old bitterness on my friends and romantic partners, but my anger wasn't their fault at all.

Today the focus of my Al-Anon work in relationships isn't on my father, but on my completely non-alcoholic boyfriend. I use the word "today" as a subtle but helpful tool. For example, when I find myself thinking, "He makes me so mad," or, "I can't stand it when he does that," I try to remember to add the word "today." He makes me so mad today. By doing this, I put the focus back on myself—why am I so easily irritated today? He's the same sweet guy—what's different about me today? Often times this little word helps me detach momentarily, so I can see my part. If not, the word "today" also reminds me that there will be a tomorrow too, when I may feel differently.

Maybe my task today is to resist doing or saying something I would need to make an amends for tomorrow.

When I arrived in the rooms of Al-Anon, I didn't know who I was. I was whatever someone else wanted me to be. I especially worked at being what the alcoholic wanted me to be. I thought we should like the same plays, movies, and TV shows, vote for the same political candidates, enjoy the same sports, and eat the same types of food. You name it. If we really loved one another, we would be alike.

Since coming into Al-Anon, I have learned who I really am, what my favorite color is, and what type of movies and TV shows I like. I've learned it's okay for me to be me. How can someone else love me unless I love myself first?

Today I know with all of my heart that I am a really special person. I have many talents. It's okay to acknowledge the good things about myself, recognize my shortcomings, and love myself anyway. As I work the Steps, I become who my Higher Power wants me to be.

I was sexually impotent through most of my marriage. Lovemaking practically ceased after the birth of our second child. Desperation, sexual desire, wanting to be loved, pride, and the idea that I could make her happy—these thoughts bounced continually through my mind. My manipulations rarely worked, and when they did, the experience wasn't mutually satisfying.

As I continued in my old ways, I experienced impotence again and again. For nearly 14 years I waited for her to change. I wanted a wife who would love me, but I was simply unwilling to change myself. Al-Anon is changing my thinking. When I put my Higher Power first in my life, miracles happen.

After my wife came back from treatment, I faced divorce. I used the slogan "One Day at a Time" to get me through this process. In doing a Fourth Step, I was able to see the common threads in all my previous relationships. I found I was attracted to women who dressed fashionably, liked to drink, and could not pay their bills. Today I am still magnetically attracted to a woman wearing sunglasses, sitting in a high-class bar drinking a martini. I can laugh at myself and know this is not a healthy place for me to be.

I also found that I was unable to tell a woman "no." I was obsessed with trying to make someone else happy. I made her my God. I lost me. When she was gone, I recreated my marriage over again. Old habits die hard. I am grateful my Sponsor had the clarity to help me see through my fog.

⌐⊛⌐

To me the word "relationship" used to be a four-letter word. I cringed whenever I thought of how I related to others. I thought I was supposed to change myself to fit what other people wanted me to be. I used to believe that other people would only be happy if I acted the way they wanted. Of course, my goal was to make others happy.

Learning to relate—and not to mirror or mimic—was something I learned slowly in Al-Anon. The idea that helped most was to keep the focus on myself. What was my favorite color? What activities did I think were fun? By embarking on a path of self-discovery, I learned that there were many gray areas about myself—pieces that had only been partially discovered. With the help of my Sponsor, I began the life-long journey of discovering who I am, because each day I change and grow. Discovering who I am has set me free. Today I know that I love the color green, but I don't like to wear it. I also know that my assets can become defects if I let them gain too much importance. I am grateful there is not a time limit on when I need to know myself. I pass on this gentle way of living from my Al-Anon friends to others with another four-letter word: love.

⌒◯◯⌒

My wife has been sober for 19 years. A year ago she told me that she needed some distance from me, so I moved out. A few days later, another man moved in. My whole world broke apart and I hit bottom. I desperately needed help. Eventually I realized that I belong in Al-Anon, and that it is not my duty to change my alcoholic wife.

The crisis I went through—and am still going through—is about me. It's an opportunity for me to wake up and become aware that I'm responsible for all of my emotions: anger, happiness, resentment, joy, fear—you name it. If I let others push my buttons, especially my alcoholic wife, then I'd better not complain about feeling lousy.

I am learning to detach with love. Whenever I realize that somebody pushed a button, I go back to program literature, get down on my knees, and remember that I have to stay focused on myself. In other words, "Live and Let Live." It's a wonderful awareness that nobody can take away my trust in my Higher Power, or God as I call Him/Her/It.

The program has become a powerful guide toward my spirituality. Whenever I let go and let my Higher Power do the job, I enjoy life to its fullest. Then it doesn't matter whether I am alone, in a relationship, or married. The program has helped me find a healthy solution to living—everything is good just as it is today. I let God guide my life and stay excited about the surprises my Higher Power puts in my life. He will never put more on my plate than I can handle.

In alcoholic families there are rigid rules to follow: don't notice, don't talk, don't feel, and don't trust—other people or my own perceptions. Those rules required that I keep secret, from myself and everyone else, the truth of how this disease affected and disabled me. I am now disobeying those rules.

I have learned to trust. I can be vulnerable, emotionally safe, and available because many of my Sponsors have shared themselves with me openly and honestly. I try to do the same for the people who ask me to sponsor them.

I now have acceptance and love for myself as I am. I can accept and love others by listening, being compassionate, and welcoming them. I avoid scolding, controlling, or interfering with the process each person I sponsor is going through. I realize that sponsorship is an effort of honesty, courage, and intimacy. Many times when I am sharing with someone I sponsor, I say exactly what I also need to hear. Sometimes those I sponsor say just the right thing at the right time, and I am able to experience more healing and recovery myself. It is a win-win relationship.

A Sponsor once told me that we travel through recovery together. It is only through close, intimate relationships with others that healing and recovery can take place. Only through sharing my story as it changes and evolves, and listening to others' stories, am I able to leave isolation and actually be one among my fellows.

Every romantic relationship I have had has been with a person whose drinking affected me. I used to think I had a sticker on my forehead that read, "Let me fix you." As a lesbian, a gay bar is one of only a few places I know to meet a potential life partner—so that's where I went to find Ms. Right. I like to laugh and have fun, so when looking for potential prospects, I would always look for the woman who was having the most fun. The person having the most fun in a tavern is usually drinking.

I believe my Higher Power teaches me lessons, but also answers my prayers, and sent me an angel in one of my searches. This woman ended up being my best friend. She was a member of Alcoholics Anonymous who showed me that people could still have fun without drinking. I went to open A.A. meetings and enjoyed socializing with recovering people. I learned a great deal about the disease of alcoholism and how it can destroy the grace and decencies of life. Still, I was firm in my belief that if someone loved me enough, they could change—that our love would fix everything. So I continued on my journey to find Ms. Right.

Instead, I found Ms. Wrong, Ms. Mistaken, and Ms. Almost Right. I learned that people who have been affected by someone else's drinking are sometimes sicker than the drinker. I tried to fix my loved ones by arguing, threatening, jumping on moving vehicles, hiding keys, staging crime scenes, and anything else I could think of to convince them that they needed to stop drinking.

Finally, in my wisdom, I decided to find a mate who didn't drink, and by that I meant someone already in recovery. I figured if I was going to continue to pick drinkers, I might want to try one who had been sober for some time. Ms. Right directed me to the doors of Al-Anon and probably just in time to save our relationship. In Al-Anon I learned I had a controlling nature and that my illogical belief that I could fix everything could also destroy a relationship—even when no drinking was involved. I learned that drinkers don't drink because of me; they drink because they are alcoholics. Nothing I could say or do could cause them to drink or stop drinking. I learned that the only control I had was over me and my reactions. I learned not to start a crisis on purpose just to be able to have my way, and how to stay peaceful in the middle of heated discussions. I learned that there is more than one right way to do things and that my other half may be right too.

Today I go to meetings regularly, have a Sponsor, read Conference Approved Literature every day, and do my part for the service of Al-Anon. Today life is wonderful, and I am grateful to have been attracted to those who have the disease of bending their elbows a little too much, because they brought me to Al-Anon. Alcoholics Anonymous gave me my Ms. Right, and Al-Anon gave her a sane and serene life partner.

After the end of my fourth "long-term" relationship in five years, I had to ask myself if *I* could be the problem. I realized I needed to take a long hard look at the way I behaved in relationships.

I pulled out my Fourth Step notebook, called my Sponsor, said a prayer, and then got to work. Within an hour, I came to realize that I did many things to keep the people I love at a distance. I built resentments and I was lazy and unresponsive in the relationship. I even created physical distance by having a job that required extensive travel. When I got divorced, I let my ex-wife take my two boys 750 miles away, even though I love them both dearly.

I also realized that having lived in an alcoholic home, I had stopped trusting loved ones. I came to equate close relationships with instability, and consequently lost the ability to commit. Therefore I made a commitment to move closer to my children and to stop traveling, and I have since done so. I have done my best to make appropriate amends to the people I love. I have learned to stop carrying resentments.

I now know that I can love the alcoholic whether she is still drinking or not. I can accept my loved ones' defects, as they have so often accepted mine. I can trust my Higher Power to guide me toward trusting others and building strong relationships in the future.

I had feelings of anger, embarrassment, fear, and frustration with my husband, who displayed deplorable behavior with his problem drinking. I managed to tolerate it for the sake of our children, but I was left with a sense of failure as a wife. Then my son became addicted to drugs and alcohol.

I had brought him into this world and loved him dearly, but I didn't like who he had become. I tried everything imaginable to fix him, but everything failed. With every failure, my self-worth as a mother dwindled. After all, I believed mothers were supposed to be protectors and healers. As he became more volatile and created ugly scenes, I became more determined to find a way to make him see that alcohol and drug use was ruining his life. I had become the only family member who would not give up on him.

I attempted unsuccessfully to have him committed, but during this process a counselor suggested I attend Al-Anon meetings. It took a while for me to realize that although the program did not give me tools to fix my son as I had hoped, it made me realize how sick I had become. After all, I had not thought about my feelings or needs in years; I was too busy trying to fix everyone else.

I can love my son without enabling him and causing more harm. He has to want to change, and I can't do it for him. By changing my own negative thoughts to positive ones, however, my relationships with others have improved.

⌒✖⌒

For years I stood on the sidelines of life, hoping someone would see that I was in desperate need of friendship. I tried to make others love me by going along with the crowd and keeping my own opinions secret. I often felt like an outsider looking in and wondered why no one seemed to consider my feelings. I didn't think my feelings were important, so I kept them inside. How could others value my feelings or opinions if I didn't value them myself?

Soon I had become my own worst enemy. I would compare my feelings about myself to what I assumed other people were feeling—and convinced myself that I was somehow a less valuable human being. I believed that others were thinking the same negative thoughts about me that I thought about myself, so being in the company of other people became a chore.

My behavior toward myself was unacceptable. I would berate myself for weeks, months, and sometimes years for simple mistakes. This internal criticism left me feeling so unworthy of love and friendship that I isolated myself from the few important relationships that I did have.

While working Step Four, it became apparent that one of my defects of character was that I treated myself poorly. I threw away potential friendships like last week's newspaper. My relationship with myself was like the half-done crossword puzzle with its missing letters and words. In Al-Anon I have been able to fill in the blanks.

I learned that I would not feel worthy of any loving relationship until I treated myself as I would treat a valued friend, family member, spouse, or child. My perfectionist ideals had held my spirit hostage for too long. The realization that my best was good enough gave me permission to ease up on myself. Only by accepting and loving who I was, right where I was, would I continue to grow.

When I reached Step Seven, I asked God to help me treat myself with love and respect. I decided I would no longer tolerate my own harsh thoughts, which damaged my self-esteem. I deserved better. I began to catch the critic—myself—midstream and I would tell my negative thoughts to go cool off. When done in a loving way, this awareness helped me to let go of my pessimistic inner voice. Setting this boundary with myself helped me see how my own behavior, and not that of the alcoholic, was responsible for problems in many areas of my life.

After looking at these years of self-abuse, it became clear to me in Step Eight that I belonged at the top of my list of persons I had harmed. Making amends to myself in Step Nine has been truly rewarding. Treating myself with love and respect, taking care of my health in a timely manner, accepting my humanness, and allowing myself to have fun are just some of the ways I have recovered the relationship with my true self. Today I acknowledge my achievements, embrace my excellence, and laugh at my seriousness. I share honestly and rejoice in my willingness to continue my journey in Al-Anon. Allowing my Higher Power and my Al-Anon family to love me just the way I am has shown me that my spirit is alive and that I am capable of loving myself. In turn, being a friend to myself has taught me how to befriend others. As a result, I have been able to develop meaningful friendships.

～❈～

After spending 54 years despising my mother because she's an alcoholic, I went to an Al-Anon meeting because I thought it would teach me how to control her. After several meetings and hearing my story shared by others, I became open to some kind of change. I finally understood that I was angry, hateful, resentful, bitter, and dishonest.

My Sponsor helped me go through the Twelve Steps. My Sponsor taught me about life, how to change, and how to put trust back into my Higher Power, whom I call God. It took two attempts to make my graveside amends to my deceased alcoholic father. It was magical and gave me the extra boost I needed to next approach my mother. I still despised her, even on the day I went to make my amends to her, but I proceeded and kept the focus on my part. What a relief!

At the right moment, the hate and bitterness I had felt for her disappeared. What a miracle! She was 78 years old when I was finally able to give her a hug and tell her that I loved her. For the first time I heard her reply that she loved me too. It seemed as if I had finally given my mother permission to love me.

It continues today. When I used to visit her, I asked God to help me get through it. Now when I visit, I ask God to make the visit good for her. It took a lifetime to change—just in time.

～❈～

There I was in the middle of my living room, yelling at the top of my lungs and hurling things at my loved one. I had been going to meetings for five years—yet something was dreadfully wrong. I was experiencing a huge slip in my recovery, and I risked losing a very important relationship in my life. My loved one just looked at me and told me to call my Sponsor. He doesn't even attend Al-Anon and he had the answer.

Once I got past the pain and humiliation of what I had done, I called my Sponsor. It took me two days to call because I knew I had slipped badly. I was afraid of what she would say. However, she didn't chastise me; she helped me find a solution. She suggested I start a list of the things I had been neglecting in the program. One of those things was meeting attendance. I needed another meeting during the week. I also needed to focus more on my daily meditation books instead of whimpering through them. Calling people and sharing more in meetings would also help me put more into my program.

The key to getting recovery back into my relationship was to focus on my Higher Power and put the principles of the program first.

⌒◇⌒

I was six months into the Al-Anon program when I was talking with someone after a meeting. After a few minutes, she said, "Do you notice anything?" I told her no. She pointed out I was talking about myself and not the alcoholic. It was an Al-Anon moment for me. I thought, "Maybe this program does work."

A few days later, I came home from work. When I walked through the door, I knew the alcoholic was intoxicated. I went to the bedroom and she was passed out in bed. I decided to use detachment with love for the first time. For three days, I acted as if nothing happened. On the fourth day, she told me she was sorry and wanted to talk about it. She talked about her drinking, and I talked about the program. That's when I realized I needed the Al-Anon program for me, not her. That was five-and-a-half years ago. Things are better in my home, even though the alcoholic in my life is not in recovery. This program has given me my sanity back.

⌒∝⌒

One of my goals as a mother—maybe my only one—was to not be like my own mother. I wanted to be loving, gentle, and consistent with my children, but I yelled at them a lot and was unpredictable. I could complain for half an hour one day about a sock that wasn't put away, and not even be bothered by it the next. One night it could be fun to splash in the bathtub. The next evening it could be messy, hard to clean up, and might cause mold in the house. I became more and more like my mother without realizing it. At those rare times when I could see what I was doing, I justified my actions by blaming others. Of course I was miserable—look what I had to put up with.

One morning I heard myself yelling at my kids like my mother, probably over some spilled milk or something equally as earth-shattering. I had a moment of clarity. Something was definitely wrong in my home. Eventually, seeing myself more clearly brought me to Al-Anon.

Step Four, in which I took a fearless moral inventory of myself, was enlightening. I did a Step Four solely on anger, with a focus on my own temper. I learned that attacks on my low self-esteem and threats to my sense of security really triggered my anger. Mom's attacks made me feel like nothing I ever did was good enough. Good grief, she was still correcting my grammar at 40!

So I worked on my self-esteem. I learned to accept myself as I am. Mistakes are just mistakes, not the end of the world. It became important to forgive myself. I learned that I am a valuable human being even though I'm not perfect. As my self-esteem increased, attacks felt much less threatening and I had less of a need to be angry.

Part of learning to love myself turned out to be learning not to accept abuse. I began to tell Mom that I wasn't going to listen when she started on a tirade about how I had failed to meet her standards. If she didn't stop, I left the room. My choices didn't make her happy, but they worked for me.

Once, as she was yelling at me about something, I made another new choice and gave her a big hug and told her I loved her. It took the wind right out of her. I wanted to love my mother, so I decided to behave as if I did. I wish I had responded that way more often in the past. It was a much more loving way.

I learned through working the Fourth Step that I wasn't the sweetest person in the world either. I realized that I didn't treat Mom with the courtesy and respect I wanted, so I used what turned out to be the greatest tool for me—"Let It Begin with Me." I worked on correcting my behavior toward her. There were many times I bit my tongue rather than spit out an angry, rude response to her. In place of impatience, I sat and listened to what she had to say rather than discounting her opinion with a thought like, "Oh, there goes Mom again. What's she going on about this time?" I tried to think instead, "Okay, this is Mom talking. Here is an opportunity to get to know her." I tried treating her like a person I wanted to know rather than an ogre to be feared. After listening to her for some time, I discovered that she was a frustrated, angry woman who didn't feel loved or worthy of love. As a result, I renewed my efforts to let her know that I loved her.

We have a wonderful relationship now. We talk on the phone frequently. When I say goodbye, I say, "I love you." The first time I said that she responded with, "Now why would you say a thing like that?" A few phone calls later, she responded, somewhat uncomfortably, with, "We love you too," and now she says, "I love you" almost easily.

My wife left me a little over a year ago. I was an active member of A.A. and was being treated for depression. Suddenly I was a single parent with two teenage kids. Before she left, our relationship had deteriorated to a lot of verbal abuse, and recently, physical abuse as she relapsed after more than 18 years of sobriety. The kids witnessed all of this.

It wasn't surprising that one of the kids reacted to the separation in a very self-destructive way. My wife, meanwhile, was projecting all of her anger onto me. With all of this going on, I became very distracted at work. I'm a project manager for a construction company; for the first time in 15 years, I had a project lose a great deal of money. No one in the company got a bonus check that year.

Meanwhile, the separation turned into an ugly divorce, which led to both of us filing bankruptcy. As I turned to God in desperation, I was guided to Al-Anon meetings.

I decided to work the Steps and work them in order. I also latched on to an Al-Anon Sponsor. I never thought I could relate to someone that didn't have a substance abuse problem, but this guy seemed to know more about alcoholics than I did with 20 years in A.A. Some of the things he helped me with seemed so profound at the time and now seem so obvious.

After working the Steps, I like myself better than ever before, despite my shortcomings. I'm able to handle things that used to confuse me and I'm beginning to share my story with others. I've got a whole new army of new friends with whom I talk and socialize as often as possible. My 21 years in A.A. have kept me alive, but my 15 months in Al-Anon have given me back my life.

∞

After traveling a long distance to see my siblings, I was startled and taken aback by their behavior when I arrived. As soon as I stepped out of the car, they began to direct harsh teasing, sarcasm, and criticism toward me. Eager to see them and fresh from a long and beautiful drive through the mountains, I was unprepared for their behavior. I found myself reacting with old behaviors in an attempt to defend against their unexpected, crazy-making antics.

Disappointed with how I'd handled things and feeling judgmental toward myself, I called my Sponsor later that afternoon.

I knew I needed to practice detachment with love if I was going to attain a sense of serenity. At that moment, however, I was unable to feel anything resembling love toward these people. I became afraid of the volatility of my emotions and the possibility that I wouldn't be able to grasp and apply my program the way I wanted to for my own integrity.

My Sponsor gently informed me that I could still practice detachment with love; only perhaps the love I would infuse into the equation could be love for myself. In time, with willingness and the help of a Higher Power, that initial expression of love could shift and grow to encompass my family. The important thing, she told me, was that there be love and detachment involved in my own experience of the situation—my Higher Power could take it from there. In the meantime, my detachment would allow me to see things with renewed serenity and a clearer perspective. Detachment with love gave me the space I needed to connect with my Higher Power and to remember my own intrinsic worth, regardless of what family members still suffering from alcoholism may say.

⌐⬥⬥⬦∘

I first came to Al-Anon to fix my alcoholic wife and my marriage. I married a woman with a huge heart who drank too much. I made the assessment that all she needed was the love and security of a good man, a good home, and a good life. Then everything would turn out just fine. After many painful years and two tries at treatment centers, my wife is sober and doing well. My recovery, still not complete, is another story.

My Sponsor tells me to just live life, and I am slowly coming to that understanding. Some of the most difficult ideas for me to accept have been the humility found in the Steps and how powerless I really am. Yet I continue to make great strides. As a businessman, I am rewarded for the opposite traits, so I have had to unlearn a lot of what I use in my working life.

Today when circumstances challenge me, I am far less inclined to lay blame and far more likely to look in the mirror and ask, "What is my part?" I am willing to examine my motives, and I don't solicit nearly as much self-pity as I once did. I am also learning that I don't know all the answers, and I can "Listen and Learn" without giving advice.

My marriage is on shaky ground right now, but I am grateful that I'm becoming honest enough to see that I'm equally responsible for where we are today.

In a recent Fourth Step, I saw with profound clarity three or four major defects of character that were keeping my relationship with my dad stuck in a painful place for both of us. My father is a recovering alcoholic in A.A. and has consistently been a pivotal figure in my life. Working our recovery paths has not always been easy. In recent years, it became necessary to create some space away from him to see my issues more clearly without his influence.

When I visited him on vacation, we had yet another bitter fight, despite both of our best efforts. I was upset and frustrated. That night, my Higher Power whispered a challenge to me: to change some of the patterns I had recently found in my inventory when I talked to my dad. Saying a quick prayer and pushing through fear, I asked my dad for his permission to be fearlessly honest with him and to share my view of our relationship from day one. Overcoming my defect of hiding the truth from my dad, for the first time in my life I told him everything I'd felt. To his credit, he listened.

We came to an impasse that night, but something changed in me. I was no longer afraid of him. I felt a new and authentic love flow into my heart for him. I felt I could finally be myself with Dad, without forcing my agenda or identity on him in an indirect, piecemeal manner.

With my Higher Power's help, the use of honest, loving conversation freed my dad and me from the lifelong prison in which we'd trapped ourselves. Without the tools of the Fourth Step, I would have never known what parts of my behavior needed to change in order to have a different experience in my relationship with him.

⌒✖◦

I came to Al-Anon because of my concern about my older sister's drinking. I had been in the program for two years before people realized I was married. I never talked about my husband because he wasn't part of my Al-Anon life. He was doing what I thought all husbands did. He was paying the bills, taking care of the yard, and making sure the cars were working. My Sponsor said that when he did something he was "supposed to do," I needed to say, "Thank you." I started doing it, but it felt awkward and he looked at me strangely. It was a beginning. Over time I saw a change in our relationship. I was learning to appreciate him for all he did.

He's not outwardly affectionate, which always upset me. Today I know that this is how he is. He shows me he loves me with all the things he takes care of—like the yard, our home, and the cars. I've invited him to some Al-Anon events and he's even come a few times. It's so awesome to see that as I've changed, my husband and I have become friends and our relationship has gotten better.

For Thought and Discussion:

1. How honest am I when I share my feelings with others? To what extent do I mask what I truly feel? How much of what I am saying is what I think others want to hear?
2. How are my relationships, as I understand them now, a reflection of my own strengths and weaknesses?
3. How have my attitudes about sex, money, or affection affected my relationships?
4. How do I define emotional intimacy?
5. In my past and current relationships, what has been the balance between giving and taking? Do I have a tendency to do—or to expect—one more than the other?

6. If I went into a relationship expecting someone else to "complete me," what did I think I was lacking that another person could provide? How did that affect the relationship as it developed?

Chapter Eight

Learning by Example

Many of us affected by alcoholism have learned what we know about relationships from people who couldn't give what they didn't have. We had few if any positive role models. We didn't know what was missing—or what was possible—from our relationships because we had rarely if ever seen anything any better than what we had experienced.

As we grow in Al-Anon, we begin to have a better sense of what it means to be healthy. We learn to separate principles from personalities. Instead of instantly reacting in a negative way to a personality, we come to understand how to apply a principle that can help make a relationship more positive. As we seek to improve our existing relationships and create healthy new ones, we look for positive role models to show us the way.

In the past, communication for many of us was often a roadblock or a one-way street. People talked without anyone listening, or no one talked at all. Not much understanding passed between anyone. At Al-Anon meetings, however, we meet people who have learned to listen attentively and to speak honestly and openly. We get to know members who have greatly improved their relationships, even though they are living or have lived with situations similar to (or even worse than) our own. It's encouraging to find such people, because their continued progress helps us to hope that improvement is possible for us too.

At first it may seem as if these people hold some fabulous secret. We watch in wonder at their peace of mind—and even laughter—in the middle of chaos. How is it possible that they can be living with the effects of alcoholism and yet be happy?

Often their lives are still full of challenges, but they have learned how to detach from the drama. They have found a way to let go of things that they can't control. They have learned to make gratitude a part of their lives, and we notice the positive effect gratitude has on the type of relationships they have. We can see how much personal growth they have gained from studying the Twelve Steps, Twelve Traditions, and Twelve Concepts of Service.

We are drawn to these members through the common experiences we share. They prove to us that contentment really is possible. Thanks to the example they set, we start to believe that since they have learned to live happy, healthy lives, perhaps we can too. We become willing to believe that our relationships can heal. Because they give us cause for hope, these are the members whom we are most likely to consider as possible Sponsors.

Like an Al-Anon meeting, the sponsorship relationship is also guided by the Steps, Traditions and Concepts that set boundaries for mutual respect within Al-Anon. A Sponsor does not dominate or govern the relationship by giving advice and direction. A Sponsor is familiar with a wide range of Al-Anon tools and can draw from a bank of experience, strength, and hope. A relationship with a Sponsor is not a substitute for family and friends, but it is a learning opportunity that can build relationship skills—and can eventually evolve into a genuine friendship. Choosing a Sponsor is an acknowledgement that we are willing to look deeper at ourselves with a trusted friend who will share wisdom to help us on our passage. We trust them when they tell us "this too shall pass," because we know they have walked the same path.

Al-Anon service can provide us with even more models for healthy relationships. Service is all about relationships—the relationship of members to the group, of the groups to each other, and of Al-Anon to the world at large. Giving back to our group—and to Al-Anon as a whole—may sound like a selfless gift of love, but service also opens the door to receiving the gift of recovery. As we are often told, "In giving, we receive." Volunteering becomes another way to practice our new behavior and to spend time with other dedicated members who are doing the same. Al-Anon members in service are putting into practice what they have learned. Service gives us many lessons.

In time, we too can become living examples to newer members, inspiring them to learn, just as we are now learning. But we only need to focus on what we can do to improve our lives today. Al-Anon offers us a wide range of choices, including meetings, service, and sponsorship. Whatever we choose to do, we can be confident that there is good reason for hope. That's the lesson we can learn from the positive example of so many others in Al-Anon.

Personal Stories

For a long time, my program meant getting to one or two meetings a week and spending a lot of time with my longtime comfort, Conference Approved Literature. It took me more than four years to ask a wonderful member to be my Sponsor. That was a turning point in my recovery.

Trusting another human being to get to know the real me took time. I kept praying for the willingness. Walled off with fear, I separated from the rest of the world. Even though I didn't have tools for being in honest relationships, I now had a Sponsor to contact when uncomfortable feelings of confusion, resentment, and rock-bottom self-esteem shook my faith.

Instead of hiding behind the wall, I started picking up the phone and asking for help. My Sponsor and I spent time together, talked regularly on the phone, took long walks, and worked the program. My Sponsor entrusted me to a Power greater than ourselves. The God of my understanding spoke through my Sponsor and other members of the program.

Change was not easy. I found that sometimes I needed to learn to sit and do nothing about the discomfort that came up when one more relationship challenged my old way of thinking. I learned to practice awareness, acceptance, and action. If I didn't become *aware* of what I was feeling and learn to *accept* life on life's terms, the *actions* I took just continued giving me the same sick results. My life in recovery has unraveled old knots of control and fear—basic survival tools I'd been using for more than 50 years. Conflict with resolution has never been part of my relationships. If there was conflict, I fled or turned my back and closed my heart.

Thanks to my loving Higher Power, I have an inventory that includes the courage to change. Resolution begins with living the Steps. With the support of my longtime Sponsor, I have worked the Steps and Traditions one day, one relationship at a time.

As a Sponsor, I do not push and pester those I am sponsoring. Before Al-Anon, I had everyone telling me what to do, think, and feel. I will not do that to anyone else. I try to use "Let It Begin with Me" and "attraction rather than promotion." I encourage and listen. I strongly suggest that those I sponsor actively work at getting well—whether that means talking to members, reading all the literature, or attending as many meetings as possible for the first six months. I let them know they can even call me at 3 a.m., because there is no right time for problems to arise.

Sponsoring gives me as much as—if not more than—the person I sponsor. I gain patience, strengthen my own program, and learn to use compassion, laughter, and acceptance. Very often the sponsor-to-sponsored relationship becomes a friendship, which is a wonderful experience for me.

⌐◦❈◦⌐

When I was first introduced to the Al-Anon program, my partner had just recently entered a treatment center. Although he decided he did not have a problem, I felt completely lost. He walked out of his program and I stayed in Al-Anon.

As a gay man, I believed that people would not understand if I talked about "him" or "he," so I tried to keep pronouns out of my sharing. A little while into the program, a member pulled me aside and loaned me one of her books. She told me she had marked a page for me to read. Later that evening, I read what she had marked. It was a sharing from a gay man in recovery. Wow! They could accept me as I am and practice principles above personalities. I was relieved to know I was not alone and I could drop the mask. I was not unique.

After that, I shared at meetings openly and honestly about my feelings. The members loved me enough to let me be me.

After a while, I decided the relationship with the man I loved was very unhealthy. The program brought me that awareness. It was not easy to end our relationship, but I did—with much support from my Al-Anon and A.A. friends.

About ten years later, we crossed paths again. He asked why I was in the area and I shared that I was attending an Area Assembly. He responded, "Are you still in that group? Did I screw you up that badly?" I lovingly said, "I was already a mess; you just helped me find the help to be healthy." We hugged and are now good friends.

⌒⌒⌒

My Sponsor had many qualities I admired. I decided that I didn't want her to see any of my blemishes, so I tried to show her only my good parts. I soon learned that it was too difficult to try to appear perfect around her all the time. I was simply going to have to trust that she could love me with my imperfections. As our relationship grew and deepened, I discovered that she does not love me any less because I have imperfections.

In time I found myself trusting her more. One day she told me we were going to start something new. She told me it wasn't my fault that there were many things I didn't learn growing up in an alcoholic home, but it was not too late to learn them. She said she would help me.

It has not always been easy letting go of shame and learning to trust. Today I am learning to parent myself in a way in which my alcoholic parents were unable. I am learning new skills and better ways of doing things.

⌒⌒⌒

Before Al-Anon, I used my Jewish identity to separate myself from others. In Al-Anon I learned to look for what I have in common with others instead of immediately separating myself.

My Sponsor modeled spiritual openness. My partner, an A.A. member, told me to "drop my sword." Gradually my attitude changed. I became more open about my religion and found that people, including Al-Anon and A.A. friends, did not reject me. In fact, they demonstrated great respect for me. By becoming more open, I was able to be honest with myself and others about who I am.

Coming from an alcoholic home made relationships of any kind difficult. I was terrified of people. I always saw myself as growing old alone. I would be the crazy old spinster of the neighborhood, with hundreds of pets and no friends.

I came into Al-Anon knowing that I wouldn't survive being alone much longer. I was in a tremendous amount of pain, constantly preoccupied with suicidal thoughts. I needed to develop relationships in order to remain a member of this fellowship, but I was terrified. The members of my group were very loving and helped me through that difficult beginning. I learned how to treat people with the same compassion and understanding that I treated my animals.

In return I have received the gift of some very special relationships. The first one is with my Sponsor. She taught me how to love and how to be a friend. She also showed me how to laugh at myself, something I was never able to do. I learned how to be alone without being lonely, and I learned how to develop a relationship with a Higher Power. Once I found a God of my understanding, I knew that I would never be alone again. I was finally able to be comfortable with myself.

It was then that my Higher Power put that special man in my life. He is a recovering alcoholic who worked at the same place I did. There is pure joy in being with someone who isn't afraid of growing spiritually. We allow each other the space to grow separately as we continue to grow closer together. He allows me to be human and to make mistakes. I thank my Higher Power every day for putting him in my life.

Al-Anon has also helped me to improve my relationship with myself. I slowly, gently took down the walls I built as a child, which protected me from everyone and shut me off from the feelings and experiences that truly make me a complete person.

When I came into Al-Anon, I couldn't stay in a meeting room more than a few minutes. I have a problem with people and crowds. Nevertheless, I stayed in Al-Anon and got into service. When making a three-year commitment, you see the same people over and over.

When I started in service, I met someone who had been in service a long time. She was a past Delegate. She encouraged me and tried to help me feel more comfortable. One day I decided to visit her. As we got to know each other, she told me that she talks to many Al-Anon people—at least one a day. She also said that I was part of her Al-Anon network. That surprised me. I had never been a part of anyone's anything. After that, every time I saw her I felt closer to her. A wonderful friendship developed.

Then something traumatic happened that changed my life drastically. I fell into a deep depression and it took three years for me to recover. All the while, my friend gave me encouragement and kept reminding me to use my Al-Anon tools. That was what I needed to hear to start recovering from this part of my life. She has given me her love, experience, strength, and hope. I will always love her.

When a relationship ends, that deep-seeded old stuff in me surfaces and I think, "I'm finished with people." I begin to think that it's not safe to invest time and share myself with others; that no one really needs to know who I am; and that people just cause pain. Then I realize that thinking that way goes against who I am and what Al-Anon is all about.

Instead, I can thank God for what I've learned from this relationship. Then I can humbly ask Him to remove my shortcomings. Perhaps I'll do better next time.

I'm married to a recovering alcoholic. In the last year or so, he has been diligently working his program, which includes daily meetings and continuous phone conversations with other people. As a result, I found myself alone more often than usual. I wish I could tell you that I handled it gracefully, but that would be a lie. The resentment inside me soared. I told my Sponsor about this and we talked about it at length. I told her that beneath my resentment lies a fear of being abandoned and a deep fear of being alone.

My Sponsor gave me an assignment to help me face my fear. The assignment was to plan a trip somewhere—anywhere—but I needed to go alone. She asked me to plan on going to public places and restaurants, but to go alone. Her own experience taught her that going through something like that could build inner confidence and lessen fear.

I picked somewhere hot—Florida. I wanted to see nature too, so I made a reservation for a kayak trip through a wilderness park. The Web site claimed that you could see birds, turtles, and gators galore.

Since I'm not a kayaker, I thought this outing would really stretch me, and did it ever. When I checked in to start my adventure, the man informed me that I would be the only one going out on the excursion. "Excuse me, did I hear you right? I'm going out there alone?" I secretly wondered if my Sponsor had called him! He said that it's best when you're alone. As he reassured me that I would be just fine, he slid the injury or death waiver over for me to sign. What was I thinking? For every "what if" I could dish out, however, he gave me an answer to combat it.

Well, he must have had a trusting face, because I believed him. As I headed down to the river, the guide gave me several tips to keep in mind while I was out there.

1. There is only one river. I can't veer off and end up somewhere else. I may go down a wrong channel, but eventually I'll hit a dead end and then have to turn back and go back to the main

river and continue where I left off. If I go with the current of the water, I'll be okay.

2. I'm going to feel lost. Everyone does.
3. If I tip over, just stand up. The average depth is three-to-four feet.

I could see the metaphor for life that God was giving me.

With fear and anticipation, I set off. I gasped at the beauty in front of me. I was in awe at the sight of hundreds of turkey vultures, dozens of big, white birds, blue herons, alligators, turtles, woodpeckers, kingfishers, blue jays, cardinals, and a bald eagle. It was remarkable. My heart pounded out of my chest when I saw the alligators, but they really were more afraid of me.

The trek was four miles long and was supposed to take two-and-a-half hours to complete. The guide was going to pick me up, but I didn't have a watch, so I had no idea about the time. I didn't know the route, so I had no idea where the end was. I hadn't kayaked before, so I didn't know what speed was expected. I took three wrong turns. I stopped for a few minutes to rest and at times I rowed really fast hoping it would be over soon. And you know what? The guide arrived at the pickup point less than five minutes before I did. I was exactly where I was supposed to be at exactly the right time. Another life lesson.

───────※───────

When my sister and I were together for family holidays, she would usually speak to me in ways I found to be unpleasant. By the time I left her, I didn't feel like talking to anyone. I would even feel the interaction physically, as nausea, for a long time afterward.

When I first started coming to Al-Anon meetings, I couldn't imagine letting go of my anger toward her. Forgiving her was unthinkable. Despite my doubts, I kept coming back. I started making friends at my home meeting. The women there were supportive listeners who didn't blame me or themselves. I learned to listen to their stories and they did the same for me.

After about a year, I called my sister to wish her a happy birthday. She started into her usual complaints about money, how nice it must be to have a husband, and how lucky I was. She kept going, laying out how unfortunate her life was with a long litany of the wrongs that had been done to her. I simply listened and when she was done, I said, "Wow, that's rotten." To my surprise she laughed, I laughed with her, and then she asked me how I was doing.

Now I know it doesn't do me any good to take responsibility for the problems of others. As one of my fellow Al-Anon members pointed out, in the phrase "to take offense," there is a choice to be made. Today I can make a better choice—just listen and let it be.

I'm one of those members who had to try Al-Anon twice before deciding it was something that I needed. When I returned to the meeting I had attended the first time, they accepted me unconditionally. They were happy to see me back.

I got a Sponsor and went to meetings, bringing along my anger, resentment, and discontent. I was talking about getting a divorce; my Sponsor suggested I wait a year before making that decision. She suggested I work on the anger and resentment and try to get some serenity in my life first. Since my husband was in treatment, this was a good time to start working on myself and doing a little service.

When my husband got out of treatment, we didn't know each other anymore. We were strangers. I had only known him as a drinker. However, with some time and with the grace of our Higher Power, we started to get to know each other as friends. We eventually became a new couple—a better couple. It's a good relationship. It's not perfect, but it sure is better than what we had 15 years ago.

After making the wrong choices in love relationships, I was spiritually bankrupt once again. I had divorced my alcoholic husband

and plunged into another destructive relationship. I fell madly in love with an emotionally unavailable man. As a result of his repeated infidelities, I fell right back into the emotional turmoil of living my life through someone else. Even after all the lessons learned through my failed marriage, I continued to attract men who weren't able or willing to invest in a healthy relationship.

Fortunately, in Al-Anon I met a wonderful Sponsor who saved my sanity. She coached me to listen to what was happening inside rather than distract myself to avoid the pain of change. I learned that making healthy choices can be very unsettling, but with the guidance of my Sponsor, it can become less scary. I relearned how to use the simple tools of the program.

I continue to struggle with my emotional emptiness and try not to fill it with unhealthy choices. When I falter, I repeat to myself, "Okay, God, I have done all of the footwork I can. You can take over from here." I find release, and as I can let go of the problem, the solutions appear. Each challenge I face this same way helps me grow in a healthy manner.

⌐◁▷⌐

I was aware of all the wrongs my husband was doing on an hour-by-hour basis. He was never fast enough in his recovery for me, and we were sliding down a mountain faster than we could scramble up. I didn't realize then that my impatience and micro-management had anything to do with our struggle.

It was during a meeting that a wise Al-Anon member spoke about a telescope. I realized that I was looking at my husband through a telescope and examining him way too closely. I decided to turn the telescope around and look at him from the other side. He became much smaller! Taking a look at my husband from a distance changed our slide down the hill to a more leisurely hike up the mountain.

⌐◁▷⌐

When my husband became violent, I knew that I needed to leave the house and take my 15-year-old son with me. I made a phone call to someone in the program. Although she wasn't able to put us up for the night, she told me to come to her house and she would help us. By the time we arrived, she had called another person in Al-Anon who could give us a place to stay. Although my son and I visited our house daily while my husband was working, we went to our new friend's house every evening until we felt safe enough to stay in our own home.

I will never forget the strength I gained from the acceptance, love, and understanding in the fellowship. Many years later, I happened to see this person at a meeting and immediately felt that connection again from so long ago.

⌒∽⌒

I am the wife, granddaughter, sister, and in-law of several recovering alcoholics. I am also the mother of an adult son who has married a young woman just like dear old Dad. Recovery in a relationship is a journey for me.

When I came to Al-Anon, I only wanted the drinking to stop. I felt I could take care of any other problems we might have. I needed to learn to live before I could let live. I didn't know how to do that. My Sponsor loved me and helped me to trust myself. She affirmed my attempts to do better, "One Day at a Time." Our son came to Alateen when he was 11. I kept telling him that he didn't have to attend meetings because of his dad, but that he was entitled to be there because of our family disease. This helped our relationship through the teen years.

My Sponsor told me I could make amends to our son by giving him a happy mom. This effort took many meetings and still does. I find that even now, the best thing I can do is to love with detachment and to be happy with my own life. I don't give advice and I don't pry into his business.

I have learned to "Let Go and Let God" where it concerns my husband and his recovery. We stay active in our respective programs. We like each other much better this way. We had to learn how to trust each other and how to have fun together. This is an ongoing process.

⌒⌒⌒

Relationships and friendships used to be about cruelty, judgment, and being unforgiving. I believed that I needed to do something to gain the other person's approval, or to be somebody different from who I was at the time. I believed that showing up and acting as a good counselor for the other person would guarantee that we had a good relationship. In the process, the other person never saw who I was.

After a few years in Al-Anon, I began to develop a relationship with a Higher Power. I began to learn that I was God's trusted servant and that God did not want me to be abused spiritually or emotionally. As I grew in my understanding of a Higher Power's love, friendships that were one-sided and emotionally draining began to lose their thrill.

New friendships came into my life. I found women who were kind, creative, fun, loving, and caring. I found friends who asked how I was and didn't just talk about themselves. I began to notice that all my female friends had good men who loved them. Our time together wasn't filled with tales of relationships that weren't working. Instead, they would share what was working in their relationships and how they worked as a partnership through the daily process of life.

After a while, I began to look at my own life. I was still choosing men who needed me to counsel them. I was still holding on to a man who had been cruel to me for years. I kept hoping he would change and I didn't want to look at reality. I began to ask if this relationship was what my Higher Power intended for me, or if it was my own self-will that told me I wasn't good enough for relationships with kindness, respect, and dignity.

I began to believe there might be a different way for me to think about relationships. I tried out my new ideas by getting a Sponsor.

I chose a woman whom I had admired for years, but never had the courage to ask. I never believed I was good enough to have her as a Sponsor. I was afraid that she would tell me what I thought I was—a really ugly person.

Instead, she shared from the heart. She began teaching me self-acceptance and the importance of accepting God's love through His trusted servants.

Next, I let go of the male friends who were cruel to me or required that I be their counselor. I allowed myself to have men in my life who were supportive—the ones I had ignored in the past because they weren't exciting. I began to discover a great excitement in the simple courtesies—the "thank you" for small favors, the return of household items washed and cleaned, the knowledge that someone was supportive of me and I didn't have to do it alone.

It's not easy to break old patterns. When I get scared, I remember that these relationships are gifts that God extends to me, patiently waiting until I say "Yes."

For Thought and Discussion:

1. How can I recognize serenity in the behavior of another Al-Anon member? When might I have been better served by following that example?
2. What qualities do I admire in other people? What can I learn from people who have these qualities?
3. How can I begin to practice Al-Anon principles in my relationships with other people?
4. How can I give back to Al-Anon based on my current level of comfort?
5. Who in my group can tell me about sponsorship?
6. When there was conflict in my Al-Anon group, how was the matter resolved?
7. How have I been able to focus on principles rather than personalities in my relationships?

Chapter Nine

Detachment with Love

The Serenity Prayer is often the first thing a newcomer hears at an Al-Anon meeting. The prayer asks the God of our understanding for "the serenity to accept the things I cannot change." The First Step gives us the same lesson—to admit that "we were powerless over alcohol" and that alcoholism is an illness we cannot change. Detachment with love is an application of this basic lesson. With it, we can let go of trying to change what is beyond our control without blaming ourselves or the person suffering from the illness. It is possible to love the alcoholic without loving alcoholism. It is also possible to love ourselves, even though we are powerless to fix the alcoholic.

The greatest obstacle to letting go is the persistent belief that we have the power to change someone else. Step One is a simple lesson, but difficult to integrate into our lives. Before we come to understand that alcoholism is an illness, we don't always have the wisdom to know the difference between what we can change and what we are powerless to change.

Many of us justify our actions by telling ourselves that we're good people who love others, care about them, and do what we do for their own good. When we first hear about detachment, we might think it requires us to stop loving and stop caring. But detachment with love doesn't mean that we cease to care about another person. It doesn't even mean that we care about ourselves more than another person. It simply means that we let go of our attempts to change what is beyond our power to change. There is great love in accepting ourselves for who we are. There is also great love in accepting the alcoholic as a person trapped in an overpowering illness.

Trying to change what we can't control is like banging our head against a wall. It's painful, but it doesn't improve the situation. It doesn't really show that we care. It just shows that we're not behaving rationally anymore. It serves no purpose, and only gives us pain without any possible positive result. We somehow imagine that banging our head against the wall will lead us to a solution, and that it demonstrates how much we love the wall. We have yet to accept Step One.

The Serenity Prayer can be used as a guideline for healthy boundaries. It's not our fault that there are some things we cannot change. We don't have to feel that we aren't good enough just because our ability to help has its limits. There's wisdom—and serenity—in accepting what can't be otherwise. We can only be responsible for ourselves. We don't have the power to be responsible for someone else.

We can still find meaning in our lives by helping others, but it would be illogical to make the meaning in our lives dependent upon things that fall outside the boundaries of our personal responsibility. Detachment with love means letting go of unreasonable expectations for ourselves. We can continue to love people and care about them. Hurting ourselves by persisting in negative and stressful speculation, however, is not proof that we're helping ourselves or anyone else.

It's not wrong to hope for a positive outcome, but we also have to accept the limits of what we can possibly know. We don't know for sure if the outcome we desperately pray for will prove to be the most beneficial result for ourselves or the alcoholic. We do know from experience that failure and frustration often turn out to be the first steps in a process that ultimately brings more positive results. While there's no guarantee that every negative will turn into a positive, there's also no guarantee that things will turn out to be as bad as we fear. We just don't know what the long-term results will be. They are out of our control. It doesn't make sense to focus all of our attention worrying about something that may never happen—or if it happens, to worry about what the consequences will be. Detaching with love also means detaching from the outcomes that we—from our limited perspective—think will be the best.

The slogan "One Day at a Time" defines an appropriate boundary. We know that we can't predict or control the future. So why would it be difficult to detach from our own image of a future that may never happen? Yet in fact, it's quite difficult for many of us to do exactly that. Why are we so convinced that we know what will be best for everyone? What basis do we have for being so certain about what the future will bring? When we focus on a future we can't know, we prevent ourselves from knowing the satisfactions that the present day could offer.

There is wisdom in admitting that we simply don't know everything and in accepting that we don't have to have the answer to everything. There is wisdom in doing nothing if we don't know what to do. We can find serenity by accepting what we can't change.

Detachment doesn't mean giving up on love. It means opening the door to the joy, hope, love, and kindness that are available to us every day. We can detach from old ways of thinking that make our day's challenges appear to be unmanageable. We don't need to hold on to the thoughts and actions that continue to bring pain into our lives.

Personal Stories

I had set some boundaries for myself about alcohol. Since I no longer drank, I didn't allow anyone to drink in my house or car. Then I met a girl who was a dark-haired beauty and just as sick as she could be.

When I picked her up for our first date, I told her that I didn't allow alcohol in my car. Nonetheless, she insisted that we go to a store and buy some beer. She promised not to open it. I gave in and we made the purchase. As soon as she got in the car, she opened the beer, spraying it everywhere. When I confronted her, she went on and on about how uptight I was. I thought maybe she was right. After all, I didn't sober up to be miserable. I should still allow other people to drink when they want.

Of course our date consisted of going dancing at a bar, except that we weren't dancing. I was just buying her drinks. I finally talked her into getting out on the dance floor, but by this time she had had quite a bit to drink. She floated away from me and was dancing by herself. Every time I got close to her, she backed away and started twirling around by herself. All of the guys in the bar were watching her little show.

I was angry when I took her home, but I asked her out again. This time I made sure I didn't have a lot of money so she couldn't get very drunk. As soon as I ran out of money, however, she got up from my table and went and sat down with some other guys who bought her drinks.

I felt like an idiot hanging around while these guys got her drunk, but I didn't leave her there. When I took her home that night, I was again very angry but I asked her out for a third time. This time I didn't bring a lot of money and made an ultimatum. I told her that she needed to sit with me or I was going to leave her in the bar. I didn't understand that she was an alcoholic; I thought I would surely be able to get her attention. Of course she opted to stay at the bar with the other guys. This time I was so angry I had the gas pedal to the floorboard of my truck and was fishtailing around town to get home. The next day I woke up with an emotional hangover and felt awful. I no longer felt anger toward her, but I felt guilty for leaving her at the bar. I started imagining what might have happened to her, so I called her parents' house, where she was staying. They said she didn't come home. Now I was sure that my actions had caused her harm. I told her mom what I had done and how bad I felt.

I didn't understand her mom's response. She said not to worry and that this sort of thing happened a lot. I didn't understand why her mom didn't feel bad. I felt so miserable, confused, and guilty.

Someone suggested that I try going to Al-Anon meetings, along with my A.A. meetings. I asked this girl out for a fourth time and began to feel really stupid about what I was doing. I vaguely sensed that I wasn't helping her, but more important, I felt like I was setting myself up for a relapse. I decided to break off the date and go to my first Al-Anon meeting instead.

⌐◯◯◯ ᵒ

My husband was a charmer and I loved him, but he drank a lot. I thought all would be well once we were married. I ended up spending the next 16 years trying to stop his drinking. By then, his descriptions of me had changed from "lovely bride" to "bitch" and "shrew." Our marriage was on the rocks and I was in despair, with no courage, no serenity, and surely no wisdom left.

I didn't think anything was wrong with me. All the faults were his. In due course, however, I was glad to crawl into my first Al-Anon meeting. I expected to learn how to get my husband to sober up, and I was amazed to hear that I had to begin with me.

There were Twelve Steps and Twelve Traditions and at least twelve slogans up on the walls of that room. I asked where to begin. It was quite simple. I was told to start with my tone of voice, think before I open my mouth, and try to take my hands off of my husband. It felt like I had them around his neck in an iron grip.

Stern talk indeed, and as I stood there bristling, another member came to me and asked if I realized what the Serenity Prayer was telling me. "What do you mean?" I said. I doubt if I had even heard its words that night.

"It has three lines," she replied. "The first tells you that you can't change your husband. The second suggests you start with yourself since you can change your attitude and your actions." "Thank you," I said, "but you said there were three lines." "Yes," she replied, "Then you ask for the wisdom to know the difference, and that requires a lifetime walk in Al-Anon." I drove home that night with hope in my heart for the first time in years.

I couldn't believe that what I had been told would help, but I tried it. Instead of a sneer and a snarl when I heard his key fumble in the lock, I greeted my husband with a smile and said in a nice tone of voice that I was glad he had arrived home safely. I told him that I hoped his supper, which was in the oven, was still okay. I felt as if I were acting in a play, but I was soon aware that there was no noisy shouting and no one fighting. No doors were slammed, no children wakened with the noise, and there was no thumping on the piano. Instead beautiful music filled the family room. I had only changed my tone of voice and given thought before I opened my mouth. It was working!

Still, I had not dared to tell my husband I was going to Al-Anon. I had said I was taking a self-improvement course. I was preparing to go to my sixth meeting when he came home early. He had taken a drink but was not drunk. He asked me if I was going to my course. I had gained a little courage and said that I was, expecting a negative or even an abusive response. I could feel my knees shaking together in fear—and then what did I hear?

"It must be a good course," he said, "because there is a hell of a change in you already, and for the first time in years I look forward to coming home in the evenings."

So I kept going to Al-Anon. By listening to the shared wisdom of others, I learned that I was indeed powerless over alcohol and had been fighting a losing battle for years. Then I learned how, by changing my attitudes and actions, I could help my husband instead of destroying our relationship further.

The problem drinking continued for many months, but the atmosphere of our home and our marriage got better. When the miracle of sobriety came to our lives, I was no longer "that bitch." With the help of Al-Anon, I had become ready for a sober husband. He was eight years in recovery before he died of a heart attack. Often in his talks and at open meetings, he told how the change in me had made him stop and think about his problem and seek help for it.

My relationship with my parents used to be filled with resentment, sadness, anger, fear, and maybe most of all, judgment. All I could think of was how they let me down again and again. I had few childhood memories other than of my parents fighting and rarely being available for us kids. I felt unwanted. I did my best to go unnoticed so I wouldn't become the target of my father's rage. I resented my mother's resentment of me and her obsession with my father. When well into my 30s, my mother would call me "stupid." My father would question my morals and choices.

Since coming to Al-Anon, I have learned to set boundaries and to be clear and consistent about behavior I will not accept. This means gently hanging up the phone or leaving the room if necessary, but first stating clearly, "Your behavior is not okay for me. If you continue, I'll need to hang up or leave." Then I follow through with my action in order to take care of myself.

I have also learned compassion and acceptance. My parents truly were doing the best they could. I cannot change the fact that they have spent so little time with my children despite being asked to come over again and again. Now my children are teenagers and are no longer interested in a relationship with my parents. I have learned to grieve for my lost childhood as I watch similar behavior unfold in my parents' lack of interest in my children.

I have learned to love my parents as they are. I can now see their good qualities too, and I choose to focus on those. My mother recently shared that perhaps she shouldn't have had kids. I felt so grateful for her honesty. I was relieved that she was finally able to share what I have known for so long. She felt safe enough to be honest with me, I hoped. I was able to give her a hug and say, "I know, but I'm glad you did."

My father has now been in recovery 11 years. I have finally seen the loving, gentle, kind, and caring man he truly is. The resentments that kept him in bondage are few now. He works hard to rid himself of resentments each day. In many ways, he is now my role model.

I am glad to have my parents in my life today. My choice to be around them is just that—a choice—not an obligation.

⌐ ⌒⌒⌒ ⌐

What brought me to Al-Anon was that I saw my relationship with my sister in five steps that were repeated over and over again. The steps were:

1. I would find out she was drinking.
2. I would get depressed for months.
3. I wouldn't talk to her.
4. I'd start talking with her by phone.
5. I'd talk to her more and more by phone until I went to see her.

Today I have a life of my own. I see my sister once a year for only an hour or two and talk to her by phone much less than I used to. When I recently learned she was in jail, I realized that perhaps jail might be the best thing for her, and I didn't get depressed.

⌐ ⌒⌒⌒ ⌐

As I continue working the Al-Anon program, my relationships with women are more rewarding. In a recent relationship, we both enjoyed each other's company and shared the responsibilities in our relationship. We both chipped in to do things together. This relationship continued for a year, when she asked for some changes from me. Reflecting on her request, I told her I was unable to do it, and said she might need to move on. I was able to accept that she might do that—and she did. The amazing thing is that she remains a good friend of mine. I learned that my Higher Power takes people out of my life for something better. This something better may not even involve a relationship!

⌐◇◇◇⌐

As a single mother with a son to raise, I felt an enormous burden. I felt that I was totally responsible for how my son turned out, and that if I didn't do the right thing at all times, he would turn out badly.

My son had a lot of difficulties while he was growing up. I got into Al-Anon just as he was starting his senior year in high school. His grades and performance in school had suffered because he refused to do his homework. That year, I told him that I was going to let him be responsible for how he did in school and that I would no longer remind, scold, or nag him to do his homework.

It was a difficult year for me, and I had to bite my tongue almost every day. For the most part, though, I succeeded. His graduation from high school was a celebration because he knew he did it himself. He was so proud of himself, and I was able to be proud of him for his accomplishments.

Our relationship has continued to improve. I have learned that I cannot change him; I can only support him. Little by little, I have been able to let him be his own man while I stand by and cheer him on.

⌐◇◇◇⌐

Before Al-Anon, my marriage was dramatic and full of chaos. There was a lot of arguing. My husband claimed he didn't have a drinking problem. However, I had big problems: fighting, worrying, making excuses, trying to cover bad checks, and making sure he made it into the bed, as well as taking care of the house, the kids, and the finances.

Now five years later, I don't have the chaos. I have peace. He's still out there and struggles to get back into the program. I work my program in all my relationships. We don't have the fights or the drama we used to have. I have the choice to dance the dance or sit one out. I get out of his way and "Let Go and Let God." I have found peace and purpose in my life, and the program works with me everywhere I go. I am happier and have more balance and better boundaries as well. I am a grateful member of Al-Anon, which has saved my life, my sanity, and a lot of my relationships.

⌐∽⊗∾⌐

In any type of relationship, especially with alcoholics, I always used to put others' needs before my own. I didn't always look for what was best for me. Instead, I tried to figure out what was best for them.

Many times in relationships, I would try to justify my actions or try to rationalize what I was doing and why. In essence, I realized that I was just making excuses to cover up my behavior. For example, I took care of the alcoholic when he was getting sick because that's what I thought a caring girlfriend would do. At least that was my rationalization. I shielded him from the consequences of his behavior. I didn't hurt him, but I didn't help him either. I work in social services where we teach others to be accountable for their behavior, but I wasn't applying this to myself.

I have since learned that I am responsible for me and can be held accountable for my actions. When I helped him and then held resentments toward him, it was my choice to do that. Shielding others is not always best for the other person or for me. I have learned it is actually better to withhold help sometimes, because I would be doing more harm than good.

When I gave help that wasn't asked for or needed, I couldn't be the person I wanted to be. I was spending my energy mired in someone else's actions or behavior. I have learned that I need to develop limits or boundaries for myself. I need to think first and recognize how far I can go before I feel less in control of myself. I need to stick to my boundaries.

Now that I am applying this approach to my life, I feel independent and strong. I trust my decisions and my choices, and I know that I will be okay. I think the Al-Anon phrase that explains it best is, "You can't help them until you help yourself." This means that I can't think about what is best for them until I first think about what is best for me.

❈

Early in my recovery, my actively-alcoholic wife asked if I would attend a charity benefit dinner with her. She had purchased two relatively expensive tickets to an event that was to be held two or three weeks later. I was excited that she was asking me out—it seemed like we rarely did things together anymore and rarely if ever at her invitation. Then I remembered all the disappointments of the past and the resentment of finding myself in public with my wife falling down drunk.

In Al-Anon I had learned to set boundaries for myself, and so I said to my wife, "That sounds like a wonderful evening and I would love to spend it with you. But I want you to know in advance that if you're drunk that evening, I will not go with you." She agreed.

On the evening of the benefit dinner, she was drunk. When she asked me if I was ready to go, I gently reminded her of my conditional acceptance of her invitation and declined to go. She was very upset. She cried. She lamented the money she'd wasted on the tickets, and as hard as it was, I held firm. That was a turning point in our family.

It still took many years and many more Al-Anon meetings before we realized sobriety in our home. That was eight years ago, and my wife and I are still together. I continue to attend Al-Anon meetings and continue to work on my program of recovery. I also work on my living amends to my wife by trying to be the husband I've always wanted to be. Living with an alcoholic is too much for most of us—living with a sober alcoholic is sometimes too much for me. But I know my Higher Power is always there with me, supporting me, caring for me, and loving me. My wife has a Higher Power that feels the same way about her. So we stumble along, hand in hand, each in search of an ever-closer relationship with our Creator.

⌒⌒⌒

The biggest block I had to overcome in my relationship with my spouse was my fear of confrontation. Our fights were mostly about financial issues, which caused me the greatest difficulty. He got angry, so I got angry. After all, he got angry first. I was ashamed to feel this way. There was a lot of blaming and yelling, but very little progress. I felt I had to choose the exact words and the exact moment to say anything. I thought this would avoid an argument, but of course it didn't. I couldn't say what I wanted to say. I wanted to speak in a positive, kind, simple, direct manner without the underlying fear, anger, and harsh words.

I finally realized that my fear was tied into a lack of confidence in myself, and that most of my anger came from not being satisfied with my own behavior. I needed to get more honest with my feelings. My stoic front had to go. There wasn't any physical violence involved, but there was verbal abuse that I accepted. I began to see that being honest with myself was a step in my recovery.

I talked to my Sponsor, and she suggested getting on my knees and talking to my Higher Power, asking for guidance and clarity. This seemed a bit uncomfortable to me at first, but she insisted it would help. Things went a lot smoother, although somehow I felt I needed to do more.

My Sponsor brought the Fifth Tradition to my attention. I wondered if I was "encouraging and understanding" the alcoholic, or if I was still blaming him for my failures.

My Sponsor suggested I try service. I did, and I noticed later that I had an amazing, new confidence in myself. I was no longer defensive. My relationship with my spouse has vastly improved.

Thanks to Alcoholics Anonymous and Al-Anon, I have had a continuously healthy relationship with my recovering life partner for 18 years now. One of her requests from the start was that she would not have to endure drunks in our home.

Through Al-Anon, I learned about setting boundaries. I learned that although I couldn't change anyone else, I could set boundaries and limits in my life and in my home. One of the toughest things I had to do was to ask my 19-year-old son to move out. He had broken our rules time and time again because of his drinking. A few years later, he moved back in and we told him the rules hadn't changed: There was no drinking in our home, and he was not to come home if he had been drinking. We didn't see him much on weekends, but we slept better at night.

This no drinking rule has proved valuable many times. One time, my brother was passing through my town on his way to his in-laws. When I arrived home from work, he was sitting in my living room with a beer in his hand. He looked at me, held up his beer, and asked me if I minded. I said, "Thanks for asking. Yes, I do." I didn't say it mean and I didn't tell him why. I visited with his wife and kids and that was great. My brother spent most his time outside, drinking and smoking.

I care for my brother, but I don't care if he doesn't like our rules. I didn't get mad at him. I didn't tell him there was help for him. I didn't try to fix him. I just set my boundaries and stuck with them. We parted on good terms and I kept my serenity.

⸻

I came to Al-Anon because of my first wife's drinking. When that marriage ended in divorce, I began to understand that I never really had a good concept of love. I confused love with pity.

In Al-Anon I came to realize that to love someone is to let them be themselves and to accept them for everything they are—not to judge them. Once I started doing that with my second wife,

I started liking myself. Any strife that we had over minor things completely evaporated. I learned to let things go. If she wanted to do something that didn't exactly fit my plans, good for her. She was an adult, totally capable of running her own life and making all the decisions she and her Higher Power needed to make. When I stopped trying to run her life, she stopped trying to run mine. As a result, the love between us has grown and the relationship has deepened.

⌒◯✖◯⌒

I entered my marriage with the thought that if it doesn't work, we can always get a divorce. I knew my husband drank and used drugs, and I wasn't happy about that. We even went to a marriage counselor a few weeks before we were married. Despite my trepidation, I believed that once we got married, everything would be alright. I was wrong.

We quickly got into our respective ruts. We didn't talk much about our feelings—except when he came home under the influence. Then I would proceed to extract promises that things would change. I wanted to believe that they would. I thought that if only I loved my husband enough, he would stop.

We grew further apart. Our interactions revolved around day-to-day survival and whether or not my husband was going to be intoxicated. We had no discussions of the future, few goals in common, and no shared vision. The joy had left our lives and our relationship. I had begun to lose hope and to respect my husband less.

We divorced, and I entered Al-Anon the following year, desperate to regain sanity in my life. I stayed involved for a few years and dealt with my anger, sadness, and other issues. I got my life on track, went back to school, obtained a graduate degree, and moved out west. I occasionally attended Al-Anon, but since I wasn't living with an active alcoholic, I didn't feel a pressing need.

Over the years, I heard from my ex-husband a few times. I had written to express sympathy when his mother died, and I had received some cards from him through the years. We met for dinner, 19 years after our divorce. I found him charming, mature, loving, and at peace with himself. He had found A.A. more than a decade before. I realized that we both wanted to try again. I knew I needed to get back to my own program if our relationship were to work.

I went to meetings, got a Sponsor, and worked the Steps—especially Steps Four through Seven. This time the focus was on me, not on helping anyone else. I finally began to see the marvelous gifts this program offers for my spiritual growth.

I realize today that my husband's recovery is not my business, and that how he chooses to work his program is up to him. I don't have all the answers for myself, so I certainly don't know what is best for him. What a freedom it is to only be responsible for myself!

⌒⋙◯⋘⌒

My wife was very ill for a long time, but I never stopped hoping that she would get better. I did everything I could for her because I thought it was my responsibility as a husband. I didn't realize that she was keeping her alcoholism secret, and that all the illnesses she seemed to suffer from were her way of hiding the alcoholism. Over the years, my focus became increasingly centered on taking care of her. If someone were to ask me what I wanted more than anything in the world, I would have said, "I want her to be healthy." Without realizing it, my happiness became entirely dependent upon what she said or did—and I didn't see that as a problem. I didn't think I had any problems; only she did, and I was taking care of her.

The rejection and sense of failure I felt when she moved out were overwhelming. It seemed so unfair. I couldn't have tried any harder for her, yet it wasn't enough. I had a deeply-ingrained habit of thinking that everything would be better if only she could get the care she needed. Even after she left, all my happiness was still dependent on her.

I couldn't accept the idea of keeping the focus on me—it seemed fundamentally selfish. The little self-esteem I had was dependent upon my thinking that I was a kind person who cared about others and would do whatever it took to help. I wasn't about to let go of what I saw as my own integrity.

I found some relief when I grasped the meaning of Step One—that I was powerless over alcohol. If she had the flu or some other illness, my help might do her some good. In the case of alcoholism, my help was hurting her. She was the only one who could do something about her illness. She didn't want my help for the illness that she actually had—only my support in helping her deny it.

The Serenity Prayer began to take on more meaning because I attained some measure of wisdom that helped me tell the difference between what I had to accept because I couldn't change it, and what in fact I could change—myself and my attitudes. I learned to detach with love when I realized that it wouldn't be a moral failing on my part if I didn't focus on helping her, because despite my self-delusion, I wasn't helping her. It no longer made sense that there could be any moral or spiritual good in engaging at great personal cost in utterly useless activities that were doomed to fail.

Putting the focus on me wasn't selfish—it was the only realistic choice available. I find the idea more useful now because it points me in the direction of things I can change. To some extent, my happiness can still be affected by what other people say and do, but at least I recognize today that there are steps I can take to change my attitude.

When I first started attending Al-Anon meetings, my relationship with my children was strained at best. My interactions were based almost entirely on protecting my children from the consequences of their own actions and on keeping the peace in my home.

I am learning to step back and let them experience consequences. At first it was difficult. Personnel in the schools and in the legal system pressured me to make sure my kids did what they were supposed to do and to keep them out of trouble. I saw both of them go to jail and it was hard. They were angry and hurt that I no longer protected them. I had drawn boundaries and they didn't know how to respond.

Gradually they have learned to accept that I will support them, but I will not enable bad behavior. They treat me with respect and are grateful for the things I do for them. For my part, I consider every interaction I have with them a gift. Every positive moment is something I probably wouldn't have had without Al-Anon tools. As part of my recovery, my prayers to my Higher Power mainly consist of, "Please take care of my children, whatever that may mean."

 ⌐◈⌐

My Al-Anon recovery has given me many coping skills to heal my relationships with my girlfriend and coworkers. First, I have learned to have serenity and a warm, accepting, loving attitude toward myself so I can relate to others in a healthy way. I now know that unhealthy relationships can cause hurt or shame. This year has been wonderful for me because I'm confident and can detach with love.

 ⌐◈⌐

I loved my husband and he loved me, but our marriage was falling apart. I was growing and changing. I had new boundaries, and my husband didn't like some of them. He resented my going to Al-Anon meetings because that meant everyone would think he was an alcoholic. His constant refrain was, "What ever happened to the girl I married? Where are the good old days?" I guess the good old days had passed.

Out of the blue, an old friend of my husband's gave him a call. Hearing the stress in my husband's voice, he asked him what was happening. My husband told him that we were divorcing, and his friend was astounded. He said, "How can that be? You two are the only people I know who truly love each other." For some unknown reason in a mysterious God-filled moment, my husband had a moment of clarity and made a new commitment to our marriage. God did for us what we couldn't do for each other.

Eighteen years later, I have the marriage I never could have dreamt possible. We love and care for each other in a nurturing way. I work my program using the Steps and Traditions in my home, and somehow the light of this program shines on us all. We laugh, love, and grow together in a healthy way, healing each other as we go.

⟀

When I was growing up, my mother abused me—verbally, emotionally, and physically. I can't remember her ever not drinking. We fought about everything and anything. If she said one thing, I would say another. I would never agree with her on any issue. Our arguments ended with my running away and hiding so no one could see my pain or that I was crying. I would never let my mother see me crying, even when she was hitting me. Therefore she hit me harder and longer than she did my other siblings. I hated my mother. I had never heard her say, "I love you," to any member in my family.

I ran away from home when I was 16 years old because I could no longer take the verbal and emotional abuse of being told I was no good, that I would never amount to anything, or that I was stupid. When I left, I said I would never come back.

Years later, I did move back to my hometown to be closer to my family. My dad was having health problems. He died from complications from surgery, which made it necessary to put my mother in a nursing home while she recovered from two heart attacks.

My brother asked me if I would check on her daily to make sure she was doing okay. My attitude had changed a little, so I agreed to stop in and see her after work. We still fought occasionally—

more so if other siblings were around. Sometimes very little was said before I went home.

My experience in Al-Anon helped me to change my relationship with my mother. Eventually I was able to gather enough courage to tell her the things I had wanted to share with her. When we were told she was not doing well, my brother, who is in A.A. and Al-Anon, went to the nursing home with me. She was sitting up in her chair when we got there. I felt I needed to share my feelings with her and got up the courage to say, "Mom, I love you." This was something I had never said to her before.

I had given up hope that she would ever tell me that she loved me. She opened her eyes and looked at both of us and said, "I love you both." We are the only two out of six children that ever heard her say that.

After that day, our visits changed. I would stop in after work, hold her hand, and talk with her. As she continued to get worse, I would place my hand on her forehead and push her hair back. When I was leaving, I would give her a hug, a kiss, and tell her I loved her.

Thanks to Al-Anon members asking me the hard to answer questions, I got to hear my mother say she loved me before she died.

For Thought and Discussion:

1. As an exercise in detachment, can I think of something negative and reframe it in terms of its positive aspects? Can I think of something positive in negative terms?
2. Why am I so concerned about someone else's actions?
3. How can letting go of others help me?
4. What did I dread would happen that never came to pass?
5. What old attitudes can I let go of today?
6. How have my boundaries changed since coming to Al-Anon?

Chapter Ten

Choosing Happiness

Some members describe acceptance as "living life on life's terms." Acceptance means putting aside the wish that our situation could be different from what it is. It's a costly luxury to worry, obsess, criticize, or pine for something that we can't have. We pay for this luxury with what we could have: the peace of mind that is available to us today. To reach acceptance of our present circumstances, it is important to come to peace with our past and to heal old wounds. This work in turn assures us that we won't recreate our past relationships in the future.

The searching and fearless inventory of the Fourth Step prepares us for the Fifth Step: accepting ourselves as we are—imperfect, with flaws and moral failings. Step Five sharpens our focus on ourselves. We put aside the illusion that we have done no wrong. We recognize that we've played a role in creating our current life situation. We let go of blaming the alcoholic for all of our troubles. We cease to be a victim of life when we begin to take responsibility for what we have done and admit to ourselves "the exact nature of our wrongs."

But after this frank self-assessment, it's important to admit our shortcomings to another person and to the God of our understanding. It's helpful to have a Sponsor or a close friend who will be supportive and respect the confidentiality of what we say without being judgmental. We acknowledge our faults in order to bring energy and commitment to our resolve to change our lives for the better. It's a great relief to bring long-hidden thoughts to the light of day, knowing that we are taking a positive step forward with the intention of leaving old behaviors behind.

The Sixth Step is another Step of self-acceptance. When we are "entirely ready to have God remove all these defects of character," we accept ourselves as we are and hand the rest over to our Higher Power. We recognize that we don't need to fix ourselves. It's not our responsibility to do so. All we have to do is to be ready to leave our guilt and remorse behind.

In the Seventh Step, we humbly ask God "to remove our shortcomings." The humility in our request for our Higher Power's help flows directly out of the self-acceptance that we've demonstrated in Steps Five and Six. We ask for this help humbly because we have admitted our shortcomings and we know that it is beyond our power to remove them ourselves. There's a great deal of dignity to be found in the humility of asking for our Higher Power's help. We share this humble dignity with every human being; no one is better than another from God's perspective. When we recognize our common humanity, we take an important step toward building trust and intimacy with others.

It's entirely within our power, however, to make amends to those whom we have harmed. Step Eight asks us to make a list of all those whom we've harmed, and Step Nine asks us to make "direct amends" to the people on our list, "except when to do so would injure them or others." These Steps deepen and strengthen our commitment to take responsibility for our lives, take positive action that makes a difference to ourselves and to others, and leave behind the idea that we are victims who have been treated unfairly.

We can't change the past. However, we can change our interpretation of the past, which can make a difference in how we feel today. When we are willing to look at ourselves critically and admit our errors, we can regret our mistakes while also taking some satisfaction that we've grown since we made those mistakes. We earn respect for ourselves as well as from others even as we remain humble out of respect for the modest role we play in a world cared for by a Higher Power.

It is our attitudes, not our relationships, which can keep us trapped in the past. If we choose to be resentful and unhappy, it is not the fault of anyone else. As we change, the nature of our relationships will inevitably change. As we say in the Suggested Welcome to our meetings, "So much depends upon our own attitudes, and as we learn to place our problem in its true perspective, we find it loses its power to dominate our thoughts and our lives. . . . The family situation is bound to improve as we apply the Al-Anon/Alateen ideas."

Personal Stories

I developed a sense of security during the first five years of my husband's sobriety, when he attended A.A. regularly. When he stopped going to meetings, my heart sank and I began to worry. Then I read in our literature that worry is an over-exaggerated sense of my own responsibility. His sobriety was between him and his God. His decision to go to meetings was just that—his decision, not mine. My worrying about it wouldn't make one bit of difference one way or another to him, but it had the potential to paralyze me.

Fortunately, I had learned a new way of acting in life—rather than reacting. After telling him I was concerned, I let go of that worry and continued working my own program. I am not God in anyone else's life, so instead I put effort into learning and applying the principles of detachment. They have now become an automatic way of life for me.

If I had not let go of worrying, I would have wasted many years nurturing this defect. To me, Steps Six and Seven are all about what defect of character I am entirely ready to have God remove. I felt I had to develop an attitude of perfect trust in my Higher Power. I had to ask God to remove this destructive, time-absorbing defect if I were to have any serenity in life. I worked to admit I was powerless over the alcoholic's thoughts and decisions in his life, and I freed myself to live my own life as best I could. This approach actually works, even with only a little willingness to improve my own life and to keep the focus on myself. Working my own program helps me to accept our many differences.

❦

Since I've joined Al-Anon, I've allowed myself to find a friend within me. Before, I was truly my own worst enemy. I beat myself up on a regular basis. Any time I felt the courage to change the things I could, I'd quickly sabotage myself with my greater need for approval to shore up my lack of self-esteem.

I've learned to listen and participate. It's okay not to be perfect. I can pat myself on the back, even if others disagree.

I've learned to love myself even when I make mistakes. I've learned that integrity is much more valuable, satisfying, and long-lasting than the instant approval I was searching for previously. I've truly learned to be a friend to one of God's beautiful creations—myself.

<hr/>

My wife was a functional alcoholic with a good job. She was—and still is—a very good person. Yet the alcoholic babble usually set in every night after eight o'clock with circular, meaningless arguments and no resolution. She would scream at me that she wanted a divorce, which would separate me from my children—the last thing I wanted. After years of intermittent counseling and cyclical improvements and disasters, I was in a state of hopelessness. I was desperately confused and torn, wondering if I should continue in the insanity or leave the marriage.

I didn't know if I could ever make the decision when she made it for me. My wife came to me and said that we were both unhappy and should get a divorce. A great weight was lifted from my shoulders. I learned that if a decision is difficult to make, then it is not the time to make it. I had the courage to change, and we are now divorced with joint custody of the children.

<hr/>

After I had been in Al-Anon a while, I began practicing the idea of "starting my day over." Up until that point, I would hold on to any grievances against life. Any argument was a great excuse to carry resentment, anger, or worry for days. In the case of my daughter, she was never just naughty; she was doing something to me.

One day I decided to start my day over after my husband and I exchanged insults in a heated dispute. Instead of carrying my baggage around with me, I left it behind. I felt better immediately and I could enjoy my family. Later I noticed my husband was doing that as well, and soon my daughter was following our example.

I am still amazed that I could have such an effect on my family by taking care of myself. Our changed attitudes really can enrich our lives, and in the process, the situation really does improve.

⌒◠⧜◦⌒

My husband and I were surprised by the news that he had laryngeal cancer, even though he hadn't smoked for many years. We asked how it could be, and the doctor said, "The years of smoking and drinking can cause this kind of cancer."

I started to panic. My internal voices started a stream of despairing thoughts that I found almost impossible to stop. "How can I do it? How can I manage another thing? Where will I get the strength to carry one more responsibility?"

For six years, I had been my husband's caregiver while he experienced debilitating health conditions. I thought I had finally accepted the limitations that chronic illness had imposed upon our lives, but here was another challenge. I was not concerned with the outcome of the treatment. The doctors were confident that a regimen of radiation would remove the cancer with minimal side effects. I was concerned about how I could manage to cram one more very demanding responsibility into the day. How could I possibly drive my husband to the hospital every day for six weeks? I was already physically and emotionally stretched to the limits.

I decided to reach out for help. I started calling every agency in the county that offers transportation to the elderly and handicapped. Every place I called told me that for one reason or another, they would be unable to offer assistance. With every call I made, my inner voices got louder. Even when two daughters offered to take a week off from work to help, I continued my descent into despair.

I reached out to my Sponsor and to my program friends. Others who had experienced similar problems shared how they had survived living in the role of caregiver.

They said the most important thing for me to do is to take care of myself. If I am not physically, emotionally, and spiritually in balance, I am more susceptible to the negative effects of stress. What better place to turn than to my Higher Power?

I take a few minutes with the God of my understanding before I begin the day. I say a brief prayer and turn the day and my will over to God. This helps me realize that I am not alone and gives me strength. Only by staying centered on the positive and by using the tools that have helped me in the past can I live today and remember that I can do for one day what I couldn't imagine doing for the rest of my life.

When my mind does stray, I need a ready tool to bring me back so that I can center myself. The easiest tool for me to use is to pause for a moment and become aware of my breathing. I breathe in and breathe out in a slow, steady, continuous breath. As I breathe, I say to myself, "As I breathe in, I breathe in peace and serenity. As I breathe out, I release all tension and fear." I repeat this exercise several times until I become calm.

I get eight hours of sleep, eat well-balanced meals, and get some exercise every day. I make sure that I get to see the sun rise over the ocean at least once a month. I arrange for respite care so I can have a weekend retreat at least once every three or four months. This is a time to relax, to pray, to journal, or just walk around without having the responsibility for the care of another. I take time for relaxation and recreation, including time away from my husband. Nothing can wear me out faster than being on call 24 hours a day, seven days a week. This sounds basic to life, but in facing chronic illness, it's easy for me as the caregiver to neglect the basics of caring for myself.

Al-Anon has shown me how to care about another person without taking complete control of that person's life. It has helped me to keep the focus on myself.

All during high school and college, a young man lived with us. I spent a lot of time with him, but didn't really know him. That young man was my brother. He's three years younger than I am, and I could have been a mentor to him as he went through high school and college right behind me, but I wasn't. I was too overwhelmed with living in an alcoholic home to do anything more than think about how to meet my own needs and desires.

Now I'm slowly learning how to be a big brother to him. I recognize that the answer to releasing my guilt is by making amends, not by avoidance. I don't give advice unless he asks. I try to be there for him in a consistent and reliable way. As I've started to treat myself better, I've started treating him better as well.

Today I'm on Step Eight. I know some day I need to—and want to—make amends to my brother. But that doesn't mean I can't start changing my behavior today.

⌐⟋⟍○⟋

Our world crashed when both of our parents died and I became the guardian of my only sister, who is twenty years my junior. As a high school teacher, I felt secure that a 14-year-old would present no challenges or surprises. I had counseled troubled teens and their parents. I just needed to apply textbook lessons to our own home life and I would produce a responsible member of society. I had not considered the effects of growing up in an alcoholic home, which had affected both of us.

When she began using drugs and alcohol, my little sister spiraled out of control with failing grades, truancy, broken curfews, thefts, and disobedience. I battled to control the uncontrollable. I stayed up to lecture, plead, cajole, threaten, and cry. I tried enrolling her in alternative programs at school. I dragged her to be evaluated for alcohol abuse. I started counseling for both of us, looking for a cure for her behavior. I complained so much that church friends avoided us. Finally I called the police. After she had spent a week in a juvenile detention center, my sister was declared unruly. She remained quiet for a few months, but nine days after her 18th birthday, she left our home. Four years after the death of our parents, I admitted I was a failure.

I began a descent into darkness. The emptiness I felt within began to overwhelm me. I prayed every night that I would die, and I woke up crying because my prayers had gone unanswered. Everyone in my immediate family was lost to me. I struggled through the days—still teaching, but more like sleepwalking.

Engulfed in fear and terror, I dialed the Al-Anon Family Groups hotline in my area. At a meeting that night, I became aware that I had been insane and that my life was unmanageable, but that I could find help.

Three tools helped to heal my relationship with my sister. First, I found that I could only practice a single idea at a time. The slogans provide manageable bits of wisdom. I began with the slogan "Let Go and Let God." My leadership abilities had earned me praise. I could manage a classroom of restless teens, I could lead church board meetings, and I could direct dramatic productions. I had come to believe that my managerial skills would substitute for loving kindness and cooperation. I had to get out of the driver's seat. I discovered that I was not able to release or detach from those I had tried so unsuccessfully to control. However, I could turn the lives of others, including my sister's life, over to a loving Higher Power. By practicing "Let Go and Let God," I listened to my sister on the phone and curbed my tongue. I kept my opinions to myself and I offered encouragement and praise. Pregnant with her first child and returning by bus across country, she called every night asking me to take care of her. I told her that God would help her to provide for herself and her child, and that was exactly what happened.

The next tool that worked for me was using a Sponsor. I knew that I had to let someone get close enough to share my strengths and weaknesses. I had to trust another person with my true self. If an Al-Anon member could see me as I really was, perhaps I could then accept myself with all my imperfections and let others see the real me. The person I hoped would be my Sponsor was a longtime member whom I admired. I wanted to ask her to sponsor me, but when I phoned her, I sounded as if I were warning her away. I told her that I suffered from night terrors and might have to call her at three in the morning. I warned her that I might lapse into incoherent sobbing on the phone. I said she might never know if I kept up in the fellowship since we met at just one meeting per week. I warned her away and I waited. She laughed and asked, "Do you think that tears, late nights, or lies are new to someone who has lived with an active alcoholic? There are those who have been praying for you when you were unable to pray for yourself. You are going to be just fine, and I will be privileged to be your Sponsor." She became my Sponsor and I became richer for that relationship.

In my relationship with my sister, I tried to mirror my Sponsor's genuine acceptance of me. I prayed for my sister daily. I allowed her to feel her own feelings rather than telling her how she should feel. I learned to accept her.

The third tool I applied was working the Steps—especially Steps Nine and Ten. I could not undo all of the harm my strong will and domineering manner had caused to my sister, but I could ask her for forgiveness and could proceed by promptly admitting that I was wrong when I slipped into old behaviors. The slips today are less frequent. We now support each other as we face our own separate challenges in life.

⌐◅✄▻⌐

Many of my relationships have improved since starting my Al-Anon recovery. One of the most important has been with my only daughter. I grew up with the disease of alcoholism and carried many negative attitudes. I brought these, along with my good qualities, into a marriage at a very young age and passed them down to my son and daughter. My husband was actively drinking. Our lives became unmanageable.

I verbally and physically mistreated my daughter, mostly because of my anger toward my husband. I was unable to express my feelings to him, and she was the victim of my wrath. Our relationship was damaged badly and seemed irreparable.

Over a period of time, I began to heal from the past and was able to make amends to her. I have been blessed with being able to spend quality time with my daughter, and I look forward to many more loving experiences with her. Recovery is a daily occurrence, but the rewards are beyond my dreams.

⌒◯⌒

After my marriage ended in divorce, my job transferred me to a new city. I had new surroundings, new people in my life. Everything familiar to me was changed. My children did not want to leave their friends in our hometown and move with me. For the first time in my life, I chose to live alone.

After becoming a member of Al-Anon, I found that I had a lot of firsts in my life. I didn't realize that I had been using all my relationships, especially with men, to try and fill the hole in my soul made from not getting the love and affection I needed as a child of an alcoholic.

I became so eager to work the Steps and learn the program. I wanted to work the Al-Anon program at the pace I had worked everything else in my life—frantically, trying to force results quickly. My Sponsor helped me understand that I could work the Steps at my own pace and in my own way. This approach was a revelation for me. I actually had choices and options on how to learn and what to learn.

After working through the Steps for the first time, I was astounded and gratified to learn how much better I understood my alcoholic father. I did my Fourth Step on my relationship with my dad, and for the first time in my life I came to know, love, and accept him for who he was. I saw so many qualities in him I hadn't seen before. I saw how my attitudes, behaviors, and judgment of him had built a solid wall of anger and resentment that no one could penetrate. Sadly, my father had died several years before, but through the use of Steps Eight and Nine, I was able to write my dad a letter of amends. I developed a new relationship with him even after death. I felt so close to him, and I allowed myself to go back in time and let that little girl sit in his lap and hug and kiss him. I allowed myself to see us together walking hand in hand. I felt the love, nurturing, and security I had not experienced before.

⌐≪◯≫⌐

When I was ready to put Steps Eight and Nine into action, I made my list of people, places, and things I had harmed. I knew it was time to return to where my former husband lives and make amends. The years of resentment were finally too heavy a burden for me. I turned my rubber conscience and concrete heart over to the care of a loving Higher Power.

In three recovery-filled months, I found the courage to write two letters of amends. They were awkward letters, but honest and written from the heart. My ex-husband was grateful to receive them, and I felt the release of guilt and resentment crack the mortar in those walls of fear.

⌐≪◯≫⌐

I had been in Al-Anon nine years when I was finally ready to take the Fifth Step. In the alcoholic family in which I was raised, men were expected to be strong and silent, and "dirty linen" was not to be aired. Therefore it was with great fear and uncertainty that I proceeded to describe "the exact nature of my wrongs" to another human being.

The person I chose to share this with didn't bat an eyelash. In hindsight I am amazed she could stifle a yawn for so long. When I was finished, or thought I was, she asked the one question I really did not want to hear: "Is there anything else?"

How did she know I was holding back? As much as I wanted to answer "no," I also wanted to live up to the honesty encouraged by our program. I stumbled my way through as I revealed the one secret I had kept hidden all my life from everyone—including myself.

"Well," I said faintly, "I have these feelings."

"Most people do," she replied.

"Not *these* feelings," I countered. "I feel attracted to other men."

I had said the fatal words. I was sure that now she would bolt out the door, screaming in horror, so strong was my own self-loathing. Yet she remained nonplussed, adding only a single word. "So?"

"But I don't know what to do with these feelings," I explained. She responded, "Have you considered feeling them?"

That was the one thing I hadn't done. Until I wrote my Fourth Step, I had been only vaguely aware of their existence. Yet as I let myself feel these feelings, I soon realized they had been with me for a very long time. I had often heard in Al-Anon that the chief symptom of the family disease of alcoholism was denial. Now I could see how far my denial had extended beyond my family's drinking.

Step Five allowed me to step out of denial and move forward with my life, no longer hiding in the darkness. It provided the initial action that brought me to a more intimate, honest, and real relationship with everyone in my life—including myself.

⌐⌐∞⌐⌐

I thought I was being a good ex-wife and making amends by leaving my former husband alone. It seemed to fit the part of the Ninth Step which reads, "except when to do so would injure them or others." We had no children, and once I came into Al-Anon I no longer had contact with any of our mutual friends, so I left him alone.

Over the years, opportunities involving people, places, and things that were tied to my ex-husband crept up, but I turned them down. I lost touch with friends because I never wanted to return to the same town where we had lived when we were married. Why would I want to reawaken memories of either good or bad times or be with people who would see me as the former wife?

I had become comfortable with my single life. It was as if my marriage was something that never happened. I had changed my last name back to my maiden name, had several career changes, moved away, and went on with my life. Imagine my surprise when my ex-husband and I began communicating by e-mail—brief "happy birthday" and "happy holidays" messages. A crack seemed to open in my "it never happened" facade, as if my Higher Power were saying, "Get ready; get willing..."

I eventually made several visits to the "home state of my heart" to visit my Al-Anon family that was so related to my recovery and my life there after my divorce. Prior to the most recent visit, I prayed to my Higher Power for guidance about making a direct amend to my ex-husband. I e-mailed him saying that I would like to meet him for lunch, but that I did not wish to intrude upon his present life and would understand if he was not comfortable in meeting me.

Although I expected rejection, he agreed, leaving me a voice-mail message. It was hard to believe that I had moved on with my life so much that I didn't even recognize his voice. I wondered if I had healed or had just calloused over.

Although divorce had legally ended the marriage 27 years ago, I felt the need for both closure and to make amends for my part of the failed marriage. What went wrong in our marriage was tied not only to his alcoholism, but to the fact that we were both adult children of alcoholics. We had been incapable of having an adult relationship because neither one of us had reached out for recovery.

What followed was amazing. My Higher Power took over at just the right time. I reached across the table and held his hand as I told him, "I have always been sorry for what I brought into our marriage. My father was an alcoholic and I didn't know it at the time." None of this surprised him. He acknowledged his awareness of my father's drinking. I was amazed at the details he remembered that I had forgotten long ago. I shared how sorry I was that I had hit him, and that it had taken me years to understand who I was really hitting.

I said all that I really needed to say about my behavior in our marriage. I didn't hear the words, "I forgive you," from him, but I didn't need to. All that mattered is that I had said what I needed to say.

He made some apologies too, but my Ninth Step was not about hearing what I would like to hear from him. I had learned to forgive because Al-Anon let me know that I didn't have to stay sick by holding on to pain. It didn't mean that what he had done was acceptable. All my forgiveness meant was that I was no longer choosing to be sick.

Knowing when to end a Ninth Step is as important as arranging a time and place to set it up. God helped with that too; we simultaneously stood up and hugged each other goodbye. Our lunch turned out to be an end and a beginning. I felt like I had reclaimed a long, lost friend. Whether or not we ever see each other again, I understood that he was a part of my life and most of all, that he helped me to find Al-Anon and my Higher Power.

When I got home, I received a message from my ex-husband telling me that our lunch was the nicest thing that had happened to him in the past three years. I told him how grateful I was too. While I didn't tell him about the Ninth Step and Al-Anon, I was grateful in both my heart and my head that I had been able to recognize God's voice telling me it was time for a direct amend and giving me the courage to follow through on my instincts. It took time, but it was worth the wait.

⌐⌐∞⌐⌐

Shortly after coming through the doors of Al-Anon, I realized that I needed to learn as much as possible about the disease of alcoholism. After all, I didn't want to control my life partner anymore; I just wanted to be informed. I read and studied everything I could get my hands on, so when she talked about her disease, I could carry on an intelligent conversation with her.

I soon learned how my knowledge could be used to my family's advantage when we went on vacation to visit my family in another state. The first day of our arrival, we found ourselves waiting for my older brother to get off work and come to my parent's home so he could see me. As the hours ticked on, it was obvious that he had stopped for a few drinks—probably to settle his nerves before seeing his little sister. When he arrived, I let him know that there was a program out there that could help him. I was so knowledgeable about what scientists were discovering about alcoholics and so informed about the program of Alcoholics Anonymous that I just had to tell him. Well, needless to say, my brother started yelling at me. Then my whole family got into it. I told my sister-in-law, my mother, my sister, and anyone else who would listen that there was a program for them too, and it was called Al-Anon. I could not understand why they wouldn't at least give it a try. After all, look what it had done for me!

The next time the family got together for dinner, my mother took me aside and asked that I please not disturb the whole family again by badgering my brother. How dare they? My brother was the one with the problem. My brother was the one who was drinking. So I stayed home and played martyr. My Sponsor told me a martyr is someone who suffers greatly due to his or her beliefs. He didn't say they suffer greatly due to someone else's beliefs. He gently directed me back to Step One. I had to admit that I was powerless over my brother's drinking, and powerless over my family's reaction to it. I am so grateful to my Higher Power and my Sponsor for their gentle ways of helping me discover the lessons I need to learn in life.

Several years later, I had the opportunity to make amends to my brother by letting him know that I love him. I made amends to my family by keeping my nose out of their business. Last, I made amends to myself by forgiving myself for my reactions. I have found the serenity in my relationships with my family that can only come from working a good program, talking with my Sponsor, and going to meetings.

A coworker and I had very different religious and political beliefs, and I was surprised to find myself resenting and judging the "close-mindedness" I assumed her values represented. I used work time to strike up controversial conversations, and I took every opportunity to voice my opinions in condescending tones to her. At the end of a long week, I acted out in this way and watched my colleague quickly pack up her things for the day—visibly upset.

Not surprisingly, something nagged at me all weekend, and when I reviewed my behavior with my Sponsor, I was horrified to see that I was doing all the things that I was being critical about in my coworker. It was I who was close-minded, prejudiced, and self-righteous, not her.

Humbled, I used the Ninth Step to make amends to her, and over the years my Higher Power has used this person to serve as one of my greatest teachers. As a result of my willingness to look at my own behavior toward someone different than me, I gained a beautiful friend and have been able to apply these rich lessons to many other areas of my life. Today when I perceive differences between myself and others, my Higher Power helps me see that we are more alike than I might realize.

⚭

There is such a fine line between jealousy and hope. I remember looking at my Sponsor and her husband and wishing that I had what she had, which was a husband in A.A. I was sure that would fix all that was wrong between my husband and me. What I didn't see was that our relationship was damaged by the disease of alcoholism, and not only by my husband's behavior. My reactions had also harmed our family deeply, but I was so far into blame and denial that I couldn't see my part. I was still trying to get other people to change so that I could be okay.

I wrote out an encyclopedic Fourth Step and took it to my Sponsor. We met at the park and sat on a bench watching our children play as I hauled out this huge stack of paper. Her eyes got so big before she laughed and said, "I have an idea. Why don't you just tell me what's *not* in there?" Perhaps she was half-joking, but I took her at her word and told her what I had been ashamed to include in that litany of complaints about my husband. Oddly enough, my omissions had nothing to do with him. I haltingly told my Sponsor what I had never told anyone else: My dad had sexually abused me. Then I told her how I had been raped as a freshman in college and had given up the baby that resulted for adoption. She held me and cried with me. I felt such relief that I was sure I was brave enough to go home and tell my husband. I had never told him. My Sponsor cautioned me to let him know in my Higher Power's time, not mine, and that Steps Six and Seven, and the readiness and humility that go with them, were very necessary first.

In my self-will, I was sure that I was ready. I never asked my Higher Power, and instead I went home filled with self-righteous "honesty." That day a pattern started that continued after several Fifth Steps: I would come home on a pink cloud and announce I wanted to talk to my husband. He would run for the bathroom and lock himself in. It just never seemed right when my nose was pressed to the crack in the door.

I eventually learned in Al-Anon that I would know when the time was right, and I prayed to be able to know when that time came. In the meantime, I began to practice new and uncomfortable principles in my life: honesty, humility, and humor. I began to see my part in things and to be responsible for only that—no more (which is martyrdom) and no less (which is denial). I began to see that my life and relationships with my husband and others in my family were just as good as I made them today. When I let go of my expectations and didn't take things personally, I was able to just enjoy the other person without expecting tomorrow to be just like today or yesterday.

The time came when I had to learn the principles all over again. Our youngest son was drinking and using drugs, threatening suicide, and out of control. By this time, my husband had gone to an A.A. meeting while he was on an extended business trip 1,500 miles away. Again I learned it wasn't about me.

When he came home, we decided to try some family counseling to help deal with our son and the crisis that surrounded him. On the way home from a session, I began ranting about how we all needed to be honest or we wouldn't get anywhere. My husband turned to me and in a gentle voice said, "If you see a problem, you're probably part of the solution." I felt so angry and threatened. How dare he be so balanced and talk about recovery to *me*, who had been in the program longer!

I was so angry, I moved out of the bedroom and into another room. Of course I took my Al-Anon books with me, and was sitting up reading them with self-righteous fury when my husband appeared in the doorway. He had a rose in one hand and a card in the other. He tentatively handed me the rose. When he saw that I at least accepted that, he handed me the card. It said, "I know you have been trying to tell me something . . . I am ready to listen." In that moment, all my fear and anger fell away. I knew that this relationship would endure or not, according to our Higher Power's will. I just had to do my part.

I began to tell this man, who had stayed by me in my insanity and my sickness without ever knowing the exact nature of my past, that if after I was finished he wanted a divorce, I would understand. Then I told him everything about the sexual abuse by my dad, the rape, and having to give up the baby. At each step of my story, he moved closer from where he had sat down at the foot of the bed. Finally, he was holding me in his arms and crying with me. Then he began to laugh. I stared at him in disbelief, tears still welling. He hugged me, his body still shaking with laughter. "Honey," he said, "Every time you came home from a Fifth Step wanting to talk to me, I thought you wanted a divorce!"

<hr />

I spent most of my life trying to get approval and acceptance from my family. I never felt good enough to meet their expectations. On the flip side, I did not know how to make friends or be friendly. I pushed everyone away and treated most people I met gruffly. Sometimes I was downright mean. I was never nice to anyone, even if they were nice to me, including waiters, waitresses, store clerks, and toll booth collectors.

When I got into Al-Anon and started working the Steps, my Fourth Step revealed what I had hidden from myself. When I got to the Eighth and Ninth Steps, I had to make amends to people I didn't really remember or know. My Sponsor gave me a great idea: I could make amends by changing my behavior today. I practiced smiling and being pleasant to every person I met each day. I can now even be pleasant to people who are not nice to me because I can remember a time when I was like them.

As a result, I have lots of friends today. Waiters, waitresses, store clerks, and tollbooth collectors are now people who are happy to see me. Today all my relationships are important because people are important to me.

⌐◦⊗◦⌐

When I first met my wife, I didn't know she was an alcoholic. I suppose that the ever-present jug of wine in the refrigerator should have been a clue. However, I didn't grow up with alcoholism and was naïve. I did grow up, though, in a family in which we thought we knew how to control and fix everybody and everything. Not surprisingly, I thought I could do the same—until I came face-to-face with active alcoholism.

My wife became gravely ill with liver failure and was in and out of treatment centers. I had to run a business and care for a four-year-old daughter. My wife and I nearly divorced, but fortunately a mental health professional suggested Al-Anon. I was desperate to try anything. From the first meeting, I knew this program could help me to deal with the issues of sadness, grief, anger, loneliness, frustration, and isolation. I worked the program diligently. At the same time, my wife found sobriety without A.A. That lasted six years. Unfortunately, I made a common mistake and gave up going to Al-Anon meetings.

When she started drinking again, it was like reliving a nightmare. By this time, my daughter was ten years old and well aware of what was happening. I quickly found my way back to the program, got a Sponsor, and worked the Steps. After more than a year of fits and starts with sobriety and my filing for divorce and custody of our child, my wife hit bottom at a rather unpleasant detoxification center.

Today she has a wonderful Sponsor and has been going to one and sometimes two meetings a day. As a family, we have a lot of healing left to do, but thanks to Al-Anon, I can see now that miracles happen. By turning my life and my will over to a Higher Power and letting go, things sometimes work out for the best; albeit, not always the way I might want, and not without some pain.

I cannot surmise to know whether we will survive as a healthy and intact family, but I do know that with both of our programs and by living "One Day at a Time," the home situation has already improved dramatically. Only when I "Let Go and Let God" have I been able to keep my sanity. When things are stressful, I repeat the Serenity Prayer and turn things over to my Higher Power. Al-Anon is like a compass, keeping my spirit on the proper course.

⌐⊂∞⊃⌐

After three failed marriages, I hooked up with a wonderful man and was crazy about him. I was sure that this time it would work. After only a few months, it wasn't working. Fortunately, he is a member of A.A., and he suggested Al-Anon.

I cried a lot during my first meeting as I realized how lost, lonely, and frantic I had been. For years I had been working hard and fast at covering up my feelings of failure and trying one more time to make things go right, on my own. So it was a tremendous relief to take the First Step and surrender. Step Two helped me to reclaim my relationship with the God of my childhood and start letting Him help me again. God then sent me a wonderful Sponsor. We laugh, cry, and work this program together and have a special relationship.

As I have proceeded through the Steps, my other relationships have dramatically improved. I recently finished my Ninth Step and experienced a wonderful sense of freedom. I was able to see those things I kept doing over and over that for all my good intentions, did not give me the results I wanted. After working through the Steps, I noticed with wry humor that the people closest to me have certainly begun acting a lot better.

I now believe that with God's help my current relationship can be the one I have been longing for all my life. But my expectations are much more realistic now. I have been able to kindly set the boundaries that I must have for my own serenity. I do not have to give my opinion about everything he says or does. I have begun learning to honestly tell him things that I would have held back or tried to work around before, for fear of his negative reaction. Amazingly, he does not react in the angry way I had feared. Most of that turned out to be in my head. I continue to work the program because it is easy to slide back into my old habits.

⌒⟨⟩⌒

Lately I've had some conflicts with people at work, which is very rare for me. In one instance, I knew I needed to confront a colleague, but if I had done it right away I would probably have blown a gasket. So I used the slogan "Think," which reminds me to wait. I don't have to do anything I'm not ready to do. Another piece of wisdom from meetings helped a lot: "When in doubt, don't." It took a week of sitting with this problem and talking it through with others before I was ready to talk with my colleague. I prayed to my Higher Power for guidance and for my coworker to be receptive to what I had to say. An opportunity presented itself, and I sat down to talk.

Not only did I find the words I needed, but my colleague was grateful that I had approached him, and he met me more than halfway. A few weeks later, a company reorganization threw me into a tizzy. I wasn't happy with my new position and expressed some of my concerns. Then I became worried that my bosses would perceive me as a negative influence. My thoughts quickly snowballed into the certainty that I would be fired. I wrote in my journal and talked with program friends. Then it came to me: I am not defined by outside conditions. It is not my boss's responsibility to give me serenity. I must believe in myself.

When I know my own worth and trust that my Higher Power loves me, I can let go of the need for approval from other people, no matter how important they may seem to my survival. As it turned out, my bosses heard my concerns and responded with kindness and understanding, not disapproval and censure. I am happier than ever in my job. I am a work in progress.

⌒◯✕◯⌒

My exposure to alcoholism, first as a child and then as a husband, produced a formidable accumulation of resentments against people with alcoholism and against the whole world. Out of a fear of destructive retaliation, I avoided contact with my family, sold my shotgun, and walked long distances to dissipate my anger. Without recovery, I experienced nightmares and severe skin problems. I was barely able to function as a provider for my wife and children.

I managed to avoid physical harm to myself or others, but I developed scorn and a blistering sarcastic tongue as weapons between myself and my alcoholic wife. I felt occasional relief and a feeling of superiority when I was able to cut her down to size. Verbally destroying others was a tradition from both of our families.

I finally landed in Al-Anon, and through the fellowship and principles of Al-Anon and Alateen, my family experienced recovery. After a year of growth, I was able to start contributing to meetings.

The program's literature taught me that there are clear consequences to harboring resentments, such as living joylessly in the past, obsessing about the possibility of revenge, and thinking of myself as a victim. I became motivated to let go of old anger.

At the same time, I learned that I didn't have to accept violence. I realized that I might have to make choices to ensure safety for myself and my children, such as calling for police protection, keeping money and spare keys in reserve, or going to a safe house until the offending person has recovered enough to participate in reconciliation.

As I continued to attend meetings, I became more comfortable with myself. By getting outside of my own skin, I have begun to deal with the challenge of forgiving past abusers. At first I wasn't able to discover why I should move beyond just letting go and actually forgive. Then I received a long letter from one of my grown children. He used graphic language to paint a picture of the suffering he had endured as a child because of my failure to deal with our situation constructively. As I read and re-read the list of his fears, embarrassments, and deprivations, I recalled my own confusion and despair at the time that lead to the neglect of my obligations. It gave new meaning to being powerless over alcohol and to my life being unmanageable. Thanks to the program, I understood that I had done the best I could with what I had at the time.

I also understood that past abusers also did the best they could at the time. We were all human and subject to countless, mostly negative influences. Our guilt had to be diminished by the other factors that had operated in our lives. With this flash of understanding, I was able to forgive myself and use this new understanding to forgive my offenders.

Through my son's letter, I was fortunate enough to see my moral shortcomings from a victim's perspective. It opened me to a better understanding of the nature of my own wrongs, the need for me to seek forgiveness, and the imperative for me to extend forgiveness in the interest of reconciliation.

⌒⊗⌒

While my husband struggled in and out of sobriety, we had an awesome sex life. When he drank, he could dance, have fun, and perform sexually with a sense of freedom and abandon. Once he finally became sober and stayed sober, he no longer would dance, nor would he engage in a sex life with me. He couldn't, he said.

The fear of being judged for his performance created an obstacle that so far has lasted for the rest of our relationship.

It has been many years since we have had a sex life, and yet we have grown together in ways I never would have imagined. The loss of a sexually intimate life with my husband has been very painful for me, but much to my surprise, I have chosen to accept this "One Day at a Time," while never giving up hope that we will once again have a sex life together.

I have grown in numerous ways in Al-Anon. I have learned to love unconditionally in spite of the ebbs and flows, ups and downs, and occasional crises in our lives, including relapses, medical illnesses, and an interest in someone else on my part, which thankfully was short-lived. Through all of this, with the help of Al-Anon, A.A., and outside help as well, my husband and I have grown together in a very intimate, yet non-sexual way. We are loving and warm with one another much of the time. We touch each other frequently in sensuous ways and know each other like only people who have been together forever do. We have a private language of our own and are very playful with one another. We express that we love each other daily.

Though sex is wonderful—an experience and feeling that can never be replicated—I am grateful to have emotional intimacy. I have a sense of connectedness and a true commitment with my husband, despite that for today I cannot have a sexual relationship with him. Life is full of challenges and opportunities for growth. Most days I feel happy and full of gratitude, and this I can achieve through my ongoing commitment to Al-Anon.

<hr />

By the time I came to Al-Anon, my relationship with my daughter seemed totally destroyed. She would say to me, "Mother, the thing about you I cannot stand is that you know everything about everything."

I was absolutely miserable and devoid of spirituality. It was then that my Higher Power led me to my first meeting. Of course, most of my initial efforts to help my alcoholic son were misguided. I further alienated my daughter because I could not detach from him.

Slowly I began to recover emotionally and physically. I realized that I could try to make living amends to my daughter and rebuild our relationship by showing her my unconditional love and recovery.

Several months ago, my daughter asked for my advice on something. Since I didn't want to be responsible for the results, I told her that I was sure she would be able to figure it out in time. I mentioned that she had choices. She became quite irritated with me and said, "Mother, do you know what I can't stand about you? You never have an opinion." I realized that I have arrived. We talk now several times a week, and we have a great time together.

⌒⤫⌒

Shortly after filing for divorce from my wife, I entered another relationship and soon was sexually active. After we became engaged, my fiancée stepped back and inventoried whether sexual activity was really what she wanted this soon in the relationship. One of her concerns was about modeling appropriate behavior for our teenage boys.

After a lot of prayer and meditation, and with the help of our Higher Power, we decided to change our behavior. It was easy to make amends to my fiancée, but I had two sons at home who were aware of the sleepovers. That night, when they returned from visitation with their mother, we talked about the choices I'd made. I told them I had made a mistake by asking them to do as I said and not as I did. I said I didn't feel I had been a good model for them, but that I was changing my behavior. Making amends to my children went very smoothly and was an example of working the Tenth Step by continuing to take a personal inventory and when we were wrong, promptly admitting it.

Removing the sexual component from our developing relationship has also allowed my fiancée and me to focus on the spiritual intimacy of our relationship. We practice the Eleventh Step by praying together daily, whether it's in person or over the phone. As a result, we have been able to reach a higher level of intimacy.

I raised two children in the throes of their father's alcoholism, when I was preoccupied with my anger and frustrations. I was emotionally absent due to the struggle, trying to maintain the illusion of keeping it all together. My time was spent cleaning the house so that all the things would be in order. My mind was elsewhere, my heart was heavy, and my spirit was slowly dying.

Today my children are adults. Sometime when they were growing up, I grew up too. I have made amends to them verbally. Each time the opportunity presents itself, I also make living amends by being the kind of mother I wasn't able to be years ago. It is a gift today to be able to be present in the moments I share with them. I listen to them, give them the dignity to live their own lives by minding my own business, and most important, I refrain from being critical of them. I acknowledge their achievements and support them in their decisions.

Recently while retrieving my young grandson from school, thoughts of his dad (my son) lingered in my mind. Looking so much like his dad did years ago, my grandson approached me with pure joy on his little face. He was so excited to see me, and as I greeted him with "Hi, happy guy," I wondered if my son was happy when he was eight years old. My thoughts stayed there for just a moment. This is today, I thought, I can't undo anything, but I can love my son's child to the best of my ability.

It's just that simple. Now I listen to every word my grandson shares, whether household chores are piling up or not. My heart is full of love for him. The time when we're together is ours to make memories. We laugh and share ideas and dreams. We play and have lunch in the park. He keeps my spirit young and alive, and I am grateful for a second chance.

For Thought and Discussion:

1. What are the rewards—and consequences—of thinking of myself as a victim?
2. What can I learn about my character from my personal grievances or resentments?
3. What can I do today to better accept myself as I am?
4. How has a Sponsor helped me gain a realistic view of the share of responsibility that I have for certain problems?
5. How can working Steps Four through Eight help me make changes that can bring more happiness into to my life?
6. Where do I still need to make amends? What is holding me back?
7. How does holding onto the belief that other people should make amends to me cause me unhappiness?

Chapter Eleven

Through Prayer and Meditation

Many of us came to Al-Anon with hardly a spark of hope left, and with little or no faith. It's not uncommon to find new members who are angry and disappointed with the God of their understanding. They are angry and disappointed about their life situation. They blame God.

Our personal concept of a Higher Power often evolves and develops in a way that we cannot anticipate when we first arrive in Al-Anon, when our lives are unmanageable. As we work the program and the Steps, we can gradually establish a broader foundation to stand upon. Anxiety and fear need not play so large a part in our daily experience as it once did. We can become more confident and trusting in our relationship with a Power greater than ourselves.

Step Eleven states that prayer and meditation can "improve our conscious contact with God *as we understood Him,* praying only for knowledge of His will for us and the power to carry that out." The message of these words is not to give up, but to let go. When we surrender our will to the care of God, we drop the limiting barriers of our own past experience and make allowance for future possibilities that we cannot anticipate. We let go of our limited ideas of what could be, and open our hearts to opportunities that we might not have dreamt possible.

This Step requires patience. Taking the time to pray and meditate could prevent us from taking hasty action that might make our situation worse. We wait for a sense of what our Higher

Power's will for us could be, hoping to feel in our hearts what we come to believe is the most appropriate path to follow.

We don't ask for outcomes that we would like. We don't pray for others to change their ways. We approach our Higher Power within the limited role that we have on this earth: to be responsible for ourselves and our own actions. Just as we learn to let go of wanting to play our Higher Power's role in the lives of others, we also let go of asking our Higher Power to take direction from us. Instead, we seek to discover how we can accept what we believe to be God's plan for us.

The Eleventh Step reminds us that just because we can't see how things might work out at the present moment, it doesn't mean a way won't reveal itself later. We don't have to know the answers in advance. We're not responsible for the answers. As we learn to let go, however, we can see how things can be resolved, seemingly on their own. Eventually, we learn to trust the process. Over time, we gain confidence that everything will turn out for the best. Many of us eventually find that we've developed what some people might call faith.

The Eleventh Step helps us to maintain our spiritual foundation. Regular prayer and meditation helps us keep our hearts open and receptive to a Higher Power's plan. We quiet our minds and keep the focus on ourselves. When we do that, we allow ourselves to change. This opens the door to changes in all of our relationships, including our relationship with the Higher Power of our own understanding.

Personal Stories

I was experiencing the pain of an intimate relationship ending, by my own choice, due to unacceptable behavior. I lamented yet again my lack of fulfillment with a fellow human being. Nevertheless, I felt that by saying "no" to this relationship, I was also saying "yes" to a higher standard of what I believed I deserved in a relationship.

After spending time working the Steps, I have gained inner fulfillment and contentment through my relationship with my Higher Power. I no longer feel I do anything alone, since I have my Higher Power with me at all times. I can acknowledge beauty around me, eat dinner at a restaurant, take in a movie, air my concerns and fears about any issue—including sex and money—and live in my home without feeling alone.

As I practice Step Eleven and make conscious contact with my Higher Power, I also check in with myself and take the opportunity to care for myself.

I won't compromise the relationship I have with my Higher Power. If I were to meet someone, I would take it slowly so that I could pay attention to both relationships. My first commitment, though, is to my Higher Power. I intend to fulfill my hopes and dreams—not put them on hold for another person.

⌒✦⌒

Prior to Al-Anon, I believed in a Higher Power. I meditated, but not consistently. I didn't pray, however. The program brought the love, learning, and encouragement I needed to pray and meditate regularly.

For me, prayer means talking to God and meditation means opening myself to be quiet and listen. I believe God speaks through people, so I really listen with my heart when someone else is talking. Attending meetings helps me keep on track with God and others.

I pray several times daily. Each morning, I invite God into my life to show me what to do. At night, I thank God for the day and list what I'm grateful for as I take my daily inventory.

I came to Al-Anon the first and second times to get my husband sober. But as soon as he stopped drinking, I stopped coming. The third time I returned to Al-Anon, I came to save myself. My disease had also progressed. I was on the verge of a nervous breakdown, and I knew I could no longer live the life I was living. A member volunteered to be my Sponsor and listened to my tales of hurt, anger, and resentment. My Sponsor told me to drop "yes, but" and "what if." from my vocabulary.

My inferiority complex developed when I was a child growing up in a home with strict religious tenets and no drinking. I did not know until after several years in the program that my father was from an alcoholic home with a lot of child abuse. My mother was abandoned as a child by her parents. They decided it was more important to be missionaries in a foreign land, and left her with strangers.

My spouse joined A.A. and was very active for a few years. Life was better, but there were still many problems as our children grew up and became addicted to drugs and alcohol. We pulled together as our children needed us, but the crises kept us focused outside our relationship. As the crises became incidents, it occurred to me that I was alone in my recovery in my household. My husband no longer attended A.A. meetings. I didn't notice at first, but we didn't talk the same language anymore. The distance between us grew. I was living with someone who was no longer drinking, but he was not recovering either, and my pain grew.

I could not leave the marriage with hate, anger, and resentment. I had to accept my past and then let go of it all. I needed to love myself and believe that I did not deserve to be emotionally abused. I had to process my worst fear: the fear of being alone in my senior years.

My pain sent me for outside help. I asked, "Why me?" The answer came back that I deserved recovery. The damage from the abuse of my childhood began to heal. Facing the grief I felt with the loss of the fantasy marriage I thought I had was not fun. It took time. The God of my understanding does not give me a hard time, test me, or cause bad things to happen. My Higher Power is loving, caring, and with me always. My Higher Power walks with me through each day, even when I forget I have a Higher Power. Sometimes my Higher Power does for me what I cannot do for myself.

At meetings I was introduced to a Power greater than myself who was completely different from the God I had brought there. As I learned how to work the Twelve Steps, I discovered how to build a relationship with my Higher Power.

I use prayer to talk to my Higher Power. I have learned that although I can say anything I want, it's best if I pray for His will to be done. The Higher Power I've come to know has my best interest at heart and can see the outcome of everything, though I cannot.

Meditation helps me hear what my Higher Power says to me. I've learned over years of practice to sit still and quiet my mind. My Higher Power has so much to say to me.

I can only guess at what my answers ought to be, but He *knows*. This relationship is the most valuable thing I have. No matter who enters or leaves my life, my Higher Power will remain.

For many years, I suffered from not having an open, honest, and loving relationship with God. As I worked the Twelve Steps, the belief that God truly loved me began to grow. Finally, I thought, this is what I want: a God who loves me.

One day my Sponsor—who was also developing a loving relationship with her God—informed me that she could not sponsor me anymore because I am a lesbian, which was not okay with her vision of what is right in the eyes of God. I lost other friends that year and decided to leave the program. After months of not going to meetings, I returned in a great deal of pain. I then started on a path that has changed my life forever. What I started to see was that God loves me. I have developed a relationship with God that I never thought possible.

Whatever relationships I choose in my life doesn't change the relationship I have with God. What changes that relationship is when I choose human beings before God, or when I forget to ask for knowledge of His will and the power to carry it out. The relationship with God changes when I do not take time to talk to Him, wait for His answers, or trust that He truly knows best. I don't want to forget to count my blessings or that it is only through His grace that I am where I am today. The only person who can change the relationship I have with God is me.

It is amazing to me how years before I found Al-Anon, I had made up my mind that God was punishing me. I thought God didn't love me or care about me because I was gay. What I know today is that God doesn't care if I am gay. That is what the world cares about. God cares if I put my trust and faith in Him. God cares if I am hurting myself or if I am hurting others. God cares if I carry the message of grace, hope, and love. God cares if I believe in Him. God cares if I help others. God cares about my dreams and my disappointments. God cares if I will make it or not. God cares if I choose to call on Him in the midst of my worst storms.

Tradition Twelve reminds me to take what I like and leave the rest. I cannot allow outside issues to keep me from focusing on my primary spiritual goal. It reminds me that God is within me, and that everyone has God within them. I do not have to believe what others say, support, don't support, judge, or tell me is right or wrong. I need to have a personal relationship with a God who loves me and who will guide and direct my life.

By reminding myself of Tradition Twelve, I am open and free to embrace the spiritual foundation of the Al-Anon program. When

I apply principles above personalities, I am able to have a relationship with God and with others that I never thought possible. I have heard it said that God either is or isn't. I know with every single cell in my body that God is, and I am so grateful.

I was unable to identify or share my feelings and would obsess over a particular woman. Yet I couldn't be direct or vulnerable with her because I was trying to impress her with a good image of myself. Instead, I could have been myself and could have allowed my Higher Power to guide the relationship according to His will.

I still experience some of these defects from time to time, but I have also had some victories. I've learned through prayer to turn over the woman I'm obsessing about to the care and will of God. I've noticed that I can be vulnerable in meetings with my safe Al-Anon friends. I have used that experience to set up temporary boundaries (such as no kissing) to develop friendships with women. I had noticed that once I kissed someone, I would become obsessed and want to impress them rather than be vulnerable. This boundary has helped me to be true to myself and to get to know more than one person, which has also helped dissipate some of the need to obsess.

I've had the courage to ask for a hug when I felt I needed one. I've been able to share with my best friend that I was afraid of getting closer to her because I anticipated the pain of losing her. I was able to tell her that I had just cried on my way over to her house after seeing a play that had revealed to me how it seemed like I had lost every person in my life. She shared that she had experienced the same thing and understood how I felt. I was so relieved and felt connected with her in a new way. Without having to ask for it, she gave me a great, warm, loving hug.

In a meeting that night, I got direction from my Higher Power that showed me what would be necessary to go beyond a friendship. I have to be settled in my relationship with my Higher Power first, in His acceptance of me. I have to trust in His control over things so that I can be accepting of His will for my relationships, instead of feeling like I have to run everything. I can trust and wait on Him to reveal things and to guide me one step at a time, knowing that I'm okay with Him regardless of how my relationship develops.

I was raised in an alcoholic home, with what I thought was a normal way of life. The God that I knew gave out rewards and punishments for whatever I did. He was a God to fear, whom I had better not upset or I would be in terrible trouble. God seemed a lot like my alcoholic father, only much more powerful.

I suffered from blinding guilt every time I did something out of the ordinary, no matter what. I was obsessed with the thought of what might happen to me. What was God going to do to me? If I did something, I just knew I was going to be punished for my actions. If everything seemed to be okay for a while, I figured I had gotten away with something. I could only identify with the black and white of any situation. All the gray areas caused me grief. I carried this perspective into my adulthood, and my health suffered from all the stress I placed on myself.

When I first came into Al-Anon, my relationship with God was a one-way street. Then I gained a whole new image of Him. I discovered a loving God who cared for His children. I learned that I could have a direct connection with Him and could talk to Him as a friend. I could count on an answer of some kind even if it might be "no." I learned that no matter what, God loved me and I could trust Him.

I believe that the gift of a relationship with God has been the richest thing I have gained in Al-Anon. I still have matters to deal with, but it is so much easier with the trust I have gained in my Higher Power.

I was afraid of the God I was introduced to at an early age—a punishing, authoritarian God; an old man with a white beard. In Al-Anon I was introduced to a God of my own understanding. I saw Him in the faces of friends and in nature. I saw Her as present for me, comforting and ever-knowing, sending me messages during hard times so I'd know I was not alone.

God is all the best qualities of the people I love; all the peace and serenity available; all the hope, courage, love, and joy I possess. In hard times, I return to my first ideas about God. I get fearful and forget myself and God, and that we are connected. Then I am reminded again that we are one, by an Al-Anon friend, a bird, or a pink glow in the night sky.

⌒◯⌒

I went to my first Al-Anon meeting a couple of weeks after my wife came home from a rehabilitation center. To reach the meeting room, I had to walk through a huge room where an A.A. meeting was about to begin. I thought of it as running the gauntlet. When I finally reached the Al-Anon meeting, I discovered a room with about 20 women and one other guy. Needless to say, I felt out of place. I asked myself, "What have I stepped into? Why me? My wife has the problem." The best thing I ever did for myself was to sit down, shut up, and listen.

I didn't know what I was doing there, but I was willing to try anything to help my wife stay sober. I didn't realize that I had taken a first step that would help me completely change my life. At that moment in time, I didn't know my life was about me. I believed it was about everyone around me.

Eventually I understood that I was sick, and that if I wanted recovery like the other members had, I would need to develop a spiritual connection. I had no Higher Power. I didn't really want one, but I recognized how that concept was working in others. I began to test the idea of a Higher Power. One of the first tools I used was the slogan "Let Go and Let God." It was easy to remember, it helped me get out of my whirling thoughts, and it worked in little short-term ways. It showed me possibilities. It gave me hope.

I am not perfect, but I make progress every day. I learn something I need to know every day. Al-Anon is the foundation of my life. Al-Anon opens door after door for me, and each one displays something more wonderful than the preceding. I know that as long as I continue to work the Al-Anon program, keep an open mind, deal with my fears, and be willing to follow the paths my Higher Power reveals to me, I will continue to learn and grow in my relationships with all the people I love and all the people I encounter on this beautiful journey of life.

The most difficult relationship I have right now is the one I have with myself. When I focus on myself, I experience a feeling of great fear and abandonment. I am ready to stop running from my thoughts and feelings. I cannot allow myself to be overcome by my fear, yet I must take some time and look at it.

Each morning I remind myself to stop and ask for God's direction when fear and confusion overwhelm me during my day. I read my Al-Anon meditation books and pray for His direction and His will in my life. There must be a reason I am going through this place. I can remind myself that I am not alone—God is with me. The outcome is up to Him; I just look for His direction. The fear and anxiety subside in time when I ask God to show me His will.

Growing up in my family, no one was there to be with me when I was mad, sad, glad, or afraid. They couldn't be—they had nothing to give. Today my recovery is my responsibility. God will be the long-lost parent I have needed to help me overcome my fear and help me move through it. As I begin to trust that God will show His will for me, I also trust that this experience will mold me in a way to be of help and service to others.

Before Al-Anon, my emphasis was on trying to change everything. I was discouraged and disappointed that God didn't change the things I wanted Him to change. I wanted my wife to be well, and God didn't answer my prayers. My relationship with my wife was similar. Neither of them met my expectations; they didn't give me what I wanted. Over the years, my path to acceptance wasn't quick and easy, but it changed my relationship with a Higher Power of my own understanding.

I had given up on prayer by the time I reached Step Eleven, but I thought that meditation might at least offer some health benefits. At first I assumed that meditation meant that I should try to control my thoughts, to force myself into a state of heightened relaxation. It doesn't sound logical, but that's what I tried to do—force myself to relax. I found that I was mostly powerless over the thoughts I had, and trying to control them wasn't working out. Learning how to observe my thoughts with loving detachment turned out to be a more positive approach. It taught me acceptance.

I used the slogan "One Day at a Time" in my meditation. Almost every stray thought that brought me anxiety or pain had to do with an imagined future or a painful memory. So in meditation I practiced reminding myself to bring my focus back to the present moment. My thoughts were engaged in the "past" or the "future," but in fact I was having those thoughts "today." Bringing my thoughts back to today was a way to detach from what seemed to be the compelling reality of my imagined future and remembered past.

Acceptance comes from letting go. Letting go of what I couldn't change opened the door to a serenity that brought with it an entirely different perspective on life. Over time, I gained a measure of confidence in the results I would get if I let go. That's when letting go led to a faith in the God of my understanding.

While my difficult relationship with my wife negatively shaped my perception of God, today a more positive relationship with my Higher Power shapes my expectations for an intimate relationship. I keep my hopes and expectations within the limits of today, remember to let go of the things that are beyond my power to control, but have faith that things will happen as they should.

⌒ ∝◦ ⌐

I was at a retreat where the facilitator talked about the concept of God within us. Through Al-Anon I came to believe that God is with me. But within me? I wasn't sure. I went for a long walk to think about this idea. I tried to remember the times God was with me.

First, I remembered when my husband was so sick with alcoholism. I knew that if I didn't earn more money, I'd lose the house because of unpaid bills. So I worked toward my master's degree. In looking back at my comprehensive exams and papers, I realized that I hadn't done all that alone. God was working with me.

Second, when my husband was living on the street and would call asking me to let him come home, I wanted to give in. Instead, my voice said, "You're sick, please get help. I love you. Goodbye." That was God speaking, not me.

After years of recovery, I went to see my mom. Once again, she and my sisters were arguing. During the long drive I kept asking God, "Help me to say everything with love. Let me say what is mine to say and leave the rest. God, let your love work through me." With the help of this program, I had forgiven my mom and moved on. My mom asked why my sisters were so sarcastic and angry, and why I was not. I was able to tell her that I had forgiven myself and her for our past. I never mentioned the word abuse, yet I heard my 83-year-old mother say, "I know I abused your sisters, but I thought my actions the last few years would make up for it."

Only God within could go on and talk with her about making amends, healing ourselves and others, and taking a daily inventory. Only God within me could get us through that conversation with no yelling, no anger, and no hostility. We ended with love and hugs.

I now know that God is within me: I am shown through the tears in my eyes and the ache in my heart when my husband speaks at an open meeting. I am so grateful he found A.A. I know God is within me when I watch my grandchildren sing and dance. The intensity of love I feel could only come from God. I know God is with me when I can look at my aging face in the mirror and say, "You are beautiful," because God's love is reflecting back at me. God is with me and within me each and every day.

◦⨭◦

When I first came into Al-Anon, I had no spiritual life because I felt I had no need for it. Religion was unnecessary; it was only for the brainwashed. At the time, I didn't know the difference between religion and spirituality. To me, God didn't exist. I thought this was only a tool used to control those less powerful. Ironically, I came into Al-Anon knowing that I expected the alcoholic in my life to save me, just as a god would. Even more ironically, I knew that no human being could ever be—nor should ever be—God. I was only setting that person up to fail in my eyes.

That small insight let me know that if I were to find recovery in Al-Anon, which I desperately wanted, I would not only need to find a Higher Power, I would need to develop a personal relationship with a Higher Power—*my* Higher Power. But I had no idea how to begin.

The only thing I knew to do was to go to meetings and share about my quest. I heard, "Fake it until you make it." That is, if I acted as if I believed in a Higher Power, I eventually would. I started small, remembering when I could to choose to believe that good things that happened to me were the result of my Higher Power. I read in *Paths to Recovery* that if I was having trouble believing in a Power greater than myself, I could make a list of "coincidences" and attribute that to my Higher Power. I did that too.

I spent a long time acting "as if," and turning things over, even though I didn't believe it would do any good, while attributing coincidences to my Higher Power. I don't know how it happened, but I can honestly say that now I have a daily relationship with my Higher Power. Whenever I feel angry, scared, lonely, or indecisive, I say, "God, you handle this because I can't." Whenever something really great happens, I say, "Thank you, God." For everything else in between, I say, "God..."

Life is not always easy when you are a woman whose soul mate and life partner is another woman. When that partner is an alcoholic, things can get even more complicated. I entered Al-Anon because I thought I needed to be supportive of my partner's struggle toward sobriety and recovery. I stayed because of me.

Both of us are well-educated professional women who were previously married and have grown children. When we met, the attraction was instantaneous and something neither of us had experienced before. Social drinking became a way to communicate openly with each other, but before long drinking became a nightly pattern.

Eventually, we stopped living together, but working the principles of the program has given me new hope. The slogans are my favorites—quick and easy reminders in a hurried moment. I have learned to detach from the problems of my partner and my children, without detaching from them or feeling like I have to be doing something for them.

Daily readings and recitation of the Serenity Prayer keep me closer to the serenity and sense of peace I have longed for. I have been able to reconnect with a Higher Power I thought I had lost, who is personal, caring, loving, and rides on my shoulder as I go through my days. I am never alone again, no matter what the future holds.

My partner and I have a long way to go both individually and together, but we are on the right path. Once I learned to trust my home group, it was so much easier not to keep secrets. I didn't think disclosure about my life was going to be possible, but it has been. The love and acceptance of my group didn't change one bit. The relief and increase in my self-acceptance is truly a gift.

⟨⟨❤⟩⟩

I grew up in an alcoholic home and proceeded with a marriage and several other relationships that failed. I arrived at Al-Anon two years ago. I was distrustful, angry, bitter, and very lonely. I had always acknowledged a Higher Power in my life, but the slogan "Let Go and Let God" was a challenge.

One weekend as I was wallowing in self-pity and loneliness, I felt led by my Higher Power to travel. I packed an overnight bag and embarked on a journey I will never forget. I arrived at a small town an hour and a half from where I lived, completely dependent on my Higher Power for direction.

After some shopping, I looked at the bulletin board with advertisements. A poster announcing a gospel concert stood out, and I asked someone for directions. After I left town, I realized I was hungry and needed to clean up, but I decided to eat and find a motel only after I found where the concert would be held.

I started driving and continued until I felt that I surely must be lost. I stopped and asked if I was close. "Oh, yes," a man replied, "just a few more miles down the road." He also informed me that the motels and restaurants were not open this time of year. I continued driving and found the little country church. I then said to my Higher Power, "I'm hungry and I have no place to sleep."

I turned at the church and remembered seeing a store a mile back down the road, but when I went back I found that it was closed for the day. I decided to clean up and change my clothes as best I could in the car. I arrived in front of the church a few minutes later. I was moved to tears as I noticed people getting out of their vehicles with containers of food for a social hour following the concert. I said, "Thank You, Higher Power. I now know you are going to feed me. Now where will I sleep tonight?"

During the first intermission a man sitting in the same pew asked, "Where are you from?" When I answered, he said, "Oh, my wife is from down in that area." During the next intermission, I explained that I had set out from home that morning not knowing where I would end up. I told him I knew my Higher Power was taking care of me because I hadn't eaten since that morning and I saw the ladies arriving with food. He then asked where I was staying. I told him I wasn't sure. He replied, "You're going home with my wife and me. We just finished a little cottage and you'll be the first one to stay in it."

I walked into that church enveloped in the love of and trust in my Higher Power. I enjoyed the concert and fellowship of people I had never met. I learned that I don't have to be lonely whether I'm home or away. I can trust my Higher Power to always be there at my side, because He loves me and will provide all my needs if I ask. I can "Let Go and Let God."

I recently purchased a new car and traded in a vehicle at the same time. During the heat of the intense purchase negotiations, I forgot to have my county tax sticker removed from the windshield of my trade-in. Without it I'd have to pay the county for a new sticker. I called the salesman and asked him to remove the sticker, which he did.

When I went back, I placed the sticker in an envelope that contained paperwork from the purchase of the new car. Later in the day, it occurred to me that I should double-check that I still had the tax sticker. I pulled out the envelope and to my horror the sticker was missing. I began to rant and rave at my irresponsibility. There was a blue cloud of profanity swirling around me in the car. Then the thought occurred to me that I had lost my serenity. Was I going to allow a $20 tax sticker to control my serenity? The slogan, "How Important Is It?" came to mind. A peace came over me. I continued to think about the sticker and where it might be, but I was no longer frantic.

I couldn't find it at home or back at the dealership. Surprisingly, the peace remained with me. At that point, I accepted the fact that the sticker was lost and that I would have to buy a new one. God had given me a level of acceptance and peace about the situation.

That night as I was putting on my shoes to go to a meeting, I felt something sticky on the bottom of my shoe, the same one I had worn earlier in the day. I lifted it and there, stuck between the heel and sole, was the missing sticker. Indeed, the sticker had fallen out at the dealership, and my Higher Power saw fit to have me step on the sticker at the precise place on the shoe where it would not be damaged or scraped off.

If surrendering to God in this small way brought such miraculous results, I wondered what God could do with my life if I totally surrendered it to Him. Today those shoes remind me that God is concerned about every aspect of my life.

For Thought and Discussion:

1. What changes do I need to make in order to integrate prayer and meditation into my daily routine?
2. When I reach out to my Higher Power, how patient am I for what I believe to be an answer?
3. How do my ideas about "control" affect my concept of a Higher Power?
4. What would I have to change in order to have a different relationship with a Higher Power?
5. How difficult is it for me to put my relationships into the care of a Higher Power, without knowing how their future will unfold?
6. How has the Serenity Prayer changed my concept of a Higher Power?

Chapter Twelve

In the Care of a Higher Power

The stress of trying to do everything ourselves brought us to a point where our lives had become unmanageable. We can find relief in Step One by accepting that we can't reorder the world to suit our wishes, no matter how sincere or well-intended they are. In Step Two we can find hope in coming to understand "that a Power greater than ourselves could restore us to sanity." Step Three allows us to deepen our serenity as we gain confidence that a Higher Power is guiding our lives according to a plan, even if we don't understand it fully. In short, we find peace when we turn over anything that is troubling us—the behavior of the alcoholic, a difficult situation at work, parental disapproval, an awkward conversation we would rather not have, or another relationship issue. We give the problem to our Higher Power, the God of our own understanding, and then use Al-Anon tools and resources to help us focus on ourselves.

Step Three can be challenging, though it offers a rich reward: a serenity that grows deeper over time. We are ready to "turn our will and our lives over to the care of God, *as we understood Him*" when we begin to understand the difference between what is within our power to change and what is not. Much of our frustration comes from our unwillingness to accept what we can't change. Much of our fear comes from our inability to force a solution to our problems. Step Three is an opportunity to remind ourselves that we can "Let Go and Let God." We can let go of our frustrated wish to control the future as well as our futile inner resistance to the present moment. Instead, we can find peace of mind in bringing our will and our lives into harmony with a Power greater than ourselves.

Letting go of a problem doesn't mean that we don't want a solution. It simply means that we won't deplete our inner resources by struggling with something that is beyond our power to accomplish. Of course we want loving relationships in our lives. As with any aspect of our lives, we can't force a solution if the ability to change it is out of our hands. We can be comforted to realize, however, that we can find meaning in our lives by playing an active role within the scope of our Higher Power's plan for us. By using the tools of the program, we can bring focus to our spiritual lives.

When we turn over our lives to our Higher Power, however, it is important that we turn over every aspect of our lives—including personal intimacy. Sexual relations may be one of the last areas where we want to surrender our intent to control and invite our Higher Power into our lives. As a celebration of love between two people, physical intimacy can have a spiritual aspect as well.

Step Three transforms our inner life, and consequently has a powerful effect on our relationships with other people. It releases us from our fixation on ourselves, as well as on others. We can nurture a loving acceptance of ourselves that we can extend to others. It allows us to release the tension that comes from trying to fix everything, and to concentrate our energies only on issues that we can handle "One Day at a Time." The slogan "Easy Does It" captures the spirit of this approach: We take on a relaxed presence that is open, welcoming, and loving. We don't "need" other people in ways that we did before, so we look for—and tend to attract—personal relationships at a different level.

Personal Stories

Before my wife went to a rehabilitation center, I was biding my time, waiting for our youngest child to finish high school, before I left the marriage. I grew up with alcoholism in a family where my mother left, my father drank more, and the children were left mostly to fend for themselves. I didn't want my children to suffer as my siblings and I had, so I stayed in a marriage that was lonely and painful.

"Let Go and Let God" helped me get my foot in a spiritual door. The Serenity Prayer propped that door open for longer periods of time. With the help of these two Al-Anon tools, I was able to quiet my mind enough to see solutions that I never could have seen if I had allowed my mind to work in its usual chaotic and frenzied state. By turning over little problems and looking for solutions, I began to learn how to trust.

Slowly I learned how to deal with the problems I had with other people and myself. The slogans helped me to keep my foot out of my mouth when silence was the best route. The Serenity Prayer gave me pause and often allowed me space to think how to act and not to react in any situation.

The more I was able to step back from my old behaviors, the more I was able to see myself in the people around me. It was then I discovered that the most difficult people for me to deal with were the people who behaved like me. I began to learn from the situations that made me uncomfortable. I began to know myself, accept myself, and love myself. I began to trust myself, and then I began to share at meetings.

I am a very different person today than when I first stepped into Al-Anon. My wife and I are still together, and we have a wonderful relationship. I have good relationships with my children. I have friends at work. I have many friends in Al-Anon. I still keep my distance from my other relatives. Watching their pain is difficult. I pray for them and ask my Higher Power to look after them.

Maybe one day they will find Twelve Step programs to help them learn how to live comfortably with themselves and others.

⌐✦⌐

I run into obstacles whenever I try to resolve difficult issues with another person without consulting my Higher Power first. Relying on my will alone often produces confusion and an even more strained relationship with the other person.

I now approach a challenging relationship issue by first asking God to be the third party present while I'm with the other person. I ask my Higher Power to give me the words and intonation that will make our communication the most effective. I pray that God control the course of the conversation and that the outcome be the best for all concerned. Sometimes I pray that my Higher Power guide me as to whether or not I should confront someone. Sometimes talking to the other person no longer seems necessary after these prayers.

Recently I developed some resentment toward my mother, believing that she had been overly critical of me in one of our conversations. I was obsessed and decided to pray about whether to speak with her. Several days passed, and my mother gave me a call out of the blue. She rarely calls me and seemed to be feeling down. As I talked to her, I realized that I didn't want to hurt her by bringing up the issue I had been dealing with. Somehow it was no longer important. I remembered that she had told me once that when she gets tired, it is hard for her to watch her words and things sometimes come out wrong. As I got off the phone, I felt profoundly grateful that I had not confronted her. I also realized that my mother really does love me.

I was able to let the issue go, thanks to consulting my Higher Power, who always seems to have a better sense of timing and what is appropriate than I do.

⌐✦⌐

Once I accepted the powerlessness in my life, it felt natural to turn my life and will over to the care of God as I understood Him. I eagerly read all I could find about Step Three and was excited when my Sponsor told me I was ready for Step Four. Still, in my heart something was missing. I wanted a revelation, an enlightenment, or any kind of sign that would clearly say to me I had arrived at spiritual awareness and would always have the direction I hoped for.

About this time, my spouse brought home a seven-week-old kitten. The kitten epitomized for me a joy for life and a sense of wonder. I envied those qualities and wanted to cherish and protect them. Traveling in cars had been traumatic for our other cats because it always meant a trip to the vet, so it seemed wise to take him for a ride with no particular place to go. I placed him on the seat beside me in the car. He immediately began to plead his concern as his eyes grew wider. With all the comfort I could gather in my voice, I responded, "Trust me. I won't let you down."

At that moment my Higher Power showed me what I was looking for in Step Three. How many times and in how many ways had He said those same words to me? Like a rush of fresh air, it became apparent to me that the missing element in my Step Three decision was simple trust. Without trust, my Step Three was an earnest statement. With trust, it could become the action and spiritual growth I was seeking. The first application I found for my evolving trust was in recognizing that my Higher Power would always find ways to reach me as long as I contributed the willingness.

⌐⌐⌐⌐⌐

My struggles with a fear of abandonment were coming out in my relationship with my boyfriend. He asked for some time alone, and I instantly shut down emotionally. I took it personally, got angry, and was very cold. I met his attempts to console and reassure me with bitter brush-offs and an icy attitude. We spent the night in separate rooms, and I struggled to sort myself out.

I was so frustrated that I couldn't meet his simple request for some time alone without trying to make him feel guilty. I was also frustrated because the exact same issue between us had occurred only days before. I had spent the last week turning my problem over to God, praying for the will to forgive my boyfriend for abandoning me, and praying that he would forgive me for acting so unfairly. After days of feeling spiritually drained, I was faced with the same problem again. I knew I was reacting equally irrationally, yet I lacked the energy, motivation, and will to turn it over all over again. I cried in bed and told God I just couldn't do it tonight. I couldn't turn it over. I didn't have it in me on this night. I fell asleep in mid-cry and mid-prayer.

I dreamt I was apologizing to my boyfriend for treating him unfairly, and I reached closure in my dream. I awoke feeling as if the drama from the night before had never existed. I gave my boyfriend affection and an appropriate apology. God had seen me through the night. He picked me up where I had fallen, carried me through the night, and dropped me off in a safe, loving place the next morning. I didn't have any work to do. He did it for me when I couldn't do the work myself. I had a lovely day and a newfound trust and reliance on my Higher Power.

⌒✣⌒

Alcoholism is a confusing disease. I need Al-Anon to remind me that I only live "One Day at a Time." I need a Sponsor who reminds me to ask myself what the problem is, whose problem is it, and what I can do about it. I need a Higher Power who can be present when my focus is on the past, the future, or the never-shall-be. I need meetings to remind me that I am not unique.

In recovery, I am trying to take care of myself by doing things I enjoy, even if they take me away from spending time with my girlfriend. Through my Higher Power, I am learning to do this with love. I am even learning to pray, "God, help me to be loving and gentle with this person," before I answer the phone. My phone calls have improved a lot.

I was having a problem with letting go and letting God. My Sponsor suggested that when I was having a problem with a Step, I needed to look at the previous Step because I had not gotten that one yet. In that way, I worked backward to Step One before I started forward again. My moment of realization came after I reached Step Three. My life has not been the same since.

I'm a very visual person. One day in meditation I got the image of a person riding a bicycle on a very high wire with no safety net. The bicycle had a basket, and there was someone serenely sitting in it while the person riding the bike peddled across the wide expanse of thin wire. I was amazed at the serenity and the complete trust of the person in the basket. Then God revealed to me that He was riding the bike, and that I must be willing to be the person in the basket. But God gives me choices. I don't have to get in the basket. I can try to walk the high wire by myself. However, I am not skilled or trained in that area. I will likely fall and hurt myself. Often, I do.

When I am willing to get in the basket and just trust God, I safely reach the other side. My part is to trust, be willing, and do as God tells me. I do the footwork and leave the results up to God.

My younger sister started drinking when I was a teenager. I hated her back then and shut her out of my life completely. I ignored her when she spoke to me and turned my head when she walked into the room. This continued when I left for college and beyond.

Years later our lives crossed again. My wife, whose drinking was really bothering me, had become good drinking buddies with my sister. One day my wife came home from a conference and called my sister. My wife excitedly told her she hadn't had a drink that day. My sister had been attending A.A. meetings for two weeks and invited my wife to her first meeting. Since then neither one of them has had a drink, and they continue to be members of both programs.

It was God's grace that used the sister that I hated as a teenager as the tool to bring my wife and me into these wonderful programs. I am grateful that my program shows me how I can make amends to my sister for how I treated her. I am grateful that I have a Higher Power that works in my life to restore relationships in ways I couldn't have conceived.

⌐⊗⌐

Before I join my husband in the bedroom at night, I turn to my Higher Power and say this prayer: "God, please help me stay in the moment. Please take away my worries about my history. Please take away my curiosity about my partner's history. And please take away my fears about the morning after."

In this simple act of prayer, I invite God to be with me in the most intimate and personal time I spend with another person. If I can truly be present in the moment and let go of the past, as well as the future, then miracles can happen.

⌐⊗⌐

I went for more than a year without dating anyone, though that wasn't my will. I ran the gamut of emotions—insecurity, loneliness, and feeling sexually starved. During this time, I became aware of the power I do have: to be of service to others and explore the creative talents that God has given me. I had a change in attitude. If it is God's will, she would appear. This was a pressure reliever.

⌐⊗⌐

Whenever I was with my husband, I would try to remember that I was dealing with a family disease, and that I needed to apply the principles of the program instead of reacting. Lies from my spouse and unconscious lies to myself had created an emotional hell of distrust. I not only couldn't trust my husband, I couldn't trust myself. I simply did not know what was real anymore. I practiced the program and slowly began to see improvements. I was not so reactive; I could say what wasn't working for me without making my husband wrong. I wanted to love my spouse, and I found I could act as if I did feel love.

I continued to struggle with the question of what was real. How could I trust my husband when there had been so many lies, so much manipulation? Then a new awareness finally came. I looked up the word "trust" in the dictionary. It said that trust was something you placed in someone or something. I realized that I was placing my trust in my spouse to be the way I wanted him to be, which was an expectation he could never fulfill. Instead, I needed to trust him to be human, living and struggling with a disease. I could trust God to be God, a Power greater than ourselves that could restore us to sanity. I could trust us to be powerless over alcohol. I could trust me to be me too—also human, also living and struggling with the disease of alcoholism. Today we are both in recovery, our lives are flourishing, and our family is healthy and happy.

⌒⟨⟩⟩⟩ ⌐

I hated my husband because I thought he was being intentionally destructive, trying his best to drive me crazy. He wanted me to be miserable. What else could explain his behavior?

If I could just bring him to his senses, he could live up to the potential I fell in love with. Then everything would be just fine. I knew the alcohol was messing him up; I thought that if I could just do the right thing at the right time, he'd wake up and realize that he didn't need it anymore. But it didn't matter what I did. I bought him toys, thinking that a distraction from alcohol would help him see what great things there are in the world. I went along with some terrible financial decisions, thinking that if he learned some responsibility, his behavior would improve.

After years of trying to force solutions, I was completely insane. I could not form a coherent thought. I couldn't follow the plot of a half-hour television show. I couldn't read a paragraph in a book and understand the meaning.

The madly-in-love couple we had been was no more. The relationship that was left was distorted beyond all recognition, warped and twisted by a disease I lived with but did not understand. I came to Al-Anon utterly defeated, completely hopeless, and desperate for an end to that way of life. All I had left was anger and hatred.

Fortunately, in Al-Anon I have learned many wonderful things. First, my beloved is an alcoholic, and it's okay to love alcoholics. They are wonderful, sensitive people who have a catastrophic illness. Then I learned that my expectations were way too high for anyone to fulfill—even me. That explained my frustration. I was so entangled with my husband's problem that I had lost myself and my ability to make a decision or think clearly. For all of these years, we had been one disease with four legs.

I learned that there is a difference between the person and the disease. Now I can separate the two and love the person behind the disease. I can politely remove myself from the behaviors of the disease and maintain my own mental sobriety. I am learning to "Live and Let Live."

Minding my own business can be difficult at times. I still think I can fix his problems, even though I now know better. When I become miserable because I am trying to live his life for him, I work the Third Step and give it all to my Higher Power. My husband has a Higher Power too, and I have no idea what his Higher Power has planned for him. Even when the path seems too painful for me, it's his path and I can't walk it for him. However, I can understand and encourage his efforts.

I have learned when I can and when I cannot trust an alcoholic—and that his actions are not about me. My feelings are not hurt as much as they used to be. I do love my husband, but the damage done to this marriage by the disease is vast and deep-rooted. We may not live long enough to have a truly happy, healthy marriage, but it gets better every day. I like him again. I respect him for who he is today. I want him to walk his path, and I want to walk mine.

～⌒∞⌒～

Accepting that alcoholism is a disease has done wonders for my sanity. When my wife got drunk and did something crazy, I would tell myself that this is the alcohol—not the person I love. This helped me avoid getting angry, screaming, and doing something that I would later regret. It allowed me to continue to love her although I hated the alcohol and what it was doing to her. I learned to stop and ask myself what I have learned in Al-Anon that would help me deal with this situation.

It was easy to accept that my life had become unmanageable due to alcohol. That just seemed very obvious to me. It took longer for me to accept that I am powerless over alcohol. Actually I don't have any problem with alcohol. It is the alcoholic in my life with whom I have a problem. With Step Two I learned that while I am powerless, my situation is not hopeless. Hope lies with the God of my understanding. I always turn to Him for help. Now when something dreadful happens, I return to Step Three. I ask God what His will is for my life and for me now. Somehow I always get an answer in due time. It usually happens that new possibilities arise that had not occurred to me. I still have to do the footwork. God just provides the opportunities so that I can take advantage of them.

While Al-Anon has not produced a perfect relationship with my wife, I am at least making progress. When problems occur in the future, I know that somewhere in Al-Anon there is something that will help. Now I just take it "One Day at a Time."

～⌒∞⌒～

My dad is an alcoholic. He usually only has one or two beers, but recently I saw him drunk for the first time. I wasn't mad at him for getting drunk, because I figured that was his problem anyway.

I think I'm good at detaching, because if someone makes me mad, I go to another room without even thinking about it. Detaching is part of Step One, which says I'm powerless over everything and everybody.

The next Step is about believing that my Higher Power restores me to sanity. I can thank God who has helped me get through many things at school, with friends, and with other people.

Step Three is turning my life and will over to God. Sometimes I think about how amazing it is to be alive and to have so many privileges. Gratitude helps me stay in the solution, not the problem.

⌐◦◦◦◦◦

Before the program, I was beaten down by events. I felt worthless in the eyes of my husband. My marriage was a failure, my friends were gone (we had moved so many times), my God had abandoned me, and the church was not there for me. I felt that nothing could reach me.

At Al-Anon meetings, the members talked about asking for God's will to be done and about letting go and letting God. With some bitterness, I thought I'd apply this approach to my problems—starting with my husband's refusal to let me lock the farmhouse door before I went to bed for the night. Once he had kicked the door down, so I was afraid to lock it, yet fearful as a young mother not to lock it. So I prayed for God to work on this problem (sort of a test), and I left the door unlocked.

The next day as we were sitting outside together, a strange truck pulled up. The driver came out and apologized profusely for entering our house late the previous night. His truck had suddenly and inexplicably stalled by our lane, and he had knocked on our door for help, but no one answered. He walked into our house to use the phone for this emergency. He said he hoped he hadn't frightened us and was sorry for dirtying my clean floor. My children and I hadn't heard a sound.

After the stranger left, my husband looked at me in alarm and told me from now on to lock the door. I just chuckled to myself and did just that every evening. Asking God for His way was a lesson I learned well.

Since then my relationship with my Higher Power has changed. I trust Him with my life. My love for myself has grown, and I take care of myself. I know that with my Higher Power, I can change and become even better.

My relationships with others have changed, too. I don't keep relationships peaceful no matter what the cost to me, but I do have deeper, more loving friendships now. I am committed to my spiritual and emotional growth. This commitment has led me away from a life of failure and despair to the kind of relationships that build me up and bring me joy and happiness.

⤜⟷⤏

These past few days have been overwhelming and difficult. My pain and defensiveness triggered my husband's anger and need to control. In turn I fought for control. As a result, we both stood on the edge of the cliff looking at the imminent destruction of our relationship.

I cried out in the night to God, "Convince him he is wrong." I asked God to fix him. My desire to control increased and I cried, "Heavenly Father help me—what am I supposed to do?" The answer I got was, "Work on yourself. Go to the Steps."

Finally I gave in and went to work on Steps One through Three. As I admitted I was powerless, my heart softened. As I trusted in God's power, my anger subsided. Peace and hope were restored as I decided to surrender and turn my husband, my marriage, and my future over to God's control, where God wanted me to be. His answer to my cry for help was enough for today.

But God wasn't finished. Four hours later, my husband came to me and shared how God had been at work in him. He had seen his selfishness, he accepted responsibility for his behavior, he admitted his character flaws, and he validated my pain. God did what I could not do. He changed my husband—and more than that, He changed me too.

"Just for Today" we are in agreement, and we both see God at work in each other and in our marriage. We realize that although there has been a lot of progress, we have a long road ahead to wholeness. If we continue individually to allow God to work on removing our character defects, we will each draw nearer to God. The result will be that we will draw still nearer to each other.

⌐✧⌐

I met my wife when I was 20, and we lived in an alcoholic relationship. I was always doing everything I could so that she would do the things I wanted her to do. My whole life revolved around her. Everything I did was for her. When things didn't go the way I had planned, I would always point out that she could have done it my way. I was going totally insane, and I am sure life wasn't very pleasant for her either.

When I came to Al-Anon, I started learning that life wasn't all about demanding that she do the things I wanted. But I heard what I *wanted* to hear and left what I *needed* to hear. I tried new ways to manipulate her, and it still wasn't working. Once again I was disappointed because my expectations were not being met. I was becoming more and more insane. I became so frustrated and angry with my wife that I prayed to God to take this relationship and do with it what He wanted. If He wanted it to work, let it work; if it was supposed to break up, then He needed to do it because I couldn't.

Things started to change after that. I wasn't controlling things anymore. I truly believe the slogans "Let Go and Let God" and "Live and Let Live" really came into my heart and mind. Last year we celebrated 20 years of marriage and renewed our vows. I believe that as long as I "Keep Coming Back," I will be able to stay out of the way and let it go the way it's supposed to go.

⌐✧⌐

Lots of people around me drank too much—my father, grandfather, brothers, uncles, aunts, and friends. The drinkers weren't the worst of it, though. Those who didn't drink often seemed to cause even more distress than the ones who did. As a kid, I constantly felt suffocated and dreamt of being able to take a breath of fresh air.

There was no escaping. My father would grab the just-baked biscuits off the table and throw them out to the dogs. My mother would run shrieking from the dining room, sounding mortally wounded. Grandfather would come home drunk, railing loudly at Grandmother to unlock the door and let him in, while she sat immobile reading her Bible. She looked up only occasionally to shout at him to get off the porch and never come back. There was a lot of arguing and screaming and wailing. It frightened me and made me anxious. I was never sure what would happen next.

After one of my father's drunken indiscretions, Mother fled to my bedroom, where she locked herself in my closet for ten hours, sobbing loudly at first and then making no sound whatsoever. I thought she had died. I called to her and rattled the doorknob again and again. No response. When she finally emerged, she placed an opened suitcase on my bed and told me to pack it with anything I wanted, because we were leaving for good. I was heartbroken. This was my home. Everybody and everything I knew and loved was here. Where would we go? What would we do?

With tears streaming down my face, I slowly and carefully chose my favorite possessions, along with a few clothes, and placed them in the luggage. Finally, I secretly tucked a photo of my father beneath my socks at the bottom of the bag. I wept some more. I knew I would never see him again. I looked around the room and said goodbye to my books and my dolls and the frilly pink satin bedspread that I loved. I went out on the balcony to gaze one last time at the park across the street. I had never felt so sad and alone—or so afraid. I thought I might burst.

Then suddenly she changed her mind. We weren't going after all, she said. I was to come downstairs and set the table for the evening meal. Apparently the storm was over. Life was now supposed to continue as usual. But I was left totally drained and confused. My nine-year-old mind grasped none of it. All I knew was that I was relieved that we were not going and that my stomach was tied in knots.

It happened again and again—the anger, the noise, the uncertainty, and the inconsistency. Little was predictable, except that it would happen again. I had to be prepared for it, whenever that might be. It left me jittery. I didn't want to be caught off-guard.

The odd thing is that despite the turmoil, I loved these people. I guess I believed that all households were like this, and that the constant upheaval was just part of the daily agenda that everyone had to learn to live with. These could actually be great folks. My dad read poetry to me and made me laugh. My mom was artistic and gave me a love of cooking. They were both smart and hard-working. I tried to remember the good and erase the bad, but I always had a stomachache.

As I grew older, nothing changed except that I expanded the circle of alcoholism that surrounded me. I seemed strangely drawn to guys who drank too much, and as a result, I went into action exactly as I had been taught by example when I was a child. I'd tiptoe around trying to be perfect so as not to upset the drinker. When this didn't work, I erupted by shouting and sometimes throwing things. Mealtimes were especially difficult. It didn't seem possible to sit down to eat without black memories of my youth creeping in with every bite I took. No matter what, I was miserable. I was a physical and emotional wreck.

I believed that drunks were the source of all my distress. All I had to do, I determined, was to stay away from drinkers. I wanted peace in my life, and I was sure I knew how to get it. When my future husband came along, I put my new scheme into action. It's either me or booze, I said, you can't have us both; make up your mind. As easily as that, I extracted a promise from him to never drink again. I thought my problems were over.

Before long I turned into my mother. My husband was eerily like my father. Our household reverberated with echoes of my youth. I developed colitis and the deep melancholy that accompanies watching someone you love withdraw into the bottle.

I got lucky after 15 chaotic years of marriage with an active alcoholic. A crisis threw the two of us into programs of recovery. As I began to attend Al-Anon meetings regularly, the real heart of my problems became clear to me. It wasn't that I had somehow gotten caught up in an uncommon number of wretched relationships. Other people weren't causing the disorder in my life. The source of my misery was me.

I realized that to heal, the primary relationship in my life has to be with God. Although this was clearly the solution to all my woes, this relationship was very rocky. What I knew about God was merely what I repeated, things I had heard others say. I felt no connection to a Higher Power. I lacked what it took to create a spiritual partnership with anyone. I couldn't have the kind of relationship I longed for with my husband, my parents, or anyone else until my relationship with God improved. I learned that my relationship with others is a reflection of my relationship with God.

I knew what I wanted. I wanted serenity and happiness in my life every day. I wanted an end to the tumultuous atmosphere of our home. I wanted freedom from the prison of this disease of alcoholism. I wasn't sure how to get these things, or even if I deserved them, but I knew somehow that the answers lay with my Higher Power.

This program tells me that if I turn my will and my life over to the care of God, He will give me the power I need to do His will. All I have to do is ask. I wasn't sure what His will was or if I would recognize it when I saw it, but I wanted to try. I decided to take the Al-Anon principles as my guide. Surely these were God's will.

The miracle began to work. One by one, principles replaced my frustrations. I discovered that when I am kind, respectful, and generous rather than snarling and shouting, calm surrounds me. When I can be pleasant and open-minded, rather than being critical and stubbornly insistent on having my way, surprisingly fruitful resolutions result. When I don't expect others to do for me, I gain independence and become my own person. When I step out of the situation and my husband makes his own decisions and leads his own life, I no longer feel trapped.

There is always a payoff: I get what I give. What I hope for is God's will and spiritual growth. These are my choices, and they are mine if I want them.

⌒◯◯⌒

I had to rely heavily on the Steps and Traditions when I was divorcing my wife. Her alcoholism was progressing rapidly. Out of concern for the safety of our sons, I had to set and keep strict boundaries. By using Tradition One, I was able to clearly see that unity and progress for the greatest number meant their mother couldn't be a part of our family group any longer.

During the divorce process, I filed for full custody of our boys. As her disease progressed, I found it necessary to ask for her visitation rights to be cancelled until she could complete a treatment program and demonstrate sobriety through regular testing. The decision wasn't easy, but by using the messages of the Steps and Traditions, I was able to work through it all without being burdened by guilt or doubt.

I had given up trying to fix my ex-wife. It was time for me to fully "Let Go and Let God." In losing her husband, her home, and her children, my ex-wife was left with only her Higher Power to help her. She sought treatment within weeks of losing visitation rights.

My boundaries brought out a lot of her anger toward me. I knew I acted only with kindness and love for her and our children, so I managed to maintain serenity through her multiple outbursts of anger.

It wasn't too long after completing her program that she called me. She thanked me for the divorce, saying that she knew without the actions I took, she wouldn't have found sobriety. I was pleased, but knew this was her miracle and I was happy for her. We've got a long way to go, and we might never be close friends again, but those amends and the continuing work we each do in our programs is allowing us to rebuild a broken relationship. Through the process, we are also becoming better parents for our children.

⁃ ⌾⊰⊱⌾ ⁃

I remember stopping by the local recovery hangout with my infant son shortly after I had started attending Al-Anon meetings. I was introduced to this handsome young man who had an infant son too. As those little boys played on the floor together, we sized each other up. I liked him right away, and despite the fact that he had only been sober for three months, I would have attempted to jump into a relationship with him if he had given me any sign of encouragement.

The only thing that held me back was that I had heard at a meeting not to start any new relationships for a year. I really had no idea how much he liked me until a year later when we went out to the movies, and then began seeing each other regularly. That is when I found out he had been interested in me all along, but had taken the same message to heart.

Looking back, I am in awe of what we did. We each came into Twelve Step recovery beaten and broken, no longer willing to live life by our own power. We knew our ways were not working and we surrendered to this new way of life. We surrendered so much that we were willing to take direction, even when it went against our feelings.

I believed we had everything going for us. I had Al-Anon, and he was clean and sober for a year and a half. I thought that was such a long time! We thought we had the perfect marriage. I was not going to screw things up the way my parents did. I mistakenly believed that recovery would be pain-free. It did not take very long for me to realize that I was living in a dream world.

I knew alcoholics needed a lot of meetings, because my mother and stepfather were both recovering alcoholics. But before long I felt myself getting angry that he was going to so many meetings. We had worked out a deal. He would watch the boys on my meeting nights. I would be there for the boys whenever he went to his meetings. The time we spent together never seemed to be enough. Instead of being grateful for a sober husband, I was so resentful that I couldn't enjoy the times we were together.

I was driving him away and didn't even know it. Not only was I bitter and critical, I was just starting to come out of the denial of long-suppressed childhood abuse. I had a lot to recover from. I gradually realized that when I didn't feel okay within myself, I focused all my energy and attention on making my husband give me what I thought I needed.

I was so difficult to live with that for a while our sexual intimacy stopped completely. At times I thought our marriage was so broken that not even God could put it back together.

One weekend I decided to take the kids and pitch a tent in a friend's yard. I remember my husband calling from work as I packed to go. Over the phone he said, "Don't do this." I told him, "All my life I have been chasing after someone for love and attention and all I ever see is their backs as they run away from me. I need to get away and try and break that cycle." It was scary to leave under those conditions, but I prayed and left.

Step Three told me I needed to surrender, plain and simple. I handed myself, my husband, and our relationship over to God that night in the tent. I cried for many hours the deep tears of acceptance. I saw myself as God sees me—as His child who has value and worth for no other reason than having been created. I saw my husband in the same light—not as an adversary to be taken on, but as a fellow child of God, bumping along on this journey with me. I saw our marriage as God's creation. I needed to get out of the way and let Him work His miracles.

I went home the next day and things were tentative for a while. I redoubled my commitment to my program. I found that as long as I kept the focus on me, our relationship continued to grow. I became more aware of the times when I would start to criticize my husband, even in my mind, and I realized how much more work I had to do on me.

I discovered an amazing paradox. The things that I thought were so broken in our relationship—our communication and intimacy—began to heal without me trying to fix them. I only needed to work on *myself*!

Over time I have begun to understand what unconditional love is. It is doing things for my husband and sons because I want to, not because I expect something in return. I would be a liar if I said I was good at it, but I can say that I am working on it with God's help. I used to expect those around me to anticipate my needs and meet them. Now I know I must ask for what I need. With the help of Al-Anon, I continue to work on taking the risk of being vulnerable.

⌒⊗⌒

I asked my Higher Power to bring into my life the sexiest, most fun person, which He did. We spent a year having fun, arguing, breaking up, and pushing buttons I didn't know I had. I accepted unacceptable behavior like cursing, shouting, losing myself, and forgetting everything that was important to me so I could be with this woman. I came to Al-Anon uncomfortable in my own skin, angry, and afraid. I am still in a relationship with this woman today, and she just started coming to Al-Anon with me.

I learned in Al-Anon to focus on myself and set boundaries. I'm doing my best to accept her as she is and love and accept myself as I am. Relationships are always evolving and I don't know what will happen tomorrow. I try to remember to hand this relationship and my life over to my Higher Power.

⌒⊗⌒

I grew up in a family riddled with the disease of alcoholism. In learning how to cope with my family environment and in watching the examples of my family members, I learned a great many behaviors and beliefs that were harmful when I applied them to other relationships.

I became a people-pleaser and an approval seeker. I was somebody who would do anything—even lie, cheat, or steal—to gain the approval of others. If I couldn't gain approval, I would do anything to avoid their disapproval. All of my relationships were based on attempting to please others in order to gain their recognition, their approval, or their respect. As my own disease progressed, I stretched myself further and further, trying to do more things for more people. Inevitably I promised more than I could do, and I ended up disappointing people rather than pleasing them.

My first marriage was unsuccessful and left me a single father with two small girls. I got remarried to a woman from another sick family, and we both became sicker. I tried to medicate the family disease of alcoholism by being a workaholic. I was constantly listening to the radio and reading newspapers and magazines. I played computer games obsessively. In fact, I would do almost anything that kept me from taking an honest look at my marriage and my life. This behavior served to isolate me further from the people in my life, creating yet more pain and conflict and requiring ever more effort to distract myself. I finally broke down when, one by one, my methods of coping all stopped working for me. Finally nothing could distract me from my emotional pain.

When I walked into my first meeting, I was a broken man. My marriage was dying. My wife was in the process of making an offer on another house, just to get away from me. I was a stranger to my children. My job was in danger, and I had no real friends left. I was physically ill; I had suffered constant headaches and chest pain for a year. I had undergone a complete emotional, physical, and spiritual breakdown. In the previous two years, I had lost two cousins to suicide, and I was contemplating the same.

In Al-Anon I found acceptance and unconditional love. These were things that I had never felt in all of my adult life. Eventually I began to hear some of the real message of Al-Anon in the meetings. I began to notice certain people with that special aura of serenity. Furthermore, I noticed that these people who had something I wanted were always people who worked a solid program of recovery based on the Twelve Steps. I heard the message loud and clear: "If you want what we've got, do what we did." So I got a Sponsor and began to work the Steps to the best of my ability.

I believe that the Third Step is the core of my program. The first two Steps are about getting me to the Third Step, and all of the other Steps show me how to implement the decision I made in the Third Step. But it was in Step Three that I began to change and to experience my spiritual awakening.

I spent no more than a minute on Step Three the first time I took it. Prior to that minute, I was a fearful, selfish, and self-seeking man who would do anything for someone else's approval. After that minute, I was a man who had turned his will and his life over to a loving Higher Power and was willing to do the best he could to live his life according to spiritual principles.

My life began to change, and over time my relationships have healed. Several members of my family have sought recovery on their own. I have a real relationship now with each of my three children. All of my daughters now know that their father loves them.

My wife has also sought recovery in Al-Anon. By applying the Steps to ourselves and the Traditions to our marriage, we've grown together as we share our programs with each other. Thanks to the healing that we've found in recovery, we renewed our marriage vows last summer. We based our vows on the Twelve Traditions as a symbol of gratitude for the program and the fellowship that saved our marriage.

My life hasn't become perfect. I still have any number of unpleasant situations in my life. However, my ability to deal with those situations has been enhanced by the serenity and self-esteem that comes with working the Twelve Steps and attempting, "One Day at a Time," to improve my conscious contact with a loving Higher Power.

For Thought and Discussion:

1. What role does a Higher Power play in my life?
2. Do I rely on God for an excuse to justify my point of view or for an opportunity to let go of something? What are some examples?
3. What outcomes would I like to control in my relationships? What negative outcomes do I fear? What would it take for me to see these negative outcomes in a positive light?
4. How has my view of a Higher Power changed since coming to Al-Anon?
5. How can I turn over my relationships to the care of my Higher Power?

Chapter Thirteen

Building Relationships through Service

Not everyone who attends Al-Anon becomes involved in service activities, but those of us who do often say that it is an essential part of our recovery. Al-Anon service draws us deeper into the program as it broadens our relationships with other Al-Anon members. Working together for a spiritual purpose, with everyone as an equal, can make our program more meaningful as a source of support and genuine fellowship. Twelfth Step activity, as service is sometimes called, often sets in motion the elements of the spiritual awakening that is the initial premise of Step Twelve, which states: "Having had a spiritual awakening as the result of these steps, we tried to carry this message to others, and to practice these principles in all our affairs." This spiritual awakening further opens us for growth in our relationships.

Al-Anon service challenges us to emerge from the isolation of our misery and build new relationships with people who are learning to integrate Al-Anon principles into their lives. First, we learn that we're not alone. Then we learn and practice relationship skills so that we don't have to be lonely. We all proceed at our own pace, without anyone telling us what to do or how to do it. We want to expand our comfort zone and learn from our mistakes.

Al-Anon service offers a wide range of choices. Setting up chairs, making coffee, setting out literature, or cleaning up after the meeting are all jobs we can perform from our very first meeting. As we keep coming back, we may be asked to greet newcomers, chair a meeting, or participate in a public outreach project.

Service positions such as Group Representative or Treasurer are not only for longtime members of the group. They represent a great opportunity to enrich our relationships with other Al-Anon members, transforming "the" group into "my" group or better yet "my home group."

Although some service roles have titles and job descriptions that might intimidate some, the people who fill those roles have endured the problems of alcoholism just as we have. Yet they are proof that Al-Anon is a program of self-discovery and personal growth. Participating in service projects with them can be an inspiring opportunity to get to know them at a different level and learn that we also have great potential for personal growth.

Probably most everyone was at least a little reluctant to take on a first service project or position. We are often unsure of our abilities and afraid of the commitment. If we haven't yet engaged in service, it's easy to think of all the reasons in the world why we shouldn't. However, the magic of Al-Anon service lies in benefits that we cannot anticipate before we've actually done any service. Those of us involved in service are grateful because it boosts our self-confidence and self-esteem—which some of us experience as an unanticipated miracle. That's why many of us look back at our early service work and consider it as a gift from our Higher Power. Members who haven't yet participated in service can't yet imagine feeling this way.

Often those of us affected by alcoholism have a tendency to isolate ourselves from others. We may be afraid or unwilling to request help. Recovery in Al-Anon is all about reaching out for help, and service is no exception. If our Sponsor is active in service, we can ask for assistance. If not, we may wish to find a Service Sponsor who can guide us. By asking for help in service, we again move toward healthy relationships and away from the outdated thinking that tells us we have to do everything on our own. No one has to do it alone. Al-Anon service is a team effort, working for a shared spiritual purpose.

As our self-esteem increases from the growth we experience in service, we are better able to take home our renewed feelings of confidence and be better partners in all our relationships. We also discover that we are capable of learning healthy forms of conflict resolution, which we can also apply in our other relationships. It's impossible to think ourselves into recovery. We have to take action to learn and experience different behaviors. Through our willingness to participate in service, we open ourselves up to new growth and the opportunity to learn new interpersonal skills. This will help us build healthy relationships both inside and outside the fellowship.

Personal Stories

The leader of the family group at the treatment center where my youngest son was recovering said that the best thing I could do for him would be to work my own recovery program. I was so devastated by my son's unexpected problems that I found myself unable to make decisions about anything.

Before Al-Anon, I cried a lot, often isolated by false shame. I tried all kinds of ways to fix other people. Today, six years later, I go to meetings and share my experiences. I especially love greeting and working with newcomers. I'm finishing up three years as a Group Representative of the very group that first gave me hope that my life could be different.

My son is now in recovery after four-and-a-half years of near-death and struggle. Except for praying for him and allowing him the dignity of making his own decisions, I had nothing to do with how he got there. Sometimes I'm tempted to tell him how his recovery should look. But then I remember that my business is working my own recovery program, and I give him back to his Higher Power.

⚭

When my husband found sobriety, we were elated and in the honeymoon stage of recovery. He was in his program, I was in Al-Anon, and our two beautiful daughters were in Alateen. How perfect was that!

However, after 18 months my husband decided he did not need the A.A. program anymore—that he could stay sober on his own. I was scared to death that we could not survive this way. Our family went through a couple of years of white-knuckled sobriety while my husband adjusted to life without alcohol or A.A.

I heard speakers at conferences who had dynamic stories about everyone in the family working a program. I did not hear dynamic stories of being the only family member with a program. Perhaps it was just my ears and my focus at that time. The stories

I did hear about households where only Al-Anon was practiced seemed to come from members living with the active disease. I wondered if I should leave my husband in order to recover. I was really confused.

I loved him so much, and he respected my program needs. So I kept coming back and put the focus on me—and not on whether my husband stayed sober. I applied detachment and determined what was acceptable and unacceptable for me, ensuring that I was living my own life.

This led to service as an alternate Group Representative and later as a Group Representative, which in turn gave me a deeper understanding of the Traditions and their use in my life and with my family. It was just the shot in the arm I needed. I gradually let go and stopped trying to force a solution and be in control. Attendance at conferences and district meetings as well as involvement in planning committees exposed me to so many people who accepted me for who I am. It gave me courage to be more independent, and I found myself taking healthy risks.

I would take a car full of members to a conference in the city or to an evening meeting some place I'd never been before. I even found myself planning trips with my children that my husband chose not to join. Once we hopped in the car and drove to a nearby city to visit my niece at the university. All this was from a woman who had lost her confidence and had been so needy and dependent on her husband to provide everything.

Today my husband is still sober, but without a Twelve-Step program. His knuckles are mostly pink now. We have a wonderful life and are more in love than when we were first married. He is my best friend and confidante. He still respects my program. Miracles can happen in relationships when we seek recovery and focus on ourselves. I am so grateful that I did not leave my marriage for fear of not having the model recovery family.

My Sponsor gave me a beautiful journal after a year of working the Twelve Steps with her. The journal was so perfect that I thought I'd display it rather than use it. I continued to journal in the spiral school notebooks I'd gotten on sale for ten cents each.

While doing Al-Anon service, I noticed a paradox. Though I wanted my efforts to be recognized, I felt very uncomfortable receiving compliments. One spontaneous compliment occurred at an Area meeting in front of about 60 people, and I wanted the floor to swallow me up. I seemed to be feeling shame and embarrassment rather than pleasure.

Al-Anon service has helped me to blossom from the shy, quiet type to someone who laughs and communicates. Part of this process has involved discovering skills I never had a chance to experience and then practicing them. Receiving compliments graciously was a skill I wanted to develop because it indicated healthy self-esteem to me. A poor relationship with myself can affect every other relationship I have.

I now make a conscious effort to hear a compliment, thank the giver, and quickly jot it down so I can remember it. Then at home, I take out that beautiful journal and write about the compliment I received. Now my journal is precious inside and out, and I'm learning to accept that I am too.

⸻

Before Alateen, I was a bitter person and didn't allow anyone to get close or to know who I was. I was always jealous of my younger brother and sister because they got the attention that I never did from other relatives. When I volunteered to be a member of an Alateen Convention Committee, I learned to hug other members and let them get to know me. We would go out to eat after the committee meetings and have a meeting while we were eating. It was great to break the limitations I had built so that I wouldn't get rejected. I am so grateful for the program friends who took me to the Alateen Convention Committee meeting and taught me to love everyone unconditionally.

Before Al-Anon, I felt like a non-person. I started out as a daughter, granddaughter, and sister—everyone else in my life was a star; everyone else was more important. Later in my life, I was known as the daughter of, wife of, mother of, sister of, or assistant to. Today I have an identity separate from all those other people in my life.

Fear kept me from reaching out to others. Shame kept me from admitting my faults or defects, even to myself. Gradually I took chances, first by doing service in the group, then by sharing. When I couldn't take another minute of loneliness, I asked someone to be my Sponsor.

Now I share the wonderful experiences of my life with a multitude of friends. I have two Sponsors—one for doing service and another for studying the Steps. I love service and stay active at all levels. The people I spend my time with know the real, honest, alive person I have become. I like me—I am a good person and I am loveable.

After nine years, I had dropped to one meeting a month and was almost on my way out of Al-Anon. Then I asked a good friend who was serving as a Delegate about my dilemma. She suggested I start attending three meetings a week and see what happened. I volunteered to serve as a Group Representative for a new meeting in my neighborhood, and asked my friend to be my Service Sponsor. I started a new journey, not knowing the abundance of personal growth it would bring to me while helping me keep my feet planted in Al-Anon. I learned a lot about trust, loyalty, and unconditional love as I ventured out to serve the fellowship. As I began to interact with other Al-Anon volunteers serving the fellowship, I noticed the gaps in my recovery. With the help of my Service Sponsor, I began to learn a lot from the Traditions and Concepts.

I learned to resolve conflicts in a healthy way—not by arguing, controlling, and manipulating, but by open discussions. I learned to convey my opinion honestly and clearly, and to allow others the same opportunity. This process is called a group conscience, as described in Tradition Two. Through this simple but effective process, I learned to communicate my thoughts honestly and openly, knowing that they would be respected and heard with an open mind. Allowing the same courtesy to others helps me build trusting relationships. I found out that while we might not agree on certain things, we could respect each other for being honest and for saying what is on our minds. We could come to an agreement through a group conscience. Such healthy interaction supported by our Traditions restored my self-esteem and self-confidence.

Serving the fellowship at the group, local, and Area level gave me many opportunities to work with newcomers and past Delegates and grasp a much bigger picture of recovery. I would not have experienced the joy of service by just attending meetings. I would not have known how important the volunteers or their contributions are in making our fellowship a better place. In return, I learned to apply the same principles to my personal relationships with equal success. I learned a lot about how to get things done and have fun while I was doing it.

Recently I was elected to serve as a Delegate. The Assembly trusted me to carry their voice to the World Service Conference. This loyalty is clearly described in the General Warranties. Through the Warranties, all Delegates, Trustees, members of the Executive Committee, and World Service Office administrative staff promise the fellowship that their conduct will be consistent with the Traditions. Serving as a Delegate was one of the most unforgettable experiences of my lifetime.

⌐⟨⟩⌐

I eventually found a Sponsor who is very involved in Al-Anon service. I received most of my growth because of the service I do. It has changed my way of thinking and my way of loving my alcoholic husband and family. Because my husband does not go to meetings and my 93-year-old father-in-law is living with us, there are times when my life seems overwhelming. I have learned that I need to go to more meetings, stay involved, and welcome the love and acceptance of this program.

⌐◌⌐

While growing up, I had the roles of caretaker, responsible one, invisible one, and victim. As an adult, I became a workaholic with low self-esteem who fearfully tried to please everyone but myself. Depression, anger, and fear were my primary emotions.

By using the tools of our program, I gradually removed myself from insane and unsafe situations with my family. Soon visits were a few years apart. I was concerned because I felt that Al-Anon should be helping me to get along better with my family, rather than not visiting them at all.

Looking back, I can now see that Al-Anon was rebuilding my self-esteem, and this growth takes time. I was learning how to treat myself with respect. My service at the Area level dramatically improved my confidence. I knew when I was ready to visit my parents.

Hope for Today was the book I chose to bring with me on my holiday trip. The words helped me to listen to my parents, rather than to seek their attention. It also helped me to find things to appreciate about them. Throughout the five-day visit, I was able to give and receive love. I was able to detach. Serenity and joy were my primary emotions.

⌐◌⌐

As a newcomer, I wondered why people would stay in the program for so many years. After being in Al-Anon for ten years myself, I didn't understand how anyone could leave. For me, it didn't take much for my thoughts, attitudes, or behaviors to deteriorate when I stayed away from meetings, avoided my Sponsor, or failed to do my daily readings. When a longtime member stopped coming, I shook my head in sadness, disbelief, and smugness. It seemed obvious to me that Al-Anon members need the program forever, and those who left suffered from some lack inside.

My pride came before a hard fall. Contentedly settled in the program, I had a great Sponsor, attended terrific meetings, and had a couple of satisfying service commitments. All that changed when my Sponsor moved to another state. Though we tried to maintain a long-distance sponsorship, it became too difficult, and yet I could not bring myself to give up and find a new Sponsor. I felt abandoned and in some sort of limbo. Another close Al-Anon friend moved even further away than my Sponsor.

My duties as an Alateen Group Sponsor were ending, and I did not know if I should commit to another two years. Then my father died, and while I was out of town for his funeral, another Al-Anon Member Involved in Alateen Service became the Group Sponsor. I felt they didn't need my participation anymore.

I felt disconnected, and after my other service term ended, I moved to another district and did not even think about attending meetings. Over the next two years, I went to a meeting here and there, feeling like I needed the program but refusing to commit.

One day I went to the local Al-Anon Information Service office. I ended up asking a woman there to be my temporary Sponsor. I felt like I was starting all over in Al-Anon, building trust and connections again. I am currently back attending meetings regularly. Today my smugness is gone, and I can be more compassionate toward those who leave the program, as well as those who return, because I have experienced both situations. I try not to take the people in the program for granted. I appreciate that each of us is on our own path.

I met my husband when I was 12 years old. He was 14, and had just recently moved to the little town in the south where I was born and raised. Something happened the first moment I laid eyes on him, and the feeling was mutual. Fifteen minutes after we met, he told me that someday he would marry me. Six years later, we eloped on a bus, and six years after that we were divorced. We nearly destroyed each other. It was a nightmare. Alcoholism had taken us to places we never dreamt we would go. Fifteen years later—with two more divorces behind me—I started dating him again. I watched him drink for more than three years before I would agree to remarry him. I wanted to be sure he had learned how to drink like a gentleman.

Even though I was raised by two alcoholic parents, I did not understand this deadly disease. I didn't want him to stop entirely—I thought people who didn't drink were rather dull and boring. I couldn't imagine going to a party where they served tea and cookies.

He was still controlling his drinking when he was with me, but being a traveling salesman, he could drink a lot on the road. After being remarried for a year or so, his alcoholism progressed and he could no longer control the amount he drank. The nightmare began again, but 100 times worse. I began breaking out in rashes, throwing up a lot, screaming, shouting, and isolating myself. I woke up almost every morning crying. Some mornings I didn't want to open my eyes at all.

A counselor got my husband into a treatment center for 30 days. The miracle began to happen. I stayed in the center for five days during family week, and it was an event I will never forget as long as I live. I began to get a glimmer of how his drinking, and my parents' drinking, had affected me. I was told to go to Al-Anon.

I went to a lot of meetings, but I just didn't get it. I had a very difficult time applying the principles of the program to myself. But I just kept coming back, talking to my Sponsor, reading our literature, going to a lot of meetings, and getting involved in service. My Sponsor is a past Delegate and one of the most incredible women I have ever had the privilege of knowing. She has always been there for me and has encouraged me in my service activities.

My husband got into A.A. the day after he got out of treatment and has continued to be very involved. He is the immediate past

A.A. Delegate from our state. We served as Area Secretary, Area Alternate Delegate, and Delegate in our respective programs at the time. What a privilege and a blessing that has been for us.

⌐⚭ɔ

I became a Group Representative when my life was at a low point. I didn't have great confidence that I could do the job well. I didn't decide that service would be a positive step in my recovery. No Sponsor suggested that I start down a service path. Instead, I sat silently week after week while someone asked for a volunteer to attend the Area Assembly. Finally, I volunteered because I just didn't have anything better to do that weekend—or any weekend. My life was consumed with grief because I was losing hope that my wife would ever get the help she needed.

I didn't have high expectations that Al-Anon service would accomplish anything much. I didn't anticipate how Al-Anon service would improve my self-esteem, open the door to friendships within the Al-Anon family, and deepen my recovery.

Al-Anon group business meetings offered me an entirely unique learning experience. While I had led business meetings in my professional life, I found that the interaction is different when everyone is there for a spiritual purpose. People still have their strengths and weaknesses, as in the business world. However, what I learned at Al-Anon business meetings gave me a sense of self-confidence and faith that I never got from my professional activities. I also received plenty of encouragement from the members of the group that I served.

It was in Al-Anon service where I most frequently had experiences that I believe were the workings of a Higher Power. I was amazed to see how things seemed to happen almost on their own. These spiritual experiences became the core of my Al-Anon recovery.

⌐⚭ɔ

My husband has been in and out of recovery, though mostly out, for our entire marriage. When he finally went to treatment,

I thought all our troubles were over. He was going to stay sober, so after going to Al-Anon for six months, I quit. Through the following years of all the ups and downs of his drinking, I still didn't think to go back to Al-Anon until a few years ago. This time my husband told me to go to Al-Anon and work my program, and that he would go to A.A. and work his. I tried a few different meetings and finally found my home group. They were looking for a Group Representative, and I accepted because I knew I needed a reason to go to the meetings and make it work this time. This time I am getting the program and working the Steps. My recovery has been a lifeline I truly needed because my husband has not stayed with recovery.

I came in wanting someone to tell me that I should stay in or leave my marriage. All anyone would say was, "You'll know the right answer when the time comes. Give it time, go to meetings, and 'Keep Coming Back!'" I followed that suggestion, kept coming back, went to Assemblies, and grew in my recovery. When I found my husband drinking this last time, I prayed to my Higher Power for guidance and decided that I had had enough and wanted out. I feel at peace with that answer. I am not a screaming maniac or a sulking kid this time. I state my views and my wants and turn over the results to my Higher Power. Al-Anon has given me peace of mind.

<hr />

Serving as an Alateen Group Sponsor provided me with the on-the-job training to make amends to a younger sister who lived her entire life with our parents who were both alcoholics. I had married and left the area where they lived. Every Wednesday night when I waited for teens to arrive I could honestly say, "This one's for you."

Currently I am the Office Manager-in-Training for an Al-Anon Information Service office. Previously, I had felt too disorganized and fearful to make a decision and carry it out, but this position has given me more confidence and discipline in keeping an office functioning, buying supplies, and making calls to repairmen. I also have the freedom to say, "I am unable to do that task. Please help me."

I'm very aware now that not all members feel ready to step into service. Just as another member patiently waited for a "yes" from me to join in the great journey of recovery through service, I can be patient and ready with a hug or two when someone says, "Not now." It is good to know service is recovery.

⌒⟨⟩⟩⌒

I came home from work exhausted, wanting just to crawl into bed. It was "birthday night" at my Al-Anon group, but I didn't want to go. I had decided to skip my meeting, just this once. Then I got a phone call asking if I would chair the meeting. The person scheduled to chair said she was too sick and exhausted to do it. Another phone call asked if I could give one of my friends her "Al-Anon birthday" token. Her Sponsor wasn't going to be there. I said "yes" to both requests, of course.

I went to the meeting early and set up the room. The original Chairperson walked in first. She felt better. The second person to arrive was my friend's Sponsor. She made it after all. The meeting went on with me just sitting quietly in the back row. Nobody said anything to me about the earlier requests. It was like the phone calls had never happened. And you know what? I felt great! The meeting was wonderful and just what I needed.

I realized that all I have to do is be willing to serve and I'm the one who benefits. I went home feeling fantastic. When I'm willing to get out of myself, life usually does get better.

⌒⟨⟩⟩⌒

I was feeling grateful about all the help I had received from my Sponsor, so I asked her what I should do to repay her. She explained to me that my desire to repay needs to reach forward, not backward. She was only passing on what she had received. In turn, someday I could pass the same gifts forward to someone whom I sponsor.

What a new way of thinking. I had always thought that there were strings attached to any gift that I had received. I certainly recognized when someone was expecting something in return for a favor. There were all those little games that were played. I was never able to accept that people would just be nice to me or help me out of the kindness of their hearts.

Now I am in healthier relationships. I am able to give without expectations of a favor returned, and I am able to receive without feeling like I owe someone something. I had the blessing of explaining to a person I helped out today that she owed me nothing, but maybe she could help a struggling newcomer someday too.

I am so thankful for those who stood willing to welcome me into this fellowship with loving smiles and open arms. I am also thankful for the newer members who continue to heed the call to service and stand ready to welcome those who are still searching. They all have done this by sharing their personal experience, strength, and hope with me in complete trust that they would be safe, without even knowing who I was. The anonymity of our program made this wonderful gift possible. It helped me to know that it would be safe for me to share when I was ready.

The first service steps I took were to just open my mouth in a meeting; to feel and know it was okay to cry; to have an understanding of the importance of finding a Sponsor; and to rise above my fear to ask for one.

I became willing to get in the car and travel to ever-expanding horizons under the guidance of my Sponsor. Later, I learned to say "yes" when asked to chair a meeting, knowing that it didn't have to be perfect. I found I could take responsibility for the meeting room key for an entire month, which entailed arriving early and asking someone else to bring the topic. I spread my wings by visiting Area Assemblies and standing for Group Representative and other positions as well. These service positions were foreign to me, but my Higher Power knew what would help me most in my recovery.

Somewhere along the line, I also became a Sponsor, which has been very helpful in my own spiritual growth. All of these steps were taken with the support of a caring Sponsor and Service Sponsor. When my first Sponsor passed away, I found it necessary to find another. This helped me keep my program fresh.

I continue to attend as many meetings as possible, knowing that my recovery depends on sharing the experience, strength, and hope of each of us. We may never know what a difference we make, but each of us will make a difference to someone else. What an awesome responsibility.

For Thought and Discussion:

1. How did I feel before getting involved in service for the first time?
2. How has my Al-Anon service changed my ideas about the program and how it works?
3. How did working on an Al-Anon project affect or change my relationship with another member, for better or worse?
4. What relationship skills did I learn from my involvement in a particular service position?
5. How has service affected and enhanced other relationships?

Chapter Fourteen

Twelve Traditions and Twelve Concepts of Service: Guides for Our Relationships

The Twelve Steps provide us with a framework for recovery, making it possible for us to have more satisfying personal relationships. The Twelve Traditions and Twelve Concepts of Service complement and augment the recovery we can attain from the Steps with principles for positive and productive interpersonal relationships. The Traditions and Concepts help people live and work together harmoniously in our groups, in Al-Anon service, and in our daily lives.

Tradition One expresses a commitment to unity for the sake of our individual growth, which is a basic premise to any healthy relationship. "Personal progress for the greatest number" brings the desire for individual progress into harmony with everyone's desire for progress. Emphasizing the common values we share can restore trust when individual interests come into conflict.

Tradition Two builds on this theme, emphasizing that we recognize only one ultimate authority for our relationships—a loving Higher Power ". . . as He may express Himself in our group conscience. . . ." We listen to everyone's concern with an open mind, and we don't make a decision until we have had an informed discussion with everyone involved. We come to accept this "group conscience," even if the final decision is not what we originally wanted. We are all equal, even though we each have our own responsibilities within the relationship.

In addition to common values, a shared purpose helps to keep our relationships on a positive track. Tradition Three helps us determine the mutual goals of our relationships and to support each other in attaining these goals. With Tradition Four, we accept that although we share a relationship, we are also individuals, fully capable of making personal decisions on our own, provided that they do not adversely affect each other.

We are reminded in Tradition Five to have a purpose to our relationships, but in fulfilling that purpose to begin with ourselves before offering support to others. In Tradition Six we accept that the spiritual health of our relationships is a top priority, and we avoid any involvements that would distract or divert us from attaining this.

Tradition Seven encourages us to be self-supporting within our relationships, "declining outside contributions," which refers to more than financial support. We also have a responsibility to care for ourselves emotionally, physically, and spiritually. Depending on others to fulfill our needs or carry out our responsibilities invites disappointment and resentment. Assuming responsibilities that others should fulfill for themselves robs them of their dignity and self-respect and upsets the balance in what should be a relationship of mutual respect among equals.

Following the guidance of Tradition Eight, which states that our Twelfth Step work ". . . should remain forever non-professional . . . ," we help those we love by sharing who we are and leading by the power of example, not by acting as experts and offering unsolicited advice. This Tradition also makes allowance for the times when a relationship needs the assistance of professional expertise.

If our relationships follow Tradition Nine as our groups do, then they "ought never be organized." While this doesn't mean they should be disorganized, it suggests simplicity. We let go of rigidity and regulation, keeping in mind that equality is sustained by order, balance, and a division of responsibilities.

Tradition Ten states that our groups have no opinion on outside issues, and thereby avoid public controversy. We can apply this to our relationships by minding our own business and not arguing about issues that have nothing to do with us. We realize that others have as much right to their opinions as we do to ours, and we give them the same dignity and respect we want for ourselves.

The principles of Tradition Eleven can also be applied to our relationships. This Tradition discusses attraction rather than promotion as our public relations policy. It translates in our relationships as simply setting a good example, rather than trying to convince, persuade, or prod.

Tradition Twelve reminds us to place principles above personalities, bringing us back to the idea that we are peers among equals, no better or worse than one another. We learn to act with humility, doing what is right, rather than seeking attention and fame. We can allow others to be as they are, giving ourselves the same courtesy. This approach is a proven way to defuse conflict, by taking disagreements less personally. With this Tradition, our self-worth can grow, and our ties to others become healthier and stronger.

It's impossible to understand the Twelve Concepts of Service without some familiarity with the Steps and Traditions. The Twelve Concepts are specific in defining the principles that guide the workings of Al-Anon world service, but these principles also apply to personal relationships of any kind.

Concepts One and Two are about the balance between personal responsibility and delegated authority. Living with alcoholism, many of us knew responsibility only from the perspective of "all or nothing." Either we were handed all the responsibilities in a relationship or none of them. Concepts One and Two remind us that we remain responsible for ourselves, but it's very practical to let go of some things and delegate them to others. Concept Three—"The right of decision makes effective leadership possible"—elaborates on this approach with a combination of trust and freedom. If we delegate a responsibility to others, we also need to give them the authority to carry out the job, without constantly watching them.

"Participation is the key to harmony," our Fourth Concept, is more involved than it may sound at first. Participation assumes mutual respect and an open attitude. In following Concepts Two and Three, which speak of delegating authority, it's clear that Concept Four doesn't suggest that the key to harmony lies in letting everyone get involved in everything. It asks for people who are not involved in a project to respect the responsibility delegated to others. Within those boundaries, participation is indeed the key to harmony.

Concept Five ensures that we are given the opportunity to be heard, even when ours is not a popular view. However, if we say something once, we are sharing our opinion. If we keep saying it repeatedly, we might be attempting to control. This Concept also makes certain that we are always willing to listen to others, even if we don't agree with them. It encourages us to listen to all sides of an argument and to "Keep an Open Mind," a principle essential to any relationship.

In Concept Six we concede once again, particularly in our relationships with others, that we can't do everything by ourselves. Through the shared leadership implicit in this Concept, we cooperate with others, using the principles of delegation, authority, and responsibility we have been learning from the previous Concepts. Balancing leadership and frequent, clear communication are essential if we are to be effective in working together in any relationship.

Concept Seven notes that relationships often have distinct legal and financial responsibilities as well as their other aspects. It is especially easy to understand when applied to the relationships within a family. While everyone within the family is equally important, it is the parents or adult guardians who sign contracts and pay the bills. They are legally accountable for actions of the family as a whole.

With Concept Eight, we learn further skills in delegating. We match up our skills to our responsibilities, so that each of us within the relationship handles those matters that are most suitable for us. Concept Nine reminds us that we are all leaders of our own lives. When we develop and show strong, healthy leadership skills, our relationships benefit. These skills include responsibility, tolerance, stability, flexibility, judgment, and vision. As we demonstrate these skills, we have a positive effect on every person and situation our lives touch.

Concept Ten gives us a helpful guide in working with others, whether loved ones, coworkers, or Al-Anon members in service. For any project in which we are involved, it is important to set clear goals and clear definitions of who is responsible. It saves us the time, money, and energy. Clearly defining responsibilities helps us avoid conflicts that can occur when people duplicate each other's work.

Concept Eleven reiterates the value of partnership and collaboration. We no longer have to work in isolation. By applying mutual trust and respect, as well as our dedication to a common goal, we can accomplish much by joining forces.

Concept Twelve contains the five General Warranties of the Conference. They can help us apply Al-Anon principles to the finances, personal authority, and decisions that are a part of our relationships. Through their application, we can apply care and good sense to all aspects of our relationships, acting kindly and democratically with everyone we encounter.

The Traditions and Concepts show how we can share common values and allow for individual expression by defining clear boundaries. We take responsibility for ourselves and respect the rights of others. It's a combination of "Keep it Simple" and "Live and Let Live."

Personal Stories

When I first came to Al-Anon, I was spending my time and energy trying to get my husband to be all things to me. I wanted him to do for me what I couldn't do for myself. His duties were to provide me with total emotional and financial support, to heal me from childhood wounds, and to jump when I said "jump."

With time I have evolved into a person who is not so needy. I discovered that I do not get all things from one human being and cannot be all things to another human being. Instead, I practice Tradition Seven and strive to be fully self-supporting and allow him to do the same.

I realize it was a huge responsibility to place on my husband, to expect his life to center around my needs. After all, he has his own needs, which are sometimes in conflict with mine. Today I am happy, have increased self-esteem, and am able to let him live his life while I live mine. Sometimes we do things together and sometimes we do our own thing. What a delightful way to live.

⌒◯≫◯⌒

There I was, a young, single man in Al-Anon, surrounded by women. However, dating someone in Al-Anon was never a consideration for me at the meetings I attended, since I was the only gay man there. When I started attending gay meetings, however, I started to realize what my single straight friends had been experiencing. Here I was, lonely and vulnerable, surrounded by eligible, attractive men who were also seeking recovery.

"Seeking recovery" became the operative words here. I'd already observed the negative effects that resulted when members used the meetings as if they were a singles bar. I'd even seen marriages break up because of interactions between members. I used these examples to remind myself that our meetings have but one purpose, as described in Tradition Three, and that I had one purpose in being there—to seek recovery. Still, I must admit that at times it was distracting.

I eventually did start dating someone from the meeting, and he has now been my partner for more than 18 years. My singleness of purpose—and his—was resolute enough that it was over half a year of participating in meetings together before we even considered dating. Neither of us were newcomers. Despite the resistance we both had to finding romance within the rooms of Al-Anon, however, the commonalities we share as we each practice the program form a powerful bond. I'm sure it has greatly contributed to the health and longevity of our relationship.

The Traditions are invaluable tools in my relationships. I am learning to be autonomous, except in matters affecting my spouse or my family or society as a whole. Major decisions require a group conscience. I am still trying to untangle our finances so I can be fully self-supporting.

I used to make decisions about my alcoholic stepson without speaking with my wife first. I showed a lack of respect by committing her to decisions I made by myself. Today we check with each other before a decision. At first, this pause in the crisis irritated my stepson, but he now knows that we communicate and that he can't play one parent against the other.

In Al-Anon we have learned to communicate with each other and even to bring my stepson into the conversation. Being in a recovering relationship means communicating, because the other person might have a better idea—even the alcoholic! Today I don't have to be right. I can have an open mind. I can grow by listening more than by speaking. We use the First Tradition to keep unity.

I have a great relationship with my wife. I have a great relationship with the alcoholic. The key was to "Let It Begin with Me." I didn't wait for them to take the first action. Today I'm tired of waiting. I'd rather move forward and grow.

Applying the Steps, Traditions, and Concepts to my life has given me the tools to rebuild myself brick by brick. Rather than demolish myself completely, as I was sometimes tempted to do, I took one old brick out of myself at a time and replaced it with a completely new one. I built a new me.

By accepting that I could not manage my life and that I had no power over others (Step One), I discovered the power of going with the strength of the flow, not swimming against the current (Tradition One). I realized that I was entirely responsible for all of my life (Concept One).

I learned to trust and surrender to a Power greater than myself (Step Three). I learned to see and respect boundaries and to mind my own business (Tradition Three). I also allowed others the same freedom (Concept Three).

By sincerely and honestly expressing my desire to change (Step Seven), I began to develop the means to fully support myself emotionally, physically, mentally, financially, and spiritually (Tradition Seven), which then made me much better able to recognize, differentiate, and support the needs of others (Concept Seven).

In coming to terms with my own strengths and weaknesses, I was able to look at how my ignorance of myself had led me to harm others, either directly or indirectly (Step Eight). This Step, in turn, helped me to recognize that I did not have all the answers where others were concerned, and that it was not up to me to solve anyone else's problems (Tradition Eight). Furthermore, I realized that I could also give up responsibility for solving the whole world's problems and allow those elected to get on with the job without spending my time criticizing them (Concept Eight).

By praying that I could work with the intentions of the universe rather than my own selfish needs (Step Eleven), I learned to be able to wait for things to happen on their own without my interference (Tradition Eleven). This spiritual perspective finally allowed me to see my role in the world in relation to everything else, without bitterness or resentment (Concept Eleven).

By finding my rightful place and purpose through my every action, I was able to let others know that they could also find the peace of living in the present moment (Step Twelve). I was able to treat everyone with dignity and understanding because I could now place my ideals before my selfish, petty needs (Tradition Twelve). This growth allowed me to be at peace and to work effectively and equitably in all my dealings (Concept Twelve).

⌒⟨∞⟩⌐

Over the years, I have learned to apply the Traditions and Concepts of Service in my personal relationships with equal success. This is how the General Warranties of the Conference, referred to in Concept Twelve, have helped me so far:

Warranty One: that only sufficient operating funds, including an ample reserve, be its prudent financial principle;

I have a goal to retire as early as possible, but at the same level of income. Recently my neighbor bought a red convertible sports car as a birthday present. Such temptations are all around me. I could easily give in to such temptations if I did not have a goal to maintain my current and future financial health. My financial goal keeps me focused and helps me decide what is good for me.

Warranty Two: that no Conference member shall be placed in unqualified authority over other members;

Over the years, I have learned to mind my own business. That means I let others be responsible for fulfilling their responsibilities the way they see fit, not the way I do. In allowing others to be responsible for making their own decisions, I am in no way giving up my authority to protect myself and my family from any harm that could possibly be caused by others' actions.

Warranty Three: that all decisions be reached by discussion vote and whenever possible by unanimity;

I am a lot more willing to have open discussions. By forcing my solution, I always lose even if I win the argument. Today the choice is clear: have open, honest discussions and seek a positive outcome. If this result is not possible, then I know when to step back and let it go.

Warranty Four: that no Conference action ever be personally punitive or an incitement to public controversy;

My distorted thinking could cause me a great deal of harm, which could be poisonous to my relationships. Therefore I have learned to negotiate rather than to be passive-aggressive or to hang my dirty laundry out in public.

Warranty Five: that though the Conference serves Al-Anon it shall never perform any act of government; and that like the fellowship of Al-Anon Family Groups which it serves, it shall always remain democratic in thought and action.

I am more focused than ever before in maintaining balance in my relationships. Outside interests constantly appeal for my time and resources. Today I have learned to politely say no to outside interests if they could become a distraction.

When I work together with other Al-Anon members for a common goal in a healthy environment, I have the opportunity to develop healthy habits, which strengthen my relationships. This reward is available to me always.

⚬⚬⚬

It was very difficult to watch my son struggle with the disease of alcoholism. He lost his job, was evicted from his apartment, and sold all he had to support his addiction. I have heard over and over in Al-Anon meetings that alcoholism is a powerful disease. But sometimes I lose perspective.

One day my son came over at lunchtime and said he was hungry. I gave him ten dollars and asked him to get hamburgers for both of us. Since it was a beautiful spring day, I thought we would have a nice lunch on our deck. Almost an hour passed, and he was not back. At first I got very angry and hurt that he would not care enough to bring me lunch even though I paid for it. Very quickly I caught myself and realized that it was my mistake in giving him the ten dollars. The thought of having a lunch with my son was so inviting that I forgot how powerful the disease is. Spending ten dollars for hamburgers was definitely not his priority, and I understand that.

Al-Anon encourages us to be understanding and compassionate to our alcoholic relatives and friends. I cannot be either if I choose to get angry when things don't go my way. I have found that our Concepts provide many indirect tools for strengthening my personal relationships.

Concept Four says participation is the key to harmony, so when I saw my son a few days later, we had a friendly discussion about this event. I told him that I made a mistake by giving him cash. I told him that I love him, but that I would not support his alcoholism. We agreed that next time when he is hungry, he would be welcome to come by the house and we would go to a place of his choice to eat, but from now on I will not give him a single dime.

Concept Seven says that the Trustees have legal rights while the rights of Conference are traditional. This Concept clearly defines the responsibilities between the Trustees and Delegates. These responsibilities provide clarity on boundaries. If I clearly understand the difference between my priorities and my son's, I can begin to set clear boundaries with love and compassion beneficial to both of us. This Concept helps me to understand and accept my alcoholic relatives just the way they are and make the best attempt to have a loving relationship.

My son eventually found recovery. He was sober for a year, just out of a halfway house, and had nothing. He had a job but had no transportation. I wanted to help him financially, but since my trust had been violated so many times in the past, I was afraid. I turned to Tradition One. We both were working our programs, and we both had common goals to get him on his feet. He found a truck and asked me to cosign his loan. I struggled at first, but I finally came to terms with what I saw.

He had a clear commitment on his part to work on his recovery and get back on his feet. I realized that if I wished to reestablish our broken trust, I needed to take a chance. Before I cosigned his loan, I had to come to a clear understanding that he has the disease, and despite his best efforts he could slip. If it happens, I won't have any resentment. I offered unconditional help with full understanding that he may slip in his commitment to recovery. I did this for me. I was willing to give him a chance without any conditions attached to my offer. My son is three years sober and doing fine. I will always love him just the way he is, and I will stand by him without interfering with his recovery.

⌐◯≫◯⌐

I became very attached to my original home group. I saw it through low attendance and difficult times. I felt that this was my group and became very possessive. When decisions had to be made, I felt they should be decided my way. If something needed to be done, I just did it, without a vote. I did every job because someone had to do it. I was glad to keep the group going, which I did, but my resentments crept through in my attitude. I did not speak nicely to other members, and my behavior in the group needed improvement, although at the time I couldn't see it.

One day another member of the group wanted to talk to me. She took an inventory, not only of the group, but also of me personally. I felt violated by what she said and no longer considered the group to be a safe place to share. Looking back, I can see where my behavior needed changing. Moving to another group allowed me to start fresh.

I attend two groups now. In my new meetings, I make a conscious effort not to take on too many jobs. If I do everything, there is nothing for others to do. Having as many people as possible participate in the group is essential for the growth of the group. Examining and learning about how I behave in a group was important. It feels good to discuss an issue and vote on it. I no longer feel it has to be my way. The group can decide, which is Tradition Two in action. Belonging to these new groups allows me to practice a better program.

⌐◯≫◯⌐

The Eleventh Tradition speaks of "attraction rather than promotion." I didn't understand that Tradition when I first came into Al-Anon. I came from a very unhealthy family. I had little self-esteem and was controlling. I tried to get my mother and two sisters into Al-Anon by buying the *One Day at a Time in Al-Anon* book for them. Any chance I got I would read it aloud to them. I went overboard on promoting Al-Anon. That did not work at all.

After several years, our family grew, adding two sisters-in-law, who were quite controlling and manipulative. My sisters felt these women took advantage of our mother because she is always the peacemaker. They also didn't like the way our brothers were being treated. I told my sisters that they were adults and would have to make their own choices. I let them know I wouldn't get into their business.

One evening I was talking on the phone with my younger sister. We had visited my parents for the weekend. She was once again wondering why a sister-in-law was manipulating our mother. I told her that was their stuff and I didn't need to know why. She asked how I stay so calm. I said, "It's Al-Anon." She said, "No, really, who are you seeing and how much are you paying him?" Again I said, "It's Al-Anon." When she said she didn't qualify, I explained that Al-Anon is for friends and families of alcoholics, and that since our father and four brothers are alcoholics, she did qualify.

By the fact that we were having this conversation, I realized she had seen a change in me, and that made me feel good. I knew I had changed, but when my sister noticed, I could tell that my progress is showing as I become the person I want to be. After the phone call, I smiled to myself and thought, "Now I understand the Eleventh Tradition—attraction rather than promotion."

Growing up in a drinking family, I have always been involved in alcoholic relationships. I didn't know anything else.

My friendships with girls in high school were all but tragic. I had no personal skills and no means to receive any. Eventually I went through a short first marriage and then a divorce. My second marriage is still mostly moving forward. My wife and I both entered Al-Anon on advice from our son's rehabilitation center. Our intention was to attend for four weeks as prescribed. After two or three meetings, we were hooked. Al-Anon was quick to show us that we needed help.

We both went our separate ways in our personal recoveries, but we came together on family issues as they arose. In the past, I always found a way out of problem areas in our relationship or in other family relationships. As I worked the Steps, I realized that I needed to take responsibility for my role as a husband and father.

I remember the Fourth Concept reminding me, "Participation is the key to harmony." I found that the more I participated in my marriage and family relationships, the better I felt about myself. We have had some awful experiences along the way, but at least the truth was revealed and amends were made, which is progress for me.

Before Al-Anon, there was no spirituality in my life. I realize today that it was a missing element I desperately needed in my life. I haven't a clue as to what my Higher Power might actually be, but I have come to believe. When I think of the insane years, I realize He protected me then as well. My relationship with my Higher Power has changed my life forever, and I have Al-Anon and the Twelve Steps to thank.

⌒⋙⊘⋘⌐

When I first started in Al-Anon, I was in a conflicted relationship with my 16-year-old son. Many of my expectations for his life had been lost in the course of his struggle with drugs and alcohol. As his dreams became less important to him, my own frustration grew, and the battle of wills began. I became depressed and anxious. I spent many hours obsessing over his choices and his future, and how that affected me. Eventually I was unable to function and enjoy life.

When I heard others share their stories and hope for a better way to live in their relationships, I was immediately encouraged to find that for myself. Slowly I embraced the principles of the Al-Anon program. The First Step was a huge relief for me. Understanding that there would be many things that I had no control over and was not responsible for gave me relief from the shame and guilt. Understanding that my Higher Power could—and would—restore me to sanity as I turned my will and life over to Him was all the hope I needed.

In Tradition Two it says, "For our group purpose there is but one authority—a loving God as He may express Himself in our group conscience. Our leaders are but trusted servants—they do not govern." This Tradition, when used in my family, really helped me let go of my urges to control my son's behavior. He has his own Higher Power, who has authority over his life. What a gift to give him back to God.

My relationship with my son has gradually improved. I've been able to give him the freedom to make his own choices and to face his consequences without my interference. We have both grown so much. We communicate more frequently and with more honesty and appreciation for each other. As I worry less about my son, I have more energy for my own continued recovery in Al-Anon. I am beginning to work toward my own goals in life.

⸙

I grew up believing that marriage was a 50-50 partnership. I became angry and resentful when I discovered that my alcoholic husband was unable to meet my expectations. I felt I was doing all of the work and receiving none of the benefits.

I see my marriage differently today. I have learned from Tradition Four, which states, "Each group should be autonomous, except in matters affecting another group or Al-Anon or AA as a whole." This Tradition showed me that I need to be a complete, healthy, separate individual from my husband, and allow him that same right. I was choosing to do all the work and not exercising my right to say no, to delegate, or to ask for help. I needed my husband to see how victimized I had become.

Today I can recognize my autonomy, exercise my choices, and allow my husband the opportunity to share in our relationship. My actions affect him. My actions do not reflect him.

⌐◯◯◯⌐

A married couple who attend my home group have been in Al-Anon for 25 years. At a meeting, one of them shared how they incorporated the spirit of a group conscience in the vows they made to each other. They agreed to remain married as long as it was their Higher Power's will for them. Through ongoing prayer and willingness, they trusted that Power to guide and direct them in their relationship each day for the greatest good of all involved—just like our group conscience, referred to in Tradition Two.

Now that I'm beginning to consider marriage for myself, their words gave me hope that I didn't have to have it all figured out before making a decision in this area of my life. This came as a great relief to me because I believed that I had to have all the answers ahead of time and had to pick a spouse who had no issues—a daunting task! This idea reflects my lingering desire to control outcomes and other people. It is indicative of the level of fear about intimacy I have had until this point in my life. I believed that by doing enough screening, I could forego life's natural ups and downs and side-step work I may need to do with another in order to grow spiritually.

With God's help and the generous gift of honest sharing from this couple, I realized that if my partner and I can place our Higher Power at the center of our relationship and trust each other to listen to its whisperings in our own hearts, I can feel much safer taking what feels like a large and sometimes frightening step toward commitment.

As long as I stay God-directed, I know that my choices can enhance my life and will not cause harm to those around me, the way they do when I'm acting on my own self-will. Just like miraculous solutions for our group's concerns flow with ease from a God-directed group conscience, so too can answers in my love relationship.

⌒◇◇◇ ◦

A while back, I served as one of the officers of our Al-Anon Information Service. During this time, our bank balance dropped and checks began to bounce. I was appointed Chairman of the Fundraising Committee to quickly restore our budget. I had absolutely no idea how I would go about doing this. I talked to my Service Sponsor, and she suggested I should first read the *Al-Anon/Alateen Service Manual*, the Twelve Traditions, and the Twelve Concepts of Service.

I found that Tradition Seven and Warranty One of Concept Twelve were there to keep our fellowship financially healthy. Our Committee developed a budget with a prudent reserve for emergencies. To solve the immediate problem and maintain long-term financial health, we decided to encourage everyone to increase the amount they put in the basket. I made a personal commitment to do the same.

I also decided to apply these same principles in my personal life and find ways to save money. At work I usually ate fast food for lunch. My doctor had been telling me to stop this, since my cholesterol was so high. I stopped abusing my body and started taking two apples to work for lunch. I have been doing this and saving hundreds of dollars per year. I have been using the savings to attend Regional Service Seminars, local conventions, and international conventions. I am also maintaining a normal weight and keeping my doctor happy.

I further looked into applying Warranty One to my personal budget. My "ample reserve," which I thought would provide healthy retirement, was only half of what I would require. I began to watch every dollar I spent and ask myself if I needed to spend it or put it in a reserve fund for retirement. I had shirts hanging in my closet that were never worn, but I bought them because they were on sale. I was wasting a lot of money because of my frivolous spending habits. I changed my ways, and in the last five years my retirement savings rate has quadrupled, which will help me attain my retirement goal.

I have also worked closely with my wife and have received many good ideas on saving money, since she is more frugal than I am. She has also set up her own retirement reserve fund and is managing it well. Applying Warranty One keeps us mindful of the need to plan our financial future, which keeps our relationship on a positive track.

⌐◦◦⌐

For a long time, I had been treating my alcoholic husband as an enemy who was out to destroy me. Now sober, he was expecting me to work with him and be a partner. This approach was a whole new way of thinking for both of us. We had never really seen it work in a marriage before—certainly not in our homes while we were growing up or among any of our drinking friends.

Then we heard a speaker one night who talked about how the Steps were for her relationship with God, the Traditions were for her relationship with others, and the Concepts were for her relationship with the world at large. What an answer to a prayer! I could work on the Traditions to help me learn how to live with others. As I looked at Tradition One, I could see how this could work in my home as well as in my group. It was about what's good for all of us—not just me.

Tradition Two talks about who is really the boss. I had been trying to run things my way for a long time, but this Tradition says that there is only one authority and that He works through a group conscience. Tradition Two gave my husband and our children a voice in how things were going to go at home as well. We started to become a family. We started learning to talk about things. We discovered that we each had valuable talents and thoughts to add to our family unit.

Tradition Three talks about discovering that we *are* a family and that alcoholism has affected each of us. I thought I had protected the kids from alcoholism so well that they didn't know what was going on. Imagine my surprise when they started opening up at family meetings.

In Tradition Four I learned that it was okay for each of us to do our own thing. I learned that when I was doing something that affected the whole family—for instance, attending an Assembly—it was my job to let them know where I was going and when I would be home. I also learned to consider that how I spent money would affect everyone else in the family.

I learned in Tradition Five that alcoholism had not only affected my family, but my extended family as well. I found that in order to be of any help to others, I had to first take care of myself. I realized that my husband's mother was not the cause of his alcoholism. She was just as affected by it as I was. I found a new understanding, compassion, and respect for my extended family.

I discovered in Tradition Six that our primary purpose was spiritual. I was so focused on how I looked to everyone on the outside that I had neglected to take care of my insides and my relationship with God. My Higher Power was a stranger to me. Taking the time I needed to get to know the God of my understanding became a top priority for me.

Tradition Seven helped me learn the importance of taking care of not only my finances but also my time. Being fully self-supporting means more than just money. It's also about what I'm doing with the hours I've been given each week. Am I doing my fair share within the family, my group, the district, and the Area?

Tradition Eight says that I don't know everything and sometimes may need to hire someone to help me. My mother died; several months later I suffered a miscarriage. It all led to severe depression. I kept trying to work the Al-Anon program while thinking that I must be doing something wrong. I finally went to my doctor who referred me to a professional. With the help I received, I was able to work through my grief and depression.

With Tradition Nine, I learned that I don't have to be responsible for absolutely everything. I might be good with the paperwork of running a home, but don't put me under the hood of a car. My husband is very good with cars, so he takes care of them and I stay out of his way.

Tradition Ten tells me to stay out of other peoples' fights and to mind my own business. Tradition Eleven reminds me that I can share how I have received help, but only when I am asked. It also reminds me of the importance of respecting everyone's right to privacy. At our family meetings, I have been confronted about sharing too much about us with others. It's hard to hear, but I am learning to keep the focus on myself.

This brings me to Tradition Twelve, where I learned the humility and spiritual power of working this program. My grandmother was a bitter, unhappy, and critical person who was deeply affected by this disease. Although I never liked her when I was a child, I have learned to have compassion for a woman who never received the benefits of knowing about a different way of life through the Al-Anon program.

For Thought and Discussion:

1. How do I work with those around me, whether at home or at work, to come to a decision that benefits each of us and all of us together?

2. When have I allowed public controversy, drama, or gossip to affect my personal relationships?

3. In what ways am I fully self-supporting? In what situations have I expected others to rescue me?

4. How often do I participate in discussions with those I love, allowing my opinions to be heard and extending the same courtesy to others, even when they disagree with me?

5. Once a mutual decision has been made, whether at home or at work, how willing am I to abide by that decision without resentments?

Chapter Fifteen

Al-Anon Literature as a Resource for Relationships

The Al-Anon program is deceptively simple. Sometimes a slogan—just a few words—is all we need to take a positive step toward recovery. The slogans represent a deeper wisdom that is interconnected with a body of thought and a range of tools, resources, and growth opportunities that is more far-reaching than many Al-Anon members realize.

So it is with Conference Approved Literature. It is only one part of a program that includes sharing and listening at meetings, participating in service, and experiencing many other growth opportunities that the fellowship offers. All these elements work together toward a single spiritual purpose: to help the families and friends of alcoholics. Al-Anon recovery doesn't come from only reading literature. Al-Anon literature is a recovery tool that's most effective when it's part of the complete Al-Anon program.

One of the advantages of Al-Anon literature is that it allows us to supplement our meetings with helpful insights and inspiring stories from thousands of members everywhere. All the Al-Anon members who send their written experience to the World Service Office collectively help to create our literature. While there may be something to be learned from a book on recovery written by a psychotherapist or doctor, that work is based on the authority of a single person. Al-Anon literature offers a broader point of view than any single writer could provide. It remains the responsibility of each of us to decide what to accept as useful and what to leave for another day or another person.

Over the years, Al-Anon literature has evolved in ways that reflect the growth and recovery of Al-Anon members. When the Al-Anon program was in its infancy, the wives of A.A. members read A.A. literature because nothing else was available. Al-Anon Family Groups had not yet emerged as a program separate and distinct from A.A. Bill W., A.A.'s cofounder, was among the first to recognize that the issues in Al-Anon recovery are different from those in A.A. He urged his wife, Lois, Al-Anon's cofounder, to write *The Al-Anon Family Groups*, first published in 1955, with other early pioneers and with his editorial assistance. They recognized early on that Al-Anon members needed literature focused on their own experience in recovery, not the alcoholic's.

The Dilemma of the Alcoholic Marriage, published in 1967, focuses primarily on one single type of relationship: a traditional marriage between an alcoholic husband and a non-alcoholic wife. That's also the basic premise of Al-Anon's first daily reader, *One Day at a Time in Al-Anon*, published in 1968. Since these books were written, our membership has expanded and times have changed, but alcoholism has not. The Al-Anon principles in these books continue to remain helpful because they apply to all relationships affected by alcoholism.

Al-Anon's more recent literature, including *Opening Our Hearts, Transforming Our Losses*, assumes a wider range of possible alcoholic relationships, and applies the principles of the program to some of the effects of alcoholism that previous Al-Anon literature hadn't explored in depth. Likewise, *The Forum* magazine presents a monthly snapshot of the Al-Anon program that Al-Anon members are working currently. There are also contemporary stories in electronic form on Al-Anon's Web site.

There is a greater wealth of recovery resources within Al-Anon literature than most members probably realize. Many members limit their study of Al-Anon literature to one of our daily readers. Undoubtedly, those books are worth reading again and again, but there are many others worthy of study. *How Al-Anon Works for Families & Friends of Alcoholics* includes sections on detachment, forgiveness, and communication, as well as the inspiring stories of many Al-Anon members from all walks of life. *From Survival to Recovery* includes some compelling accounts from members who grew up in alcoholic homes and who have had life-long struggles to build healthy relationships. *Paths to Recovery* offers personal insights into how Al-Anon's three Legacies—the Steps, Traditions, and Concepts of Service—can be applied to our relationships. The Al-Anon Web site and other Al-Anon members can suggest more literature that might be helpful.

Since its earliest origins, Al-Anon Family Groups has presented an ongoing conversation among families and friends of alcoholics that continues to this day. The insights in Al-Anon literature all have their start at meetings, where members discuss their concerns and share their progress. Then members write about their recovery based on these discussions. These writings become the basis for Al-Anon books and pamphlets. This material is subsequently used at meetings to stimulate further discussion and fresh opportunities for self-discovery. Our literature has been a reflection of that discussion, has contributed to it, and continues to move the discussion forward.

Personal Stories

Several years ago, my wife had what we and the doctors thought was breast cancer. Last week we went for her regular mammogram, and this time they found something that required a biopsy. We both did well before the procedure, but as we were driving to the doctor's office in morning rush-hour traffic, I began to be stressed out by the traffic and my fear of what would happen. My wife was beginning to lose her composure too.

We were both ready to lash out at the world when we were unable to cross a busy intersection for the second time because of a short traffic light. I knew that if I could use something from my program, I might be okay and be better able to help my wife with her real fears.

I always carry *Courage to Change* in my car. I reached over and handed it to her and asked her to read today's message out loud. I can't tell you what she read, but I can tell you how calm and peaceful I became and how my wife stopped driving the car from the passenger seat. When she finished reading, she said she knew that I was doing the best I could and that she would try to do the same. We still don't know what the test will reveal, but we ended up having one of the most peaceful and serene days in months.

⤜✦⤛

As a small child, I once screamed at my alcoholic mother, "If I had to have a mother, why did it have to be you?" By the time I arrived at Al-Anon, the antagonism between us had solidified into a wall of mistrust and mutual loathing. Yet emotionally, this woman was important to me. I knew she suffered. Al-Anon told me she was sick, not guilty.

Shortly after joining Al-Anon, I read a sentence in *As We Understood* . . . , "Gratitude changes your attitude." I saw how negative my attitude was. If I wanted to change my attitude toward my mother and end the torment of this unhealthy relationship, it was up to me to practice and feel gratitude toward my mom.

I asked my Higher Power for help. Each time I had a negative thought or burst of anger concerning my mother, I would stop and write down three things about her for which I am grateful. At first I struggled and wept. I couldn't find anything good to write. But I had committed myself to the task. I was sincere in my wish to end the pain of resentment, hate, and mistrust. My first attempt to find three things to be grateful for took more than an hour of searching. I knew that nobody in the world was all bad. Those first three were pretty feeble, but they were honest.

I'm proud of myself for persisting. Although at first I didn't want to do it, as the weeks went by I found that I was enjoying this practice. One evening, I was surprised and alarmed that I hadn't written anything about gratitude recently. Upon reflection, I realized I had not had a single negative thought about my mother all day. I'm grateful beyond words that I haven't had any since then. Thank God I had enough faith in the program and more than enough desperation to make an effort. "Gratitude changes your attitude." Now I'm aware when my attitude is negative. Then I know it's time for me to apply the magic of gratitude.

<hr>

I did not have good parenting skills. I grew up in an alcoholic home, but Al-Anon showed me that my past was no excuse for poor behavior in the present. I loved my son and was willing to go to any lengths to give him a better life. I told him, "I've not been the best mother to you, and from this day I'll start being a better mom."

I worked at being consistent. I read in *The Dilemma of the Alcoholic Marriage* to say what I mean and mean what I say. In the past, I would overreact and yell out some sort of punishment, such as, "You are grounded for life!" After all, as a teenager I had been grounded for life at least a dozen times. Then the next day, I would experience the guilt and remorse of my overreaction, and my son would give me the silent treatment—a behavior he learned from me.

My Sponsor introduced me to the *Detachment* leaflet. Now I ask myself questions based on the statements in this piece. My son needed to experience the consequences of his actions, and sometimes that had nothing to do with me. For instance, when he skipped baseball practice and I didn't cover up for him, the coach sat him on the bench. Sometimes I learned that I had the problem or that I was manipulating situations. Sometimes I needed help in figuring out the possible consequences or what my motives really were, so I would call my Sponsor.

I didn't abandon my son. Instead, I minded my own business with loving detachment. I said such things as, "You're a smart kid. God loves you, and I love you, but I can't figure this one out for you." Sometimes it was tougher for me to stick to the program than to take the easy road and do it for him. Again my Sponsor and other Al-Anon friends assured me that I was doing the right thing—that I was demonstrating more love by doing it the tougher way.

I had to make changes before I could see the past clearly. I had been so self-centered that I never saw how much I was hurting my son. My son had learned that it was easy to pressure me into a snap decision that I would regret the next day. He had little respect for my decisions or for me. But now I was sometimes taking two or three days to decide what to do. Sometimes I even admitted not knowing what to do.

Our literature tells us it is tough on family members when we start to change; it was tough on our family. He pulled out all the stops—pouting, charming, stomping, yelling, giving compliments, not talking, talking all the time, and using humor. It was tough to be consistent and follow through.

I didn't think I was making much progress, but one day my son and a friend were in the neighborhood park throwing water balloons at passing cars. A man stopped and pulled my son into his van. This stranger tore his t-shirt, yelled at him, and drove around for several minutes before bringing him home and screaming at me for being such a poor mother. I was angry and embarrassed.

This man, whom I would never see again, thought I was a bad mother. How could my son embarrass me like that? I called my Sponsor and told her how my son had done this terrible thing to me. She said, "He must have been frightened by the experience." Suddenly I realized the enormity of what he had gone through. My selfish thoughts were gone, and I realized they had only been there to mask my fear.

I went into my son's room, put my arm around him, and said, "Tell me about it." He fell down in my lap and sobbed for several minutes, saying how scared he was. We talked about how sometimes the consequences of our actions are much more dire than the initial action. We talked about decision-making. As he lay there crying, I realized something was profoundly different. I was letting my son have feelings—out in the open feelings. All those previous years, I had taught him to stifle any emotions—just as I had been taught as a child. And I was openly talking about God to my son. Things really were different for us.

We became very close and began to enjoy each other's company. I was not his best friend; I was his mother—a woman he loved, respected, and enjoyed being around. In return I gave him love, respect, consistency, and freedom to make mistakes, even when it was tough for me.

I could always find something in Conference Approved Literature that applied directly to my problem. I even did what is described in *Courage to Change*: I left my wife on the floor when she passed out and fell out of bed. I covered her up with a blanket, with love of course. Our son even put a pillow under her head. Detachment works.

I am struggling with my relationship with my mother. Today is her 65th birthday. I called her to wish her a great day, and before I knew it she was screaming at me about my relationship with the alcoholic in my life and how it's affecting the children. I grew up in an alcoholic home and wasn't allowed to talk about alcoholism. My mom still feels the same way. If I weren't practicing the tools I have learned in Al-Anon, this phone call would have turned into a nightmare. I was able to accept her opinion and move on with the conversation. Once I was off the phone, I felt exhausted and asked myself how I managed to get into such a spin again.

I remembered that I had heard a speaker say she always keeps *The Forum* in her handbag for when she needs a mini-meeting. I picked up my *Forum* and opened it. I could not believe how God was working for me when I started to read. It was all about a mom and a daughter and acceptance. The magazine reminded me how important my program is and how I need to work it into my life so I can have healthy relationships with my family.

⌒⌒⌒

I volunteered to lead a meeting on Tradition One. I didn't yet understand how this Tradition applied to my life, but I was inspired by a talk I'd heard about performing service in whatever small way possible. I thought this was a good place for me to start.

I began preparing for the meeting by reading several books. My favorite was *Paths to Recovery*. There I found a passage that hit home with me. It said that Tradition One speaks of unity—something lacking in my home. It suggested that I look at my part in the lack of harmony in my family.

I had tried for years to take control away from my Higher Power. In doing so, I made decisions that often led to despair and insanity for me and my family. My relationship with my alcoholic daughter seems to have suffered the most. Al-Anon has given me tools to use to change this behavior and to recognize my own insanity.

⌒⌒⌒

My dad is an alcoholic and my mom is a binge drinker. They split up when I was three. As a child, I used to envision Daddy coming to rescue me. He was never around, so I didn't see him drinking.

I only saw Dad once when I was ten and then not again until I was grown. When we met, he said he wanted to be totally honest with me. He told me he was an alcoholic, and had started drinking at the age of eight. He told me I was his child and that I needed Al-Anon, which was for family and friends of alcoholics. He also told me that as my children got older, they would need Alateen.

I thought he was silly, but Dad pointed out how things had been with Mom: how it was before he left, how his brother sexually abused me, and how I had ended up in an alcoholic marriage. Dad said all he wanted was to try and make amends for not being there.

But Dad relapsed, and I blamed myself for everything in my life that had not gone well. I thought I had made a recovering alcoholic begin drinking again. My husband went off the deep end and became violent, and I blamed myself for that too.

Still, I kept remembering my dad telling me that I needed Al-Anon. I finally looked up the local meetings and found we had just one. I checked it out so that I could fix Dad and my husband—and make all of my memories go away.

Instead, Al-Anon helped me deal with Dad's relapse and his phone calls in the middle of the night. I was able to share what was happening, find suggestions, listen to stories from other members, and read Conference Approved Literature. *One Day at a Time in Al-Anon, Courage to Change,* and *From Survival to Recovery* helped me tremendously.

Today, thanks to his return to A.A. and my continued presence in Al-Anon, we are able to have a father-daughter relationship, and he is able to know his grandchildren and great-grandchildren. We are able to talk and relate. I owe it to my Higher Power who sent Dad to tell me about Al-Anon.

⌒⟨∞⟩⌐

Having a relationship means having a connection with other people, places, or things. But as a result of living with an alcoholic,

I was caught in a cycle of blame, denial, self-doubt, and bad habits, such as gossip and dominance. I formed unhealthy relationships.

Today I know to align myself with God in every relationship and to use the principles of honesty, faith, courage, integrity, humility, forgiveness, perseverance, and love. I can develop my relationship with God first, then with myself, and lastly with others.

The chapters on communication in *How Al-Anon Works for Families & Friends of Alcoholics* and *The Dilemma of the Alcoholic Marriage* helped me develop healthy habits for listening and examining my motives. The topics of acceptance and forgiveness were powerful in their impact on my attitudes.

Sponsorship and service have given me the opportunity to practice relationships, truly putting love into action. I have learned to accept the guidance of a Higher Power, forgive others for what I think is wrong, and accept and forgive myself for not being perfect.

My task in relationships today is to listen, keep an open mind, forgive, and keep my hands off and my heart open.

I grew up with an alcoholic father who died 18 years before I walked into my first meeting. I felt nothing. I had stopped loving and respecting him years before he passed away.

One day I read in *Courage to Change* that alcoholism is a disease that has varied symptoms. For the first time, I put together my father's behavior, alcoholism, and my inability to control the disease. At that moment, I had a spiritual awakening that gave me back the ability to love my father. I was able to forgive him and love him for the first time since my childhood. I was given back a father who was simply a man with a disease, deserving of my compassion, forgiveness, and love.

My ex-husband wanted my teenage son to come and live with him and his new wife. They had a new little girl, and they wanted our son there also. They lived more than a thousand miles away and wanted him through the end of high school—five years. All our relatives lived near there too. Initially I said no. Then one day, as if God were sitting next to me, I heard, "It's time." I argued with God, but the answer was the same, "It's time." I went to my Sponsor's house, and we cried together. I realized that I could not be the mother I thought I was without giving my son and his father the chance to have this great relationship like we had. This was the toughest, most painful thing I had ever done, but I was willing to go to any lengths to be a good mother. I let him go with love. Only Al-Anon could have given me that.

I had no idea what would fill this huge void that had been created. My life had lost its direction. I couldn't drive by Little League games without breaking into tears. I thought of going back into the bars and seeing if the old gang was still there. Whenever my son called, I kept a brave front because I was not about to guilt trip him like I had been taught.

Life may be tough, but I had to learn to live my own life—for myself, not for someone else. Two weeks after my son left, I went to the Alateen state conference. I was given the privilege of serving as the Conference Committee Sponsor for the next year's conference. God had replaced my son with the 15 teens on the Committee. It was a wonderful year with these kids. I owe them my life.

Less than a year later, my ex-husband and his wife decided they didn't want my son to live with them anymore—sort of like returning a dog to the pound. The boy who returned to my home was not the boy who left. Things got tougher. This young man was angry, hurt, rejected, and manipulative; he drank, used drugs, and stole. I was once again fighting alcoholism.

I stopped looking for someone to blame. It didn't matter. I was his mother and I had to grow up and toughen up some more. I took parenting classes. I called my program friends who had been through similar experiences. I kept asking, "How will I know what to do?" They told me to trust God. He would let me know.

I kept several *Detachment* leaflets in my car, my purse, at work, and around the house. I relied on the Traditions as guidelines for our family. We went to outside counseling. I cried through entire Al-Anon meetings. It was the only safe place to let my guard down.

One day I got a call to come pick up my son. He had been shoplifting. The policeman said they would not arrest him because he had no previous problems. I told the officer that was because no one had ever arrested him, not because he hadn't done it before, and that I felt he should be arrested. I just knew that this man on the other end of the phone was going to tell me what an awful mother I was because I was having my son arrested. Instead, the officer said, "Ma'am, you are a very brave woman and I wish there were more parents like you." My Higher Power spoke through that officer to let me know I was doing the right thing.

Things got worse before they got better. I constantly turned my will and life over to God, not alcoholism. I didn't know what would happen to my son, but I knew that I was going to do the things I felt were right and have no regrets no matter what his consequences. I grabbed onto God and didn't let go. I prayed on my knees every morning and asked my Higher Power to talk to my son's Higher Power and to keep my son safe. Each day I gave my son to God for safekeeping.

Then one day I found my son with a large quantity of drugs. I was sure it was for more than his personal use. The next words out of my mouth surely came from God. I said, "You can't live here anymore." I was afraid for his life, but grounded with my Higher Power and knew he could not live with me.

Later that week, I was saying good-bye to my son at the airport. It had been two-and-a-half years of the toughest kind of love I have ever known. I knew without a doubt that I had done everything God and this program had asked of me. It was time to let go of him all the way. I knew my son had a wonderful, loving God who would protect and help him. I went to hug my son and said, "I love you and I'm sorry it didn't work out." He stiff-armed me so

I couldn't hug him, looked me straight in the eye with a cold stare and said, "If I ever see you again, it will be way too soon." With that he turned and walked away, never looking back.

My heart shattered. Once again our literature told me what to do. A passage from *One Day at a Time in Al-Anon* says, ". . . when anything very dreadful happens, I must think of *what I would be doing if it had not happened, and then do that.*" That is what I did. An hour later I was at a company retreat giving a 60-minute professional presentation.

After a couple years, my son and I were able to be around each other, but it was very strained. I was able to be at his high school graduation, but off to the side. At family gatherings, we never knew when or if he would show up.

Years later, I was planning a trip to my hometown. By now my son was in junior college in another part of the state. He kept calling and asking me to come and see him. I only had a few days vacation and I really didn't want to drive two hours out of my way only to be stood up or put down. My Sponsor reminded me that I was his mother and that he was not making an unreasonable request. I trusted her and made arrangements to meet him at a restaurant.

We met and talked for two hours, just as if he had never left the first time. When it was time to go, I said, "You'll be 21 soon. There were times when I thought you would never make it." He reached across the table, took my hand, looked me in the eye and said, "Thanks, Mom."

Today my son is a trustworthy, fine young man. He often invites me to his home, and we tell his wife about those old times with great humor. I thank God for our relationship each day.

⌐⊷⌐

I came to Al-Anon to change enough so that my wife wouldn't leave me. She believed I was being verbally abusive. I agreed with her that my frustrations and resentments were coming out. I was miserable and I was sharing my misery. I was convinced, though, that if I worked hard enough by working the Steps thoroughly in my first year, reading the literature, and going to at least three meetings a week, I'd make her happy.

Seventeen months later, I was thoroughly immersed in Al-Anon. I'd worked through *Paths to Recovery* and *Blueprint for Progress* with my Sponsor. I felt better—yet my wife left me.

What I did learn is that I can either be frustrated or happy, resentful or serene—regardless of my living situation. My wife will be happy or not according to her own choices.

Al-Anon has given me the means to know which choices are mine. I'm still a novice at recognizing these choices and still a novice at actually making decisions, but I'm on my path to recovery.

⤚✦⤙

My relationship with my adult daughter was one of turmoil, disappointment, and anger. When I first read the pamphlet *A Guide for the Family of the Alcoholic*, I instantly recognized us. At meetings, people shared experiences about themselves and their adult alcoholic children. I identified with them and wanted to weep with relief. Al-Anon members understood what I had tried to do to improve our relationship, and the huge sense of failure I felt as a parent.

As I continued in Al-Anon, I learned about detachment. Perhaps detachment would be easier for me with my daughter living far away. I lived 1,500 miles away and knew better than to initiate unwanted contact with her. We rarely talked on the phone. Occasionally one of us would send a brief post card.

Al-Anon has helped me change my view of my daughter. I am beginning to see her as a person who inherited the disease of alcoholism from both of her parents. She did not choose to be an alcoholic. I understand that, and I try not to personalize her anger when she calls me on those rare occasions.

Now I understand that my daughter has a Higher Power just as I do. For the first time in my adult life, I am at peace with myself. I believe that my daughter is on her path, a different one than before, but her life is unfolding just the way it is meant to be. Her Higher Power is there whenever, and if ever, she chooses to ask for help.

Al-Anon helps me simplify my expectations of any interaction with my daughter. I have also learned to set boundaries and protect myself from being manipulated. I still get hurt, but I recover faster because of Al-Anon.

⌒⌒∝⌒⌒

When I first came into Al-Anon, I had trouble knowing how I felt. Growing up in an alcoholic home, if I cried I got threatened with, "Stop it or I'll give you something to cry about," so all my sadness turned to anger. This was reinforced when I was with my first husband. His married friends told him that if he ignored my crying, I would soon stop. They were right, I stopped. The only emotion that seemed acceptable in my family and in my marriage was anger. I forgot how to cry and how to laugh. When I finally reached the doors of an Al-Anon meeting, the first thing I heard was laughter. The first thing I felt was hope.

Al-Anon Conference Approved Literature has been a lifesaver and a life changer for me. When I was mixed up inside, but didn't know what I was feeling, I went to the index in the back of our daily readers, *One Day at a Time in Al-Anon* and *Courage to Change*. There I would look up anger and read some pages. One time I saw the word "resentment" and thought my feeling was more like that, so I looked up "resentment." Then I found the word "jealousy" and realized I was feeling envious and jealous of someone. I was able to work on my feelings and make my amends.

Eventually I purchased more Al-Anon books. I am so grateful that our literature contains indexes. By discovering my true feelings, I was able to take the necessary steps to work on them by talking to my Sponsor or another trusted Al-Anon friend or by going to a meeting. Today when I need to know how I am feeling in any relationship, I start with Al-Anon literature. I've passed this on to those I sponsor and I've mentioned it at my meetings.

Conference Approved Literature is a great source of knowledge about me, thanks to the thousands of other members who continue to write parts of my story for our literature. Today I know it's not all about anger. I can laugh and cry when I feel like it, and the wonderful part about feelings is that sometimes I do both at the same time.

For Thought and Discussion:

1. What piece of Conference Approved Literature has had the greatest effect on my attitudes about my relationships?
2. When I was in despair about a relationship, what Al-Anon literature gave me hope?
3. Which pieces of our literature have helped me most in understanding "detachment with love"? In learning communication skills? In setting boundaries?
4. What Al-Anon literature could I use to chair a meeting on breaking isolation?
5. What piece could I use to chair a meeting on intimacy?
6. Which passage from Conference Approved Literature has helped me calm my fears?

Chapter Sixteen

Meaningful Relationships

There is no simple recipe that will solve all of our problems instantly. Al-Anon is a journey of self-discovery. No one can do it for us. But we can learn to apply Al-Anon principles to our own unique situations, and somehow we come to see our problems in a different light.

We begin by recognizing that someone else has a problem with drinking. As we start to understand the illness of alcoholism, however, we also begin to understand ourselves better. We come to discover that even when we have to accept what we can't change, we still have choices available to us. We also learn how to make choices that are healthier for us.

As we grow in Al-Anon, we eventually realize how little we knew in the beginning—but we see this progress only in hindsight. Even though we didn't know how to get the social skills and self-confidence necessary for healthy relationships, we find that we get what we need as we progress. It's impossible to predict what we will need next year; nevertheless, there's always a lesson that we can learn today.

We take our challenges "One Day at a Time" so that we focus only on today's problem. We learn to concern ourselves only with what we can do today, and we leave tomorrow's challenges for tomorrow. After working the program in this way, day after day, we eventually realize that our relationships—or our attitudes about them—have improved.

For some of us, this progress is unexpected. We didn't think it would ever be possible. How did we get there? What did we do to make it happen? Some would say that a Higher Power led us step-by-step to recovery in relationships. Others might simply say that the program works—as long as we work the program.

Although we may not understand exactly how we were able to make progress, that understanding isn't necessary. The examples of countless Al-Anon members show us that progress is possible. We share with these members at meetings. We meet them while doing service projects. We read their stories in our Conference Approved Literature. It isn't necessary to believe blindly that Al-Anon works, but scientific proof isn't necessary either. There are many Al-Anon members who are willing to share their program with us, and their serenity is obvious to anyone who takes the time to speak with them.

Al-Anon gives us hope because we can see the progress enjoyed by people who were once overwhelmed by problems similar to ours—and they're ready to share their experience, strength, and hope. As our Suggested Closing reminds us:

"Whatever your problems, there are those among us who have had them, too. If you try to keep an open mind, you will find help. You will come to realize that there is no situation too difficult to be bettered and no unhappiness too great to be lessened."

Personal Stories

Through the interaction and practice with individuals in my Al-Anon group, I now have loving, accepting, and compassionate relationships. I have made many new friends through the program. I have come to look upon Al-Anon as my second family. The tools of this program have helped me in all my relationships—with children, at work, and in everyday life. It has given me a safe and secure environment in which to grow and learn to love myself as well.

Today I don't have that aching, burning need to fill a void by using someone or something. I have come to understand my Higher Power's love for me. I have come to understand the difference between wanting a significant other in my life and needing a significant other in my life.

⌒❦⌒

My brother and I are completely different on the outside. He has two children, a nine-to-five job, and a big house in the suburbs. I live alone in a small city apartment and work the random hours of an artist. I am struck by the fact that two people who grew up in the same circumstances can lead such seemingly different lives.

Last year I had a tiny bit of program under my belt when I went home for his birthday. He burned himself on the coffee pot and immediately started to strangle me. I knew enough to ask him calmly to stop, and I left the party. As I drove away from his house, I cried at how painful and frightening that situation had been.

This year I sent my brother a small gift in the mail. I wished it could have been of more material substance and expressed this regret at a meeting. Someone suggested I write my brother a note as part of the gift. I meditated and prayed before attempting such a significant amends. In the letter, I mentioned alcoholism and our rage-filled, fearful upbringing for the first time. His wife called the next week to thank me for whatever I wrote in the letter that brought my brother to tears. Now my brother calls me occasionally just to say hello.

Lines of communication have been opened because I admitted my sadness in the safety of a meeting and was willing to take action based on someone else's shared experience. My improved relationship with my brother is a gift I never could have imagined.

⌐◦✖◦⌐

I was a caretaker. I did everything for everyone, whether they wanted me to or not. I was in charge, in control of it all. I worked to make sure everyone's needs were met. I never rested, I never said no, and I constantly felt resentful that they didn't appreciate me at all.

Then I started to attend Al-Anon regularly, got a Sponsor, and began to do the Steps. I worked hard at changing myself and my attitudes. It was a process—no overnight miracle, but a miracle nonetheless. When my husband was diagnosed with multiple sclerosis and his health started to decline, I used my program as I became his caregiver. I had learned to take care of myself first, so I was able to care for others. Al-Anon meetings are always a priority. Without the constant help I receive there, I'd be a mess. I am able to help others, but not to do for them what they can do themselves.

The relationships I have with my loved ones today show mutual respect. I respect their right to be themselves, make their own decisions, and live their own lives, mistakes and all. Thanks to my work in Al-Anon, they also respect me today.

I have been a caregiver for my husband for 14 years now. For seven years, I was also a caregiver for my dad, until he passed away. Having two disabled men to care for was not easy, to say the least. What I learned in Al-Anon got me through it "One Day at a Time." I never gave up taking care of me. I have learned the difference between caretaking and caregiving.

⌐◦✖◦⌐

Before Al-Anon, I was never sure what my true feelings were. I was so focused on pleasing everyone else and worrying about how others felt about me, I never gave myself priority in anything. I always gave everyone the last piece of pie or the first choice. My feelings and wants were secondary. I thought this was the right way to act. If I made a mistake, watch out: Here came guilt and shame. Forgiving myself was not an option. I did not know how to do that. I thought God was punishing me, and therefore He wasn't going to forgive me either. My attitude was very negative, and I felt bad most of the time. On the outside you might not know it, but on the inside I was dying. Shame, guilt, and resentments were eating me up.

Slowly my life has changed. By living the program, I have come to be my own best friend. By working the Steps, I have discovered much about myself and realized some greater truths.

God is not punishing me, and I deserve the last piece of pie if I want it. I do not have to be perfect—I'm excellent just the way I am, warts and all. Al-Anon gave me tools to learn to develop one of the most important relationships in my life—the one with myself.

Using these tools, I have let go of the shame, guilt, and resentments that kept me focused on the negative side of life. I take better care of myself physically, spiritually, and mentally. Most days I'm happy and free to develop into the kind of person I truly think God wants me to be. Today I trust myself as I would my best friend—and that's a long way from where I started. I like myself, and by working the program, my relationship with myself only gets better and better.

⌐◦⊗◦⌐

When I first came to Al-Anon, I was separated from my husband and we had decided to divorce. In my opinion, he was the guilty one—totally responsible for the failure of our marriage. He had gone outside of our relationship for support from another woman. I was indignant, hostile, angry, ashamed, resentful, and afraid. Looking back, I see myself as having been hard, brittle, and prickly. Making my amends list, I put my husband's name in the "never" column.

Sometime later, our oldest daughter decided to marry. Despite the tension, my former husband and I had to work together. Meeting one evening over coffee, we made a pact: We would not allow our feelings to interfere with our daughter's wedding. Happily, we remained true to that agreement. In some small way, we moved from active hatred to a simmering kind of anger.

Several years later, our second daughter announced her intention to marry. This time the energy was different. I could step back and watch my daughter turn to her father to plan her wedding. I knew my former husband was in poor health and this milestone was important to him. I didn't have to be important. We moved from simmering anger to involved indifference.

Our contact was minimal, but with lots of meetings and hard program work, my heart softened toward him. I took responsibility for my part in our divorce. I saw the things I had done or said. I became accountable for my unrealistic expectations about what he could do. I finally saw that we both had done the best we could with what we had learned in our families.

When our son announced his marriage, I was living far away and didn't think I could afford to attend his wedding. It was a difficult decision to make. My son called to tell me my ticket had been taken care of, so all I had to do was get on a plane. At the wedding rehearsal, I learned that my former husband had paid for the ticket. He wanted me to share in the joy of our son's wedding. I cried and accepted the change of heart it represented.

That night my three children, my former husband, his wife, and I sat down at the same table and shared dinner. We laughed and cried and enjoyed each other. I got to hear my former husband tell my son how proud he was of him and how much he loved him. Many times since that night, my children have told me how much it meant to them to see the healing. On that same trip, I was able to complete my amends to my former husband. I was able to thank him for the part he had played in my life and the wonderful children we had given each other. I saw love in his eyes when we spoke. That was the last time I saw him alive. I attended his funeral with a clear conscience and a heavy heart. While we had not become fast friends after our divorce, we came to respect each other. We came to a place where we felt affection and consideration for one another. It really was enough.

c⸙o

On my first trip home after finding recovery, I shared with my mother that there was a program for people whose lives and attitudes had become distorted by living with alcoholism. (My father died from this disease at 47.) My mother's reply was, "But if I go to Al-Anon, your brothers and sisters may think they have a problem." Of my five siblings, only my younger sister is not an alcoholic.

A few years later, to my amazement, my sister and my mother did try Al-Anon. However, they decided it was not for them. I knew my sister would do whatever my mother decided.

Every childhood photo shows me holding my sister's hand, trying to protect her from the misery of living in an alcoholic maze. On and off over the years, she has called me to say that she is going to give Al-Anon another try, but she hasn't. I wanted her to have Al-Anon so much that at times I promoted rather than attracted. It took talking to my Sponsor, going to meetings, praying, meditating, and working continuously on the Steps to help me remember that I cannot make someone else's well-being more important to me than it is to them.

My sister has gained a significant amount of weight and is on numerous medications. She enables her two sons, just like my mother did to my brother until he died. My Sponsor reminds me that although my siblings might not survive this disease, I need to release them—including my younger sister. In order to be the loving daughter and sister that God wants me to be, I have to stay detached and put into action every one of the Steps and Traditions.

My family is doing the best they can. As I gradually let go, however, I find that their view no longer makes the sky any less blue for me.

c⸺∞⸺ɔ

After attending Al-Anon meetings for several years, I began to attend meetings focused on adult children. A few months later, I went for a visit to see if I could love my father and hate the disease. I sat down close to my dad and whispered, "Do you want to go for a drive and look at the land?" He nodded, so I picked up the keys to his truck and we took a drive together.

This ride was perhaps the first and last real moment I had with my dad. We talked as adults. I no longer needed to criticize him, for I understood he had a disease. I was able to accept him with all his wounds. I recognized the many wonderful things he had done for me, which I had previously not seen because I had been trying to place blame.

I remembered the vacations we had, the camping trips in the mountains, and the college money that allowed me to get my degree. I remembered the freedom of living on the farm, playing in the barn, and gathering eggs with my aunt. All of a sudden I saw my father as a loving man who had a disease. Thanks to the program, I have this one very special afternoon with my dad. He died two months later at the age of 64.

c⸺∞⸺ɔ

My relationship with my alcoholic daughter has come full circle. She was always my baby who never quite fit in. We struggled at times to live in the same house. Eventually my daughter chose to leave her family and live a life on the streets. I didn't hear from her for almost six months and didn't know whether she was dead or alive. One day I got a call from the hospital saying that she'd attempted suicide for the third time. They asked if I would come to get her. My answer was no.

I knew she was right where she needed to be to get all the help she needed. She had been beyond my help for a long time. Deciding not to get her was one of the hardest things I've ever had to live with, but I knew it was best for both of us. She sobered up and started over, but we didn't speak for over a year. I knew if I just left the door open and turned her over to my Higher Power, that when the time was right, she would come to me to start our relationship over. We just couldn't rush things.

Al-Anon and A.A. have helped us once again be a part of each other's lives. We are stronger and closer to each other than we have ever been before. Because I was able to take my hands off and allow both of us to grow and heal, today we truly like each other. We are friends who enjoy each other's company. I have my daughter back in my life with love and respect. I don't know what tomorrow brings and I don't care. I am just enjoying our new-found relationship "One Day at a Time."

⌐◦◦◦

Before coming into recovery, all of my relationships were a struggle. They all involved conflict in some form or another. Usually the conflict stemmed from my desire to control and the other person's desire for personal freedom. I lacked trust and respect for myself. As for my Higher Power, I wasn't even communicating with Him. In fact, it never occurred to me to even think about my God. I had a God—not one of my understanding, but a God nonetheless. But that's all. He was tucked away in some corner of my mind, utterly useless to me, or so I thought.

Since then, I have learned that it's about progress today, not perfection every day. I still want what I want when I want it, but if it doesn't go that way, I know there's always plan B. I have learned to qualify my requests with, "If it is Your will." I make the decision each day to turn my will and my life over to the care of God, and sometimes I change my mind part of the way through. But I know I can start over at any time, and I can make that same decision again. I have choices today, and I can allow others to also have, and make, their own choices. I don't always like it, but I try to accept it today. After all, it's the only day I really have, and it is a gift.

⌒⌒⌒

It was clear from the start that my mother and I had a very special connection. We shared a similar disposition and many interests. Unfortunately, my mother's drinking added an extra sense of distortion to everything that was said or done. It could turn an "I love you" into "Don't ever leave me—I can't live without you!" or an "I'm upset with you" into "I hate you and wish I never had you!" Without Al-Anon to help me realize it was the disease talking, I had nothing to go on but the words themselves, and I believed every one of them.

I had equal difficulty interpreting her actions. They were often very unpredictable—soothing one moment and frightening the next. I was never sure which mom would be there for me. I proceeded cautiously in all of life, fearful of how my mother would react. I would tell her very little of what really happened—at school or anywhere else. Often I was more afraid of what she would do to others than to me—and how I would face the embarrassment. I was always trying to protect myself by protecting her from the truth. I was a small, skinny boy uninterested in sports. School was often a nightmare place for me, where I was teased and bullied by other kids. Letting my mom know what was really going on would only make matters worse.

Throughout high school and college, I was reclusive, friendless, and terribly lonely. Even the connection I once felt with my mom had disintegrated to the point where all we did was scream and argue. I had exhausted myself in trying to stop her from drinking, and nothing worked. By the time I went to my first Al-Anon meeting, my life had become so unbearable that I felt I had nothing to lose.

I slowly crawled out of my shell of isolation as I listened to fellow members. They constantly encouraged me to use Al-Anon's

Twelve Steps to discover who I really was. "You can't love what you don't know," they told me. As I followed the Steps, I discovered many things about myself that I had clearly avoided for years by focusing on others. As I gradually opened up to my Sponsor and other Al-Anon friends, it became all the more apparent to me how much I always held back from my mom. I was still protecting myself by protecting her. I realized that if we were ever to have the kind of relationship I really wanted to have with her, I would need to be willing to share more of my life with her. I knew this meant, among other things, letting my mom know I'm gay.

It took some time, and much prayer and meditation, before I was ready to take such a risk. By then I was already in a committed relationship with my partner and it was very clear how much we were all missing because of my inability to tell my mom the truth. Next to attending my first meeting, coming out to my mom was the hardest thing I ever did. To my surprise, she received my revelation with grace, acceptance, and love. As she said at the time, "I'm 78 years old. I've lived through a lot of things. This is just one more thing."

In my apprehension over telling her, I had not taken into account that by this time my mom had not been drinking for a number of years. She became very active in her church and local school organizations. She started dressing up as a clown and began visiting hospitals, schools, and nursing homes. She became an absolutely delightful, playful person, full of fun and laughter. This was not the mother who raised me.

Sometimes, when even I was worried about a pending situation, she would say, "Well, I'm just going to take this 'One Day at a Time.'" She became a real inspiration to my partner and me. She treated my partner as another son, and having been motherless since his teens, he was grateful.

My openness with her prompted her to be more open with me. She shared joys and disappointments from her life that she had previously kept hidden. We became comfortable just being ourselves around each other, no longer needing to be guarded or protective. The relaxed intimacy we developed grew stronger as together we explored common interests. None of this would have been imaginable to me without Al-Anon.

⌐∝≈∽⌐

During my son's teenage years, he began drinking, using drugs, lying, and stealing from me. Since I was the custodial parent, I had to deal with this insanity until he turned 18 years old. With the loving help of my Sponsor and several trusted Al-Anon members, the day after my son's birthday I removed him from my home. It was the most difficult thing I have done in my life.

I spent a lot of time on my knees turning him over to my Higher Power and doing my best to stay out of the way. I wouldn't see him very often, and I couldn't give him money. I did buy him a pair of shoes when I saw that his were held together with duct tape. I was able to hand him a couple cans of soup and tell him that I had faith that he would find his way. I always told him that I loved him, but that I disagreed with his choices.

Just before Mother's Day two years later, he came by and asked to talk. He said, "When you kicked me out, I hated you. I sometimes had to beg to sleep on someone's floor because I didn't want to sleep on the street. I worked in fast food places so I would have a meal to eat. However, it took me over two years to realize that I was making the decisions to drink and use drugs. As much as I hated you for kicking me out, I know that it was the most important thing you could have done for me. I learned to live life on God's terms."

On Mother's Day I received a card from my son. It said on the front: "They say you get out of life what you put into it." When I opened the card, it said, "But I say, you also get out of it what your mother puts into it, and you've put a lot into mine." And then he wrote, "Thanks for all your love and support. I love you, Mom."

Today my son is the father of three, working on a loving relationship with his wife. He has a job he enjoys. Things aren't perfect, but they are so much better than I could have imagined. I am able to share with them and try not to run their lives.

I have so many relationships to work on still. I know that as I apply the Al-Anon ideas, they will get better. I know that miracles happen, and I'm not going to give up until I have a lifetime of miracles.

⌒⋙⌒

I was sick and tired of what I thought was a dead relationship with my husband. I felt like I should have buried the relationship years ago. Then I started to go to Al-Anon, and four months later he moved in with his mother in another state to keep her out of a nursing home.

In my sick mind, I thought God was doing this to punish my husband for all of his years of drinking. Little did I know, God used this opportunity to open my eyes.

While my husband was gone, we were not talking unless it was necessary. I tried to make it unnecessary. I always thought it was good to have space between us. Then I began to notice the love that my husband had for his mother and how he showed it every day. He spent what turned out to be the last nine years of her life making amends for all the things he put her through as a young man. Words cannot express how my feelings changed from wishing him out of my life into being proud of his loving concern. Working the Al-Anon program gave me the opportunity to make amends to my husband.

We were there for each other when our oldest son became ill. As we faced each day knowing it would probably be our son's last, we didn't blame each other and were able to support each other. God helped me to love my husband as the person who began as my best friend and became a wonderful husband, loving father, special grandfather, and now a great-grandfather. It took our son's death to get him to stop drinking and me to be grateful and thankful each day for the blessings.

⌒⋙⌒

My dad, my knight in shining armor, drank too much some-times. He'd get mean, critical, and would humiliate me at times, but I always remember loving him so much and feeling that my very existence depended on him.

It's very dangerous to be dependent on an alcoholic. I grew up angry, insecure, and very afraid. I also grew up thinking I was responsible for everything and everybody. When I got married, I felt I was responsible for my alcoholic husband's happiness. I sup-pose I was still trying to be sure there was happiness in my home. Of course, there rarely ever was.

When my husband became violent, I knew it was time to end the marriage. I stumbled into Al-Anon during that tumultuous time. I began working the program vigorously. I wanted my life to change. Even though I didn't know how to change it, or even what I was trying to change it into, I knew I was going to die if I kept going the way I was going.

Things started to change a little at a time. Eventually, after quite a few years and a lot of hard work, I realized I wasn't angry with my dad anymore. He was still actively drinking, but I had changed. I no longer expected him to be an infallible knight who was sup-posed to run to my side at the slightest whimper. Believe me, there were many whimpers. I began to see him as a human being; a man whose life had been less than perfect. I saw him as a very sensi-tive soul who had suffered a great deal in his own alcoholic family upbringing—a person filled with sadness and broken dreams. My heart broke for him, but in my pain a wonderful thing happened. My broken heart finally began to heal. I began to forgive.

I began to notice and cherish things I had never noticed before, such as how much I resemble my dad. We have similar physical characteristics and personality traits, such as sensitivity and com-passion. From him I got my oval face, body shape, intellect, low cholesterol levels, and a love and talent for gardening. We shared a great deal, and suddenly that was wonderful.

I wanted him to know. I picked out the perfect card, and I included a note telling my dad about what I'd learned and how happy I was to have had the realization. The next time I saw him was at my nephew's birthday party. Though we were surrounded by screaming kids, my dad waited until we had a semi-private moment and thanked me for the card. He was more than a little emotional when he asked why I had done that. I said, "I thought something nice about you and I just wanted you to know it." He smiled a little nervously, hugged me, and scurried off to play with the grandkids.

A few minutes later my mom found me. She told me how my dad had reacted when he got the card. She had found him that day sitting at the kitchen table crying. After he showed the card to her, he said, "I don't deserve this." My mom had hugged him and assured him that he did, but he insisted that he didn't—something I'm sure he's felt for almost his entire 67 years.

Now every day I try to show him that he does deserve to be loved and cherished. He's my dad and I love him. But he's also a creation of God, and that's really the only requirement.

Things have really changed since I sent him that note. I can't say for sure it was the only reason, but my dad and I talk more. We hug more, and when we do, it's a little tighter and we hold on a little longer.

⌒⌘⌒

I was a very lonely person, even though I had many exciting friends. I just could not get boundaries straight. I had walls that would come crashing down when I got too lonely from overworking.

I thought I related to people well, but I was often told that I was hurtful and controlling by the people closest to me at home and at work. I did not see people as they were, but fell in love with them as I romanticized them to be. Life was exciting, but I felt hurt and lost because there were always goodbyes.

The Twelve Steps helped me to realize how lonely I had been as a child and how I was compensating for the lack of attention. I had developed patterns of looking for false connections with people.

I got a high from having my life caught up and carried away in a relationship, which usually became obsessive and eventually hurtful. With Al-Anon I have learned to trust in a new way and to develop healthy relationships and boundaries within those relationships. I can stand on my own two feet without depending too much on someone or having someone depend too much on me.

The excitement is not there like it used to be, but there is more profound joy and awe as I see my friends grow and mature, many of whom are in the program. Healthy and happy relationships can be a lot of hard work, because I have to first understand myself as a flawed and imperfect human being. With acceptance of myself comes a new acceptance of others.

⌒◇◇⌒

All of my married life I was the person in charge. My spouse had no problem with me making major decisions for our family and our home. I chose where we would live, what furniture we would have, what he would wear, and where we'd travel or spend holidays. I spent money where I chose to spend it and handled all the finances. I ran the show, and my spouse cooperated saying that he wanted me to be happy.

It was after I came into Al-Anon that I was able to see how alone I was in the way we lived. Being a one-woman show did not make me happy. Instead, it contributed to the loneliness that alcoholism kept alive. Although I had been married for several years, I had not learned to work with others. My spouse was a silent partner. Our lack of joint participation robbed us of mutual joys and shared memories.

I was in Al-Anon about a year when I attended a meeting with another member in an old area of town. The church where the meeting was held was nestled in a square of unique shops and restaurants. After the meeting, my friend and I browsed the shops. There was a jacket in one of the shops that caught my eye. It was perfect. My friend urged me to buy it. I looked at myself in the mirror, and although I loved the jacket, the reflection in the mirror looked like loneliness in blue jeans and sequins. I decided to do things differently. I didn't need another empty piece of anything in my house.

That evening I shared the experience and my feelings with my spouse. His reply was a loving one. "Let's go have dinner at the square this weekend and take a look at the jacket." I was secretly excited that I might allow myself to be loved.

I was not sure I could be comfortable shopping with my spouse, possibly hearing an opinion from him as I played the role of equal. Once at the shop, I took the jacket from the rack and said, "This is it." To my surprise, my spouse suggested I try it on and model for him. He told me I looked great in it and that he wanted to buy it for me. He took it to the cashier and paid for it. Arm in arm, we left the store.

The jacket is out of fashion now, but it still hangs in the basement closet. The memory, however, is fresh and still brings tears to my eyes. You see, I decided I could change my part and risk being vulnerable and loved. I allowed someone to give to me. I received so much more than a garment that night. It was an early step in the process of having a relationship in which we both participate in our life together. I have to take risks to have good relationships. I must be open to love and to being loved. It begins with me.

⌐✆ↄ

I was completely distraught after my fiancé broke off our engagement. At the time, I had only a small understanding of the problems in our relationship. When everything was going smoothly, I would begin to feel uncomfortable. The next thing I knew, I would speak harshly, trying to start an argument. The night he decided to call off the engagement, I once again started an argument for no reason. He lovingly said that he cared for me, but could not stay in a relationship with someone who started arguments for no reason. He suggested I try Al-Anon because he knew that my late father was an alcoholic.

I was at my rock bottom. I started attending Al-Anon meetings regularly, and within the first weeks I learned that families of alcoholics, especially the children of alcoholics, don't always know how to function in times of peace. Life with an active alcoholic brought constant turmoil that I often recreated when I started so many fights with my fiancé.

Part of regaining sanity is finding the ability to enjoy the peaceful times, which I am now doing. My fiancé and I are back together and plan to get married. I am looking forward to gaining even more of an understanding of what living with sanity means.

⌐◁◯▷⌐

My relationship with my mom has been a long process of healing. Mom enabled Dad's drinking and did all the typical things you'd expect in the alcoholic home. She poured the booze down the sink and then bought more. She argued with my dad, but when he became belligerent, she would take on the role of mother and feed him, get him into bed, and take good care of him. She fed the drunk friends he dragged home, but she was angry about it.

When I was 13, my mom would send me into the bar to talk my dad off the barstool. When I could drive, it was my job to get Dad home. I learned at a very early age to be my mom's helper. I was supposed to have all the answers.

As an adult, during a visit home, I found the memories my mother shared from my childhood to be very hurtful. They were a constant reminder that her life would have been easier if she hadn't had a third child. As a dutiful daughter, I kept my mouth shut because we had an unspoken rule about upsetting Mother and causing her stomach problems.

The next time I visited, Mom and I were finally alone. In Al-Anon I had learned about setting boundaries and taking care of myself. I had discovered that I might have something strong to say, but I could say it in a gentle yet firm way. I expressed the pain that her comments had brought me. I said I would appreciate her not sharing them in my presence. If she chose to do so, I would leave.

This was the first honest adult conversation I can recall having with her. She looked at me, acknowledged how these words could cause pain, and agreed to not repeat the behavior. She has kept her word to me. There have been many little steps in healing the wounds of my family. Now I share how I feel and ask for kindness and respect. I have always known how to push my mom's buttons and cause her pain. In my process of healing, I have honored her choices and treated her in the same way that I wanted to be treated. Today I enjoy the relationship I have with my mother. I call her almost every week and visit when I am able. I recognize that I will not have her for too many more years, and I want to enjoy every day God gives us. I also send her little cards and notes to brighten her day. I send her flowers because I want her to enjoy flowers while she is living, rather than save them for a grave.

⌐❧⌐

I met my husband in college, and we married a month after graduation. He was the star athlete—a party animal—and I enjoyed sharing his limelight. After we were married, his drinking progressed and so did my resentment. Years later, there was little love, respect, or trust left. I was obsessed with his drinking. I came to Al-Anon to find the recipe to fix him, but instead I found the strength to learn to live, laugh, and love again.

I listened to those who shared stories of hope and how their relationships eventually did blossom into something I could only dream about. They gave me the faith to stay in this relationship "One Day at a Time." Today I am so grateful for the gift of our love affair. I found that just as anger and resentment can grow, so can trust and love. We are truly blessed. My husband is now sober, and our relationship is truly special. We have grown so much individually and moved forward together. We laugh and cry together and are committed to sharing our lives. I don't need to be in his limelight any longer. Al-Anon has given me my own light.

⌐❧⌐

After 10 years of wishing my ex-husband would just disappear, our relationship made a dramatic change for the better. But he didn't change a bit. He still accused me of things that I didn't do and brought weekly chaos into my life. Friends in the program and my Higher Power suggested that I could pray for my ex-husband's well-being. Instead of wishing him dead, I could wish him well. I began praying that he could be happy, peaceful, free from suffering, and filled with loving kindness for others. I added that last part for me. Maybe if I prayed for that, some of it would come my way. Alcoholics may not always recover, but relations with them can still get better.

My ex-husband doesn't write me nasty e-mails anymore. He doesn't express negative opinions about me to anyone I know, either. He calls occasionally to say hello to his son, but the barrage of accusations has stopped. Maybe the idea of "This too shall pass" had a part in all of it. I'm glad that I never disappeared with my son to avoid his father's venom. I'm glad that I stayed in town where he could see his son if he chooses and where his son could see him.

I have chosen to use the tools of the program. I call upon my Higher Power to do for us what we cannot do for ourselves. I use this prayer anytime I have resentments. There is no greater gift to ourselves or others than prayers for happiness, peace, freedom from suffering, and loving kindness.

⌒⟨⟩⌒

I watched as the woman I loved slowly destroyed herself with alcohol. She had told me several times that she was going to drink herself to death, and she acted like she meant it. Some days I wished she would hurry up the process. Other days I worked my mind into a frenzy trying to figure out where I went wrong and what I could do so she would become sober. Most days I was just numb. I was a shell of person, functioning out of habit in a world of ever-diminishing social contact. I was living in isolation, and I had myself convinced that I was happy to be there.

I came to Al-Anon shortly after my wife found A.A. At that time, I had very little going for me in regards to human relationships. Before A.A., my wife had been drunk most of the time. Now she was busy working her program. My son was away at college and my daughter was in high school. I had no friends. I had little contact with the rest of my family. I had no spiritual life. I didn't like myself very much. The only people I talked to on a regular basis were my coworkers, but our conversations didn't extend to a social or personal level. I kept to myself. During the course of my life, I had found too much pain in relationships. I wanted to stop the pain, so I isolated myself.

It was suggested that I attend six meetings before deciding whether or not Al-Anon was for me. I thought that would be easy enough to do, so I did it. Even though I didn't say much besides my name, and even though I felt a little embarrassed by not being able to share on a topic, I continued to attend for another six weeks, and then another, and on and on. I began to feel comfortable at the meeting. Even though I didn't understand much about the program and thought that some of the regulars were a little crazy, I kept coming back. I saw something there that I wanted. I wanted to be able to open up and share, but I was too shy. I suffered from low self-esteem and I didn't trust anybody, not even myself.

When I began trusting the members at meetings, I started sharing on the topic. I was amazed that people listened. I was sure I had nothing to say, yet I found that speaking about my feelings, my pains, and my troubles helped me more than I believed possible. It pulled the monsters out from under the bed and put them in a light that allowed me to deal with them one at a time. I was mending my relationship with myself, with a Higher Power, and now, by sharing at meetings, with people.

After a while, I began to chair meetings. One day I volunteered to be Group Representative. Later, the other Group Representatives in my district asked me to be the District Representative. These opportunities and other service positions have helped me grow. I learned how to work with others. I learned how to make amends.

I learned how to trust others and myself. I learned how to deal with life on life's terms. My self-esteem was growing, and I felt very good about how I was changing.

As I began to heal and learn how to handle life as an adult, I was able to look closely at my wife's struggles. I saw how she worked her program and how this kept her sober. I understood how working my program helped me stay out of her business. I realized that I have enough to do in taking care of myself. Over time our relationship has grown and our love has deepened. It has been "One Day at Time," but the days are now numerous and the bond between us continues to develop and grow in healthy ways.

⌐∽⊗◯∽◦

The first realization I had in Al-Anon was that I was the one who had screwed up my life. Nobody else had done this to me. I needed to find out who I was. I dug deep inside to learn what I could about myself, and finally I caught on that nothing different would happen unless I changed. Ongoing change is my responsibility. Unflinching self-assessment somehow shines a bright light on where I need to be, and ultimately leads me to understand my relationship with God. With humility I get to work hand in hand with my Higher Power. Al-Anon shows me that it isn't my relationship with the alcoholic that I need to focus on. It's my relationship with God that governs my behavior and my attitudes.

Luckily, there was time before my parents died for me to make amends to them. Although their life together remained as it always had, our relationship changed. After a lot of soul-searching, I learned to talk with my mother pleasantly, chatting about everyday occurrences, enjoying each other. The anger was gone. Though ours had been a decidedly unaffectionate household during my childhood, the day came when my father told me he loved me. It had been years since I had first gathered the courage to say the words to him. I thought he would never voice them. One day as we sat in the living room talking, I could see that he had something he wanted to say. Try as he might, the words wouldn't come out. Then suddenly he burst into song, improvising a sweet little tune that allowed him to sing the words "I love you."

Saying those words is a big deal. Through all the dark years of my husband's alcoholism, love didn't really seem to exist for me. My attempts to offer love were either disbelieved or were so far removed from his interest in booze that they were ignored. Somewhere in recovery, we began to say "I love you" and mean it—many times a day. It is the recognition of what we do for each other, and the admission that we care—the pledge of our absolute devotion.

I am far from perfect. That's okay. I don't have to be perfect anymore. All I have to do is to offer my best intentions, reach out when I can actually help, accept with grace whatever comes my way, and smile with the assurance of the peace within me.

Love is so powerful. Our cofounder, Lois W., wrote in *Lois Remembers* that love is "an actual physical emanation as well as a spiritual force." She recognized that God is love and that it is love that ties us all together. It is a confirmation that my relationship with God is essential to the success of any other relationships.

Twelve Steps

Study of these Steps is essential to progress in the Al-Anon program. The principles they embody are universal, applicable to everyone, whatever his personal creed. In Al-Anon, we strive for an ever-deeper understanding of these Steps, and pray for the wisdom to apply them to our lives.

1. We admitted we were powerless over alcohol—that our lives had become unmanageable.

2. Came to believe that a Power greater than ourselves could restore us to sanity.

3. Made a decision to turn our will and our lives over to the care of God *as we understood Him.*

4. Made a searching and fearless moral inventory of ourselves.

5. Admitted to God, to ourselves, and to another human being the exact nature of our wrongs.

6. Were entirely ready to have God remove all these defects of character.

7. Humbly asked Him to remove our shortcomings.

8. Made a list of all persons we had harmed, and became willing to make amends to them all.

9. Made direct amends to such people wherever possible, except when to do so would injure them or others.

10. Continued to take personal inventory and when we were wrong promptly admitted it.

11. Sought through prayer and meditation to improve our conscious contact with God *as we understood Him,* praying only for knowledge of His will for us and the power to carry that out.

12. Having had a spiritual awakening as the result of these steps, we tried to carry this message to others, and to practice these principles in all our affairs.

Twelve Traditions

These guidelines are the means of promoting harmony and growth in Al-Anon groups and in the worldwide fellowship of Al-Anon as a whole. Our group experience suggests that our unity depends upon our adherence to these Traditions:

1. Our common welfare should come first; personal progress for the greatest number depends upon unity.
2. For our group purpose there is but one authority—a loving God as He may express Himself in our group conscience. Our leaders are but trusted servants—they do not govern.
3. The relatives of alcoholics, when gathered together for mutual aid, may call themselves an Al-Anon Family Group, provided that, as a group, they have no other affiliation. The only requirement for membership is that there be a problem of alcoholism in a relative or friend.
4. Each group should be autonomous, except in matters affecting another group or Al-Anon or AA as a whole.
5. Each Al-Anon Family Group has but one purpose: to help families of alcoholics. We do this by practicing the Twelve Steps of AA *ourselves*, by encouraging and understanding our alcoholic relatives, and by welcoming and giving comfort to families of alcoholics.
6. Our Family Groups ought never endorse, finance or lend our name to any outside enterprise, lest problems of money, property and prestige divert us from our primary spiritual aim. Although a separate entity, we should always co-operate with Alcoholics Anonymous.
7. Every group ought to be fully self-supporting, declining outside contributions.
8. Al-Anon Twelfth Step work should remain forever nonprofessional, but our service centers may employ special workers.
9. Our groups, as such, ought never be organized; but we may create service boards or committees directly responsible to those they serve.

10. The Al-Anon Family Groups have no opinion on outside issues; hence our name ought never be drawn into public controversy.

11. Our public relations policy is based on attraction rather than promotion; we need always maintain personal anonymity at the level of press, radio, films, and TV. We need guard with special care the anonymity of all AA members.

12. Anonymity is the spiritual foundation of all our Traditions, ever reminding us to place principles above personalities.

Twelve Concepts of Service

The Twelve Steps and Traditions are guides for personal growth and group unity. The Twelve Concepts are guides for service. They show how Twelfth Step work can be done on a broad scale and how members of a World Service Office can relate to each other and to the groups, through a World Service Conference, to spread Al-Anon's message worldwide.

1. The ultimate responsibility and authority for Al-Anon world services belongs to the Al-Anon groups.
2. The Al-Anon Family Groups have delegated complete administrative and operational authority to their Conference and its service arms.
3. The right of decision makes effective leadership possible.
4. Participation is the key to harmony.
5. The rights of appeal and petition protect minorities and insure that they be heard.
6. The Conference acknowledges the primary administrative responsibility of the Trustees.
7. The Trustees have legal rights while the rights of the Conference are traditional.
8. The Board of Trustees delegates full authority for routine management of Al-Anon Headquarters to its executive committees.
9. Good personal leadership at all service levels is a necessity. In the field of world service the Board of Trustees assumes the primary leadership.
10. Service responsibility is balanced by carefully defined service authority and double-headed management is avoided.
11. The World Service Office is composed of selected committees, executives and staff members.
12. The spiritual foundation for Al-Anon's world services is contained in the General Warranties of the Conference, Article 12 of the Charter.

General Warranties of the Conference

In all proceedings the World Service Conference of Al-Anon shall observe the spirit of the Traditions:

1. that only sufficient operating funds, including an ample reserve, be its prudent financial principle;
2. that no Conference member shall be placed in unqualified authority over other members;
3. that all decisions be reached by discussion vote and whenever possible by unanimity;
4. that no Conference action ever be personally punitive or an incitement to public controversy;
5. that though the Conference serves Al-Anon it shall never perform any act of government; and that like the fellowship of Al-Anon Family Groups which it serves, it shall always remain democratic in thought and action.

Index